Micro-Credit, Poverty
and Empowerment

Micro-Credit, Poverty and Empowerment

Linking the Triad

Editors

Neera Burra
Joy Deshmukh-Ranadive
Ranjani K. Murthy

 ICICI *social initiatives.org*

SAGE Publications
New Delhi/Thousand Oaks/London

First published in 2005 by

Sage Publications India Pvt Ltd
B-42, Panchsheel Enclave
New Delhi 110 017
www.indiasage.com

Sage Publications Inc
2455 Teller Road
Thousand Oaks, California 91320

Sage Publications Ltd
1 Oliver's Yard, 55 City Road
London EC1Y 1SP

Published by Tejeshwar Singh for Sage Publications India Pvt Ltd, phototypeset in 10/12 Bookman-Light by Prism Graphix, New Delhi and printed at Chaman Enterprises, New Delhi.

Library of Congress Cataloging-in-Publication Data

Micro-credit, poverty and empowerment: linking the triad/ editors Neera Burra, Joy Deshmukh-Ranadive, Ranjani K. Murthy.
    p. cm.
  Includes index.
1. Women in development—India. 2. Women—India—Social conditions. 3. Women—India—Economic conditions.
4. Microfinance—India. 5. Non-governmental organizations— India. I. Burra, Neera, 1951– II. Deshmukh-Ranadive, Joy. III. Murthy, Ranjani K.

HQ1240.5.I4M53   332—dc22   2005   2005020300

ISBN: 0-7619-3366-2 (Pb)   81-7829-509-1 (India-Pb)

Sage Production Team: Mudita Chauhan-Mubayi, Shinjini Chatterjee, Rajib Chatterjee and Santosh Rawat

Contents

List of Tables

List of Boxes

List of Boxes

List of Abbreviations

ABM	Assistant Branch Manager
AM	Area Manager
ANM	auxillary nurse midwife
APDPIP	Andhra Pradesh District Poverty Initiatives Project
ASA	Activists for Social Action
BC	Backward Caste
BCG	Bacille Calmette Guerin
BM	Branch Manager
BPL	Below Poverty Line
CASA	Church Auxillary for Social Action
CB	Commercial Bank
CBP	Community Banking Programme
CBPPI	Community-Based Pro-Poor Initiative
CCD	Covenant for Community Development
CEDAW	Convention on the Elimination of All Forms of Discrimination Against Women
CEO	Chief Executive Officer
CGT	Continuous Group Training
CV	Community Volunteer

DCB	Demand Collection and Balance
DHAN	Development of Humane Action
DPIP	District Poverty Initiatives Project
DPT	Diptheria, Pertussis and Tetanus
DRDA	District Rural Development Agency
DSSS	Diviseema Social Service Society
DWCRA	Development of Women and Children in Rural Areas
EC	Executive Committee
FCO	Field Credit Officer
FGD	Focus Group Discussion
FI	Financial Institution
FWWB	Friends of Women's World Banking
GDI	Gender Development Index
GoAP	Government of Andhra Pradesh
HDFC	Housing Development Finance Corporation Ltd
HDI	Human Development Index
HH	Head of Household
HUDCO	Housing and Urban Development Corporation
ICDS	Integrated Child Development Scheme
ICICI	The Industrial Credit and Investment Corporation
IFAD	International Fund for Agricultural Development
IFPRI	International Food Policy Research Institute
IGP	Income Generation Programme
ILS	Internal Learning System
IMPACT	Improving the Impact of Micro-finance on Poverty

INDNET	Indian Network of Micro-credit Practitioners
IRDP	Integrated Rural Development Programme
JBY	Janashree Bima Yojana
KAGB	Kalahandi Anchalik Gramya Bank
KKVS	Kadamalai Kalanjiam Vattara Sangam
LEAP	Learning for Empowerment Action through Participation
LIC	Life Insurance Corporation
LPG	Liquefied Petroleum Gas
MD	Managing Director
MACS	Mutually Aided Cooperative Society
MC-RIL	Micro-Credit Ratings India Limited
MFI	Micro-Finance Institution
MHH	Male-Headed Household
MHHMIS	male-headed household management information system
MKMVS	Mugavai Kalanjiam Mahalir Vattara Sangam
MM	Mahila Mandal
MMK	Mahila Mahiti Kendra
MMS	Mahila Mandal Samakhya
MoRD	Ministry of Rural Development
MVF	M. Venkatarangaiya Foundation
NABARD	National Bank for Agriculture and Rural Development
NBFC	Non-Bank Finance Company
NESA	New Entity for Social Action
NGO	Non-Governmental Organization
NIRD	National Institute of Rural Development

NSSO	National Sample Survey Organization
NTR	N.T. Rama Rao
PDS	Public Distribution System
PRA	Participatory Rural Appraisal
PRADAN	Professional Agency for Development Action
PRI	Panchayati Raj Institution
PVK	Pothigai Vattara Kalanjiam
RBI	Reserve Bank of India
RDT	Rural Development Trust
REFLECT	Regenerated Freirean Literacy through Empowering Community Techniques
RGVN	Rashtriya Gramin Vikas Nidhi
RMK	Rashtriya Mahila Kosh
ROSCA	Rotating Savings and Credit Association
RRB	Regional Rural Bank
SAARC	South Asian Association for Regional Cooperation
SAPAP	South Asia Poverty Alleviation Programme
SC	Scheduled Caste
SCG	Savings Credit Group
SERP	Society for Elimination of Rural Poverty
SEWA	Self-Employed Women's Association
SGSY	Swarnajayanti Gram Swarozgar Yojana
SHARE	Society for Helping Awakening Rural Poor through Education
SHG	Self-Help Group
SIDBI	Small Industries Development Bank of India
SIM	SHARE India MACS

SML	SHARE Micro-finance Limited
SPARC	Society for Promotion of Area Resource Centres
SSP	Swayam Shikshan Prayog
ST	Scheduled Tribe
TBA	Trained Birth Attendant
TBF	The Bridge Foundation
TNCDW	Tamil Nadu Corporation for the Development of Women
UNDP	United Nations Development Programme
VDC	Village Development Committee
VNA	Veterinary Assistant
VO	Village Organization
WHH	Women-Headed Household

Glossary

agarbatti	incense stick
ammavadi	child care centre
anganwadi	child welfare centre of the government (present name)
balwadi	child welfare centre of the government (past name)
basavi	Woman dedicated under the *devadasi* custom to a god/goddess in a temple
basti	settlement
beedi	locally-made, usually non-filter cigarette
chapati	see *roti*
chulha	cooking oven
coolie	porter
dais	midwives
dal	food preparation from pulses
dalit	oppressed class, particularly refers to Scheduled Castes
devadasi	lit. 'female servant of god', a practice of marrying girls to gods/goddesses
dosa	crêpe made with rice and pulses

dupatta	Indian long scarf, generally made of cotton or silk
Gollas and Mudras	Two communities classified as socially and economically 'backward' by the government
gram	village
gram panchayat	village local self-governance unit
gram sabha	village assembly
Grama Vidiyal	'Dawn of the Rural Poor'
idli	patty made of steamed rice and pulses
Jamaat	Arabic word for 'community'
jogini	see *basavi*
kalanjiam	mud bin for grain storage, used by DHAN to refer to savings and credit self-help groups
kirana	grocery
laddoo	a sweetmeat usually prepared for special occasions
mahalir	women
Mahalir Kutir	women's space
Mahasabha	forum for all groups to come together
Mahila Bank	women's bank
Mahila courts	women-run courts (not legal)
Mahila Mahiti Kendras	women's information centres
Mahila Samakhya	education for women's equality
mahua	flower with medicinal properties, also used for distilling liquor
Malas, Madigas	Two communities under the Scheduled (caste) list of the government, normally more backward than backward castes

mand	weight of approx. 4 kg
mandal	second layer of administration and local self-governance unit, comprising a few gram panchayats
melava	fair
Muthi Chawal	literally, 'handful of rice', as used in the book, refers to a grain bank
neem	sc. name Azadirachta indica, also called margosa
paan	betel leaf
padayatra	foot marches
Parvati Parameshwar	see *jogini*
patel	upper-caste group, also used to refer to a person from the upper caste
perecherla	branch (Telugu)
pucca	firm/permanent
punlukura or *gonkura*	sour greens
Rashtriya Mahila Kosh	National Women's Fund
roti	round, thin and unleavened Indian bread
sahukar	moneylender
samvad sahayak	village communication assistant
sarpanch	head of gram panchyat
Stree Shakti Puraskar	women's empowerment award
Swarnajayanti Gram Swarozgar Yojana	Lit. Golden Jubilee Village Self-employment Plan
swarozgar	self-employment
tai	aunt
taluka	third layer of administration and local self-governance, comprising a few blocks or *mandals*

thittam	scheme
vayalagams	tank farmers' associations
Vidyadeepam	lamp of education
Yojana	plan
zamindar	landlord
Zilla Parishad	District Council, an elected local body

Foreword

Around the globe, the United Nations Development Programme (UNDP) seeks to promote approaches that focus on
reducing human poverty, emphasizing the importance of
equity, social inclusion, women's empowerment and human
rights for poverty reduction. A key priority is to make a piv-
otal difference in reducing extreme poverty and hunger by
half within 2015, the first and perhaps the most critical
Millennium Development Goal of all.

Efficient financial systems are vital for the prosperity of
a community and a nation as a whole. To ensure that poor
people are included in the benefits of development, it is
necessary that these vast numbers have consistent access
to financial services, access that can translate into a key
element of economic growth and poverty alleviation. However, micro-finance is much more than simply an income
generation tool. By directly empowering poor people, particularly women, it has become one of the key driving mechanisms towards meeting Millennium Development Goals.
The UNDP-assisted South Asia Poverty Alleviation Programme (SAPAP) pilot project in three districts of Andhra
Pradesh that was initiated in 1996, relied on a three-pronged
strategy of social mobilization of the poor, skill development
and capital formation. A majority of the poor mobilized under
the programme were women. The state government has since
scaled up this approach to cover all its districts. UNDP further extended its support to the state for micro-finance and

social mobilization under the Government of India's Community Based Pro-Poor Initiative (CBPPI) from 1997 to 2001. The year 2005, declared the International Year of Micro-credit, provides us with an excellent opportunity to showcase best practices, share ideas on new and innovative uses of micro-credit and micro-finance schemes in broadening choices for the poor. This study is a contribution in that direction.

The essential goal is to strengthen and spread the word on available and viable micro-financial services, which offer the possibility to many to improve their own situations through their own efforts. Micro-credit and micro-finance will, however, reach the maximum number of poor clients with the optimal effect only when they are recognized as a national priority, integrated into the financial sector, and complemented by measures for skill development and social mobilization.

The case studies presented in this volume highlight the need for an integrated approach to micro-credit and micro-finance. The analysis of the data from the cases presented here show that holistic approaches to micro-credit and micro-finance are an important part of the answer to poverty alleviation. However, micro initiatives have to be backed by a pro-poor macro policy environment. Mainstream financial institutions have a major role to play in providing financial services to the poor and need to respond in a number of different ways, if the challenge of poverty alleviation has to be taken up. Furthermore, poverty is gendered, with women being at the bottom of the poverty scale, and micro-credit initiatives must focus on ways of empowering them.

It is my great pleasure as the Resident Representative of UNDP in India to support the production of this volume during the International Year of Micro-credit. This is a critical time to renew our shared commitment to the reduction of poverty, and to understand the role micro-finance plays in doing this.

MAXINE OLSON
UNDP Resident Representative
and UN Resident Coordinator

Foreword

The book is a collection of six case studies of governmental and quasi-governmental organizations initiated by UNDP and ICICI Bank to assess the impact of micro-finance activities on women's empowerment and poverty reduction in India.

The micro-finance institutions studied here aim to alleviate the poverty and vulnerability of their members. The case studies were based on the work of the following institutions: Activists for Social Action (ASA), Andhra Pradesh; Development of Humane Action (DHAN) Foundation, Tamil Nadu; SHARE Micro-finance Limited (SML), Andhra Pradesh; Swayam Sikshan Prayog (SSP), Maharashtra; South Asia Poverty Alleviation Project (SAPAP), Andhra Pradesh and Lokadrusti, Orissa.

The project undertaken in this volume becomes critical in the context of the debate on South Asian experiences in micro-credit and the impact of such interventions. It was aimed at identifying the contribution of 'economic empowerment' in the overall context of 'women's empowerment' and also to understand the type of social mobilization strategies suitable for sustainable empowerment.

The researchers have adopted different methods in the case studies to explore the empowerment and poverty outputs of micro-credit. The findings of the case studies have been placed within a framework that links issues of poverty with those of empowerment and illustrates how micro-credit could be analysed in terms of its impact on those issues.

The book studies and evaluates women's empowerment at individual, collective (group) and wider (societal) levels. At the individual level, the evaluative measures of the framework bring out issues of access and control, and access to labour and income are identified as critical. The measures also recognize that control over labour, income, mobility (physical and social) and their own bodies are vital to women's empowerment. At the collective level, issues of access to, and control over, political spaces, consciousness, collective strength, visibility and recognition for women's groups have been emphasized. At wider levels, the framework points to the need to track changes in the macro-economic framework, and in poverty profiles of village- and community-level institutions.

Overall, the book attempts to establish the relationship between social mobilization, micro-credit and women's empowerment and goes on to evaluate potential impacts of 'micro-credit' vis-à-vis 'micro-credit plus' approaches on women's empowerment. It also provides a comprehensive literature review on the theoretical and empirical research conducted in the area, specifically on the concept and processes of women's empowerment and reduction of household and individual (women's) poverty.

ICICI Bank's Social Initiatives Group and UNDP commissioned these studies with a view to understanding the impact of micro-credit interventions. While this is a good beginning, further rigorous research on the mechanisms of transmission between access to credit, and empowerment and poverty alleviation is required. This book will aid practitioners, banks, funding agencies and the government in getting a sense of the social returns of micro-credit interventions.

ICICI BANK

Preface

This book brings together case studies commissioned by the United Nations Development Programme (UNDP) and ICICI Bank to assess the impact of micro-credit activities on women's empowerment. The *Human Development Reports* and other United Nations/World Bank reports identify South Asia as one of the most deprived regions in the world. South Asia has the largest number of people in the world living in absolute poverty, which includes 43 per cent of the developing world's population. Sixty per cent of these are women, with limited access to basic needs. The greatest burden of human deprivation and poverty, illiteracy and health-related problems fall on its women.[1]

In India, as in many other countries, ensuring women's access to credit through micro-credit schemes is a major component of strategies for both poverty alleviation and women's empowerment. Thousands of women's self-help groups (SHGs) have been set up across the country by NGOs and through government programmes, such as the Rashtriya Mahila Kosh (RMK), the Indira Mahila Yojana, and the Swarnajayanti Gram Swarozgar Yojana (SGSY). Micro-credit through women's SHGs is also a central element of the development vision outlined in the Tenth Five-year Plan.

----

[1] UNIFEM, 1999, *Carrying the Beijing Torch in South Asia.* India is ranked 127th in the *Human Development Report 2004*, with a Human Development Index (HDI) value of 0.595. The Maldives ranks first in the South Asian region, with an HDI value of 0.752.

However, the experience of women's groups, NGOs and government agencies involved in implementing micro-credit programmes indicates that their outcomes are dependent on a range of complex factors. A rigorous analysis of these experiences and the lessons derived from them is essential to maximize the impact of micro-credit interventions. While the impact of micro-credit on income poverty has been extensively studied and documented, there are very few studies that explore the extent to which such programmes have been able to facilitate non-economic dimensions of empowerment for women.

The Ministry of Rural Development (MoRD), Government of India, in association with the UNDP, initiated a whole range of 'Community-Based Pro-Poor Initiatives' between 1997 and 2004. Under this programme, a number of NGOs were supported to strengthen self-help initiatives through micro-credit and women's empowerment. They were supported through capacity-building programmes, training in income generation activities, constructing water-harvesting structures, and through the provision of material and social assistance for land development, education, health and other non-income-related issues.

Poverty is not merely a question of lack or dearth of income, but also of marginalization, deprivation and exclusion. Eradication of poverty therefore requires sufficient attention towards these non-income-related issues as well.

It was in this context that the UNDP, in partnership with ICICI Bank, decided to commission case studies of the work done by some of its partners, such as the South Asia Poverty Alleviation Programme (SAPAP) based in Andhra Pradesh; Swayam Shikshan Prayog (SSP), an NGO based in Maharashtra; DHAN (Development of Humane Action) Foundation, an NGO based in Tamil Nadu; and Lokadrusti, an NGO based in Orissa to assess the extent to which micro-credit had facilitated women's empowerment. In addition, ICICI Bank felt it would be useful to document the experience of at least two major micro-finance institutions to provide a comparative picture. SHARE Micro-finance Limited (SML), based in Andhra Pradesh, and Activists for Social Action (ASA), based in Tamil Nadu, were selected for further research on this issue.

These studies are crucial in the context of the debate on South Asian experiences in micro-credit and its impact. Organizations in India like the Self-Employed Women's Association (SEWA), the Annapurna Mahila Mandal and the Working Women's Forum have already demonstrated the feasibility of providing small loans to poor women, primarily to support small entrepreneurial ventures, and have established, without doubt, that access to credit is vital to women's ability to earn an income. The extent to which access to micro-credit alone has led to women's wider status and autonomy is still not clear.

It is commonplace now for micro-credit to be increasingly hailed as a panacea for poverty alleviation. While micro-credit has, in some circumstances, contributed positively to women's empowerment and helped extremely poor women survive economic crises in the short term, it is now increasingly recognized that micro-credit interventions have concentrated only on the economic aspects of poverty and not addressed its non-economic dimensions. It has been rightly argued that since some credit programmes foster group formation and enable women to generate income, they offer *potential* for both political and economic empowerment. However, since credit by itself cannot overcome patriarchal systems of control at household and community levels, this potential is not always realized.

Micro-credit works when other empowerment strategies are included as part of social mobilization. These strategies have included assisting women to have increased control over their incomes and resources, helping women to define their own priorities, and ensuring their participation in decision-making at various levels: household, community, region and state.

The primary aim of commissioning these studies was to understand the role of social mobilization and micro-credit for women's empowerment. The Social Initiatives Group of the ICICI Bank backed these studies with a view to understanding the impact of micro-credit interventions, as evident from the case studies in the book.

The six chapters presented here relate ethnographic case studies at the micro level with broader issues of gender mainstreaming, equality and justice at the macro level. Both NGOs and quasi-governmental organizations have been involved in the six case studies. The documentation has tried to focus on the 'voices of the poor'. The studies have, however, been unable to address all issues in their entirety. For instance, how do the benefits of micro-credit and consequent women's empowerment filter down to the girl child? There are some reasons for this: at one level, there was not enough time to tackle all research questions; at times, the women themselves were not forthcoming with these details; and some studies were done with micro-finance institutions, which are not necessarily NGOs. Further documentation and in-depth research remains a future aim of such works. Yet, these studies throw light on the role of economic empowerment for the overall empowerment of women, and the kinds of social mobilization strategies required for empowerment to be sustainable under differing conditions.

These case studies were commissioned in 2001 and discussed in a workshop held at New Delhi in January 2002. The participants included the case study writers and the NGOs, as well as a large number of experts, practitioners, micro-finance institutions and government departments. The studies were revised on the basis of the discussions.

I would like to take this opportunity to thank all the participating organizations which provided facilities for the consultants to visit them and learn about their work. Without such collaboration, these studies would not have been possible. I wish to thank Dr Anuradha Rajivan, Ranjani K. Murthy, Soma Kishore Parthasarathy, K. Raju, Amitha Kamath, Shashi Rajagopalan, Veena Padia and Dr Kalpana Sankar for their meticulous research and analysis. Given the framework of the studies, it was not easy to keep the focus of the research.

My former colleague, Dr Kalyani Menon-Sen, provided valuable inputs in the conceptualization of the studies and facilitation of the workshop. Asha Swarup, former Joint Secretary, MoRD, Government of India, was always an enthusiastic supporter of this project, deeply interested in the ethnographic case studies and the recommendations that emerged from these presentations. But for her support to the

'Community-Based Pro-Poor Initiatives Programme', these studies would never have been commissioned. ICICI Bank, with its commitment to supporting pro-poor micro-credit policies and strengthening its public–private partnership, was very generous with its grant. Bikram Duggal and Kartikeya Saboo of the Bank were committed and interested participants throughout the process, reading and commenting on earlier drafts—their inputs were invaluable.

Joy Deshmukh-Ranadive and Ranjani K. Murthy, co-editors of this volume, took on the responsibility of putting the papers together—this volume owes a great debt to their efforts and time, and would not have come together without their efforts. Finally, I would like to thank all my UNDP colleagues for their organizational and administrative support, and SAPAP for providing additional funding support for the workshop and one of the case studies.

NEERA BURRA
Assistant Resident Representative
United Nations Development Programme

1

Introduction: Linking the Triad

Joy Deshmukh-Ranadive and
Ranjani K. Murthy

Micro-credit as a tool of poverty alleviation and empowerment, particularly of women, has gained credence in development dialogue the world over. The provision of micro-credit involves initiatives on the part of state and non-state organizations in making available very small amounts of credit to poor clients.[1] There is an acute need among the poor for credit, both for consumption and production, which often forms the deciding line between survival and succumbing to poverty. In other words, credit is sought for basic requirements such as food, as well as for income generation activities.[2] The rationale of micro-credit is based on the hypothesis that the poor can be relied upon to return on time the money that they borrow. It has been proved that the poor are capable of thrift and savings.[3]

---

[1] The focus of this book is on micro-credit as against the broader understanding of micro-finance, which includes other services such as insurance, etc. Hence, the term 'micro-credit' is used as against micro-finance. This is not to belie the fact that there are practioners who deal with insurance and other services. However, largely credit and savings are practised.

[2] It has been found that besides food, credit is also needed for health, housing and education. These needs are also critical for survival. See Stern and Stern (n.d.).; Zeller (2000).

[3] For a discussion on the capacity to save and the need for credit to the poor, see Rutherford (2000).

Poverty is a persistent problem in developing countries. Caught within vicious circles of various kinds, the poor continue to remain poor primarily because they are poor. One of these vicious circles is created due to the lack of financial resources to generate livelihoods and income creating a wheel of low incomes, lack of livelihoods and low resources. Right from the 1950s, it has been the effort of governments within developing countries, donor agencies and international funding organizations to crack this spiral by intervening with subsidized credit, which can be used by poor households to generate incomes. These institutions attempted to supervise the uses to which loans were put. Repayment schedules were based on the expected income flow from the investment. However, returns were often over-estimated, especially in the context of agricultural production which depended heavily on unpredictable weather conditions. When loans were not paid, public money was used to waive outstanding and overdue loans at election time. There was also dependence on the fluctuating priorities of governments and donor agencies. Hence, credit provision for poor people was intermittent and limited.

Over time, there has been a global trend in criticism of subsidized forms of credit. Attention has been focused on market-based solutions as against state-based solutions. Policy-makers were cautioned that the other side of credit was that it was a debt, and if subsidized credit was supplied in excess without realistic assessment of people's ability to repay, it could result in the impoverishment of borrowers. Recent developments in the design of micro-credit schemes have generated enthusiasm, since innovative features in design are supposed to reduce the costs and risks of extending loans to the poor. These innovations lie in the reliance on social collateral as against physical collateral. Small groups of poor people are formed who then engage in savings activities and rotate small loans amongst themselves. Micro-credit, as is being promoted currently, circumvents the drawbacks of both the formal and the informal systems of credit delivery. The novelty of the current system of micro-credit lies in it being seen as a poverty-reducing institution which pays for itself. It is supposed to be beneficial to both micro-credit institutions[4] as well as clients. Since the poor can be banked upon to return loans on time, it is believed that micro-credit and profits are not antithetical to each other. In fact, this intervention is being hailed as the one method that will address both development and promote market behaviour at the same time. In particular, it is seen as remarkable, since it can unite the growth and poverty agendas.

Among the real and potential clients of micro-credit, women are seen as the most appropriate targeted beneficiaries, since it is argued that in contrast to men, the entire household benefits when the loans are given to women. Women are also reputed to be more reliable than men when it comes to repayments. It is further claimed that micro-credit empowers women since it accords economic independence and instils confidence by virtue of their participation in groups as well as their undertaking and expanding economic activities.

This book aims at providing insights into the impacts of six NGO and quasi-government interventions in micro-credit on poverty alleviation and the empowerment of women. The interventions are placed in the context of the importance that micro-credit has today within development programmes as a tool of poverty alleviation and women's empowerment. The book suggests a conceptual framework within which the two goals of micro-credit, poverty reduction and women's empowerment, can be linked. This forms the basis of analysis of the six studies in the concluding chapter. The framework that has been suggested and its use in analysis in the conclusion can serve as a basis for designing micro-credit programmes that are more sensitive to the poor and

---

[4] By micro-credit institutions are meant formal institutions like banks, both commercial and non-commercial, which are in the 'business' of finance. Within the institutional mapping of micro-credit, non-governmental organizations often fall in the category of 'intermediaries' which constitute the link between banks and the clients. Hence, they are also in the business of finance since they have to on-lend and maintain their own financial sustainability. They are, however, not formal financial institutions themselves. There are no doubt organizations like BASIX where one of their institutions is a bank.

to women. It also facilitates drawing up indicators for impact evaluation exercises that are sharper in capturing processes of poverty alleviation and empowerment. In the contribution of both authors and editors, the book points to ways in which further research on micro-credit and women in the contexts of empowerment and poverty can be undertaken.

The International Legitimization of Micro-finance as a Tool of Poverty Eradication and Women's Empowerment

Officially, the intervention of micro-finance has been heralded worldwide as one of the most effective cures for poverty. Over the few years prior to 1997, a series of meetings were held to design an approach that could be followed by all countries across the globe. The meetings worked towards contributing inputs for the World Micro-credit Summit Campaign held at Washington, DC in February 1997. Four core themes were stressed as part of a 55-page Declaration and Plan of Action. These were:

❖ Reaching the Poorest: 1.2 billion people are living in absolute poverty in the world. These comprise some 240 million families. These form the group from where most of the Micro-credit Summit's target of 100 million poorest will be tapped. The Summit also promotes the use of quality poverty measurements to identify the poorest.

❖ Reaching and Empowering Women: Since women are supposed to be good credit risks, and women-run enterprises benefit their families, micro-credit is seen as a tool to empower women. It should be noted, however, that the understanding of 'empowerment' here is restricted to increase in incomes.

❖ Building Financially Self-sufficient Institutions: This theme is based on the experience of developing countries which have shown that micro-credit programmes can improve their efficiency and structure their interest rates and fees to eventually cover their operating and financial costs. The Campaign offered day-long courses at global and regional levels held from 1999 through 2001, which trained practitioners in these aspects.

✦ Ensuring a Positive, Measurable Impact on the Lives of Clients and their Families: Two impact evaluation studies conducted by the NGO Freedom From Hunger showed that current clients of its affiliate institutions in Honduras and Mali had experienced positive programme impact at the individual, household and community levels. The studies showed the higher levels of empowerment of client households in terms of larger enterprises, increases in personal income and household food consumption, savings and the feeling of self-esteem, as compared to non-client households.

These four core themes of the Summit Campaign helped to focus both on the demand side of micro-credit as well as the supply side. Papers were prepared for the Summit, which substantiated these themes. These have since been updated and are used widely as guidelines by practitioners in this sector.[5]

Micro-credit in India

Micro-credit in India has to be understood against the structure of the financial system which has evolved through two sets of financial institutions—formal and informal. The formal system consists of a multi-agency approach, comprising cooperatives, public sector commercial banks (CBs), regional rural banks (RRBs) and private sector banks. There are innumerable types of informal credit suppliers in India which consist of rotating savings and credit associations (ROSCAs), traders, merchants, contractors, commission agents, moneylenders, etc.

---

[5] Visit http//www.microcreditsummit.org/papers/papers.html.

In India the major objective of the nationalization of banks in 1969 and 1980 was to improve the flow of institutional credit into rural households, especially poor households. Commercial banks are supposed to play a dominant role in rural financial markets in contemporary India. Priority sector lending was one of the most important tenets whereby the Reserve Bank of India (RBI) stipulated commercial banks to earmark 40 per cent of their advances for priority sector lending. However, trends show that the accent on development banking of commercial banks weakened considerably in the 1980s and 1990s. Banks have generally shown disinclination to service the poor who are distanced spatially and metaphorically away from them and hence whose risk profile is difficult to assess. The formal sector consequently took the initiative to develop a supplementary credit delivery mechanism by encouraging non-governmental organizations (NGOs) to act as facilitators and intermediaries.[6] Currently the micro-credit sector is dualistic in nature. The formal structure has a legal and regulated component, which provides credit and other services to the non-formal sector. The non-formal structure largely comprising of NGOs, SHGs, clusters and federations of groups operate outside the legalized structure and have demonstrated considerable organizational flexibility and dynamism in responding to the demands at the grassroots.

Within the institutional mapping of micro-credit participants in India, the players constituting the regulatory bodies, apex bodies and intermediaries, comprise those responsible for the supply side of the intervention. The clients constitute the demand side of the intervention. The regulatory body is primarily the RBI. The National Bank for Agriculture and Rural Development (NABARD) also performs a regulatory role, although this bank features among the suppliers of bulk credit too. The apex bodies are those who supply bulk credit for on-lending purposes. They are also called wholesalers.[7] The next components of the

---

[6] At the beginning, NABARD had a pilot project in Karnataka (1991), whereby self-help groups (SHGs) were linked with formal banks mediated through an NGO. The project was apparently successful. This led to its institutionalization in 1996 by the RBI.

[7] Some of the major institutional sources of bulk credit to the Indian micro-finance sector consist of NABARD, Mumbai; Small Industrial

institutional mapping are the intermediary agencies, which comprise banks of various kinds—scheduled, regional, rural and cooperative, micro-credit institutions and facilitating NGOs.

The Indian Reality: Poverty

India has been fighting poverty through state initiative ever since Independence in 1947. However, even in the new century the picture is not very encouraging. During 1950–55, the poverty headcount ratio (which measures mainly income poverty) averaged over 50 per cent, a situation which continued (fluctuating below 45 per cent and above 60 per cent) till the early 1970s. After this period there has been a systematic decline in the headcount index, which lasted upto the mid-1980s. Subsequently, the poverty levels increased in the early post-liberalization phase of the 1990s, and after that there have been fluctuations around a modestly declining trend. In absolute terms, the numbers of the poor have increased from approximately 200 million in the early 1950s to about 300 million currently.[8]

The official measure of poverty in India is based on the concept of income poverty. Based on a calorie norm, income poverty estimates the income needed to provide individuals with a stipulated minimum of food intake per day in rural and urban areas. There are, however, other indicators than mere income, which are accounted for when poverty is conceptualized in a broader sense. These are: levels of consumption, levels of expenditure, infant and child mortality, status of health, education levels, literacy, availability of food, nutrition levels, availability

---

Development Bank of India (SIDBI), Lucknow; and the Rashtriya Mahila Kosh (RMK). The Last is a government initiated autonomous body under the Department of Women and Child Development which extends credit support to NGOs and Women Economic Development Corporations and operates from New Delhi; HUDCO, New Delhi; HDFC, Mumbai; FWWB, Ahmedabad; Rashtriya Gramin Vikas Nidhi (RGVN), Guwahati and The Bridge Foundation (TBF), Bangalore (SIDBI, 2000).
[8] There have been debates about the actual trends in poverty reduction. For a discussion, see Cassen (2002).

of adequate rest, etc. Further, other forms of discrimination that are due to caste, race and ethnicity aggravate situations of poverty between households.[9] It must also be noted that all these indicators view the household as the unit *of* analysis and not as a unit *for* analysis. Intra-household disparities that make some members poorer than others within the same poor household, cannot be identified unless gender-based discriminations are brought to the centrestage.[10] There have been studies that have used deprivation indicators that are non-monetary to show poverty levels within households.[11] These are undoubtedly region and culture specific, but the important factor to be recorded is that poverty of a household is not necessarily the same as poverty within a household and, often for women, the two compound to aggravate an impoverishment that is related to gender.

Poverty can be seen as an interlocking failure of ownership,[12] exchange[13] and consumption[14] entitlements[15] and outcomes,

---

[9] Using household level data for the fiftieth round of the National Survey's (NSS) consumer expenditure survey, Meenakshi et al. (2000) report that poverty rates are higher among scheduled caste and scheduled tribe households than among all households virtually in all states.

[10] This also applies to age-based discrimination within the household, which is not the primary focus of the study.

[11] See Cantillon and Nolan (2001). The study is based on poverty in the US, specifically drawing from a sample in Chicago. The hardship and deprivation indicators in developing and industrialized countries will not only vary, but those between developing countries will also contextually vary.

[12] Ownership entitlement refers to what one is legally or normatively entitled to own. In India, for example, one is entitled to own land (upto a limit), one's labour, livestock, productive assets and finance. At another level, one also owns a membership in one's family, community and citizenship vis-à-vis the state. See Murthy and Rao's (1997) expansion of Sen (1981).

[13] Exchange entitlements refer to what cash one can exchange one's produce and labour for in markets, what productive inputs and goods one can exchange one's citizenship for vis-à-vis the state (for example, free agricultural extension) and what resources one can exchange one's membership in the community for (for example, common property resources).

[14] Consumption entitlements refer to what basic needs one can exchange one's membership in the family and one's citizenship for (free education and, in the past, health care) (Murthy and Rao, 1997).

[15] Entitlements can be legal (enforced through rule of law), or normative (customary, that is, enforced through social pressure) in nature.

which are shaped by both the domestic and macro environment.[16] Entitlements when they are legal have the state machinery as accountable in the event of a non-fulfilment. It is the normative entitlements that constitute the trap within which all deprivation falls. Normative entitlements, since they are socially and culturally determined as per norms, are bordered perceptions of what a person should get by virtue of her/his class, caste, race, ethnicity and gender. There is also a third level to be considered, which are human entitlements. These are entitlements that every person irrespective of demarcations receives by virtue of being a human being. In the light of development being translated as a 'human right', these entitlements seem to be the common denominator, which bypass biases, both social and political.[17]

In conceptualizations of poverty, the stress is most often on the lack of resources by virtue of a failure in entitlements. *The root of the problem however lies in the mismatch between responsibilities and entitlements.* Poverty can be conceptualized as the acute paucity of entitlements in order to fulfil basic responsibilities essential to human survival and maintenance. Households have to perform certain functions through which they are responsible for their own survival, maintenance and generation. While households are different in composition, every household commonly performs the three functions of consumption, production and distribution. The household consumes goods and services, which are supplied both from within the household and also from the market. The household produces goods and services, again, both for one's own consumption and for sale in the market. The household also produces human beings. This production entails biological reproduction, social reproduction, and physical and economic maintenance. It is

---

[16] Adapted from Sen (1981) by Murthy and Rao (1997). Also see Kabeer and Murthy (1999).

[17] The Declaration on the Right to Development stated that the right to development is a human right and it was adopted by an overwhelming majority by the UN in 1986. These rights include human rights, economic, social and cultural rights along with civil and political rights. For a discussion, see Sengupta (2001).

through these that human beings are produced.[18] The household also distributes time and resources across members. This function of distribution determines consumption and production. In other words, distributive rules determine who consumes what, how much and when. Distributive rules also determine areas and hours of work, both within and outside the household. The allocation of resources is similarly determined. These distributive rules are determined by norms, which in turn are set by ideology (patriarchal or otherwise), lineage systems (patrilineal or matrilineal), kinship systems (unilateral, bilineal), religious codes, age of the household member, marital status and life-cycle of the household. These norms are invariably gender-biased.[19]

Every household functions within a socially stratified environment, which accords it a place in a hierarchy. Social, political and economic factors determine the entitlements of households. Poor households are those with extremely low levels of resources, skills and entitlements that have the responsibility of maintaining and reproducing themselves. This is a responsibility that is common to all households, but when one compares entitlements, the weight and burden of the responsibility on poor households is heavier than on non-poor households.

In economies where the responsibility of the maintenance of its population is shouldered by the state, in the existence of poverty, the issue of the failure of legal entitlements looms large. Anti-poverty programmes and schemes in India were hitherto addressed at enhancing the entitlements of poor households, on one hand, by providing employment, subsidized credit, etc., and also on lightening the

---

[18] Human beings are also produced by institutions outside and other than the household; however, here we are outlining the responsibilities of the household per se.

[19] The functional form of the household has been merged with the formal definition of the family to give a composite category of the 'domestic unit', which can be operationalized and used in research and policy. See Deshmukh-Ranadive (2001).

burden of responsibility, on the other hand, by subsidizing food, health, child care and education services. With liberalization and globalization, there has been a withdrawal of the state's role in sharing the burden of responsibility of reproduction and maintenance of households. Since there is little effort now in that direction, the only other way in which poverty reduction efforts can be made is in triggering off processes that enhance entitlements and community-based efforts to share responsibilities (though the latter is not entirely desirable). The catchword is 'self-help', and micro-credit as it is promoted today is a means of enabling the poor to help themselves to expand entitlements and share responsibilities. Inasmuch as micro-credit initiatives can close the yawning gap between entitlements and responsibilities for poor households and for different members of households, they can be said to succeed in alleviating poverty.

When we look at the four core themes of the Summit, several questions come to mind. Theoretical arguments and impact evaluation studies have together contributed towards raising contradictory issues which have hence become a matter of debate. For instance, in the context of the first theme, while it is the claim of the Summit that the poorest will be reached and while some micro-finance institutions (MFIs) also claim success in doing so, there is evidence to show that *it is not the poorest, but the poor who are reached.* The reason for such an occurrence is attributed to high transaction costs involved in reaching the poorest who are not only metaphorically but also literally difficult to reach and serve (also linking micro-credit with savings). The second issue of debate within the first theme is the capacity of the poorest to absorb credit and start enterprises. Again, it has been noticed that the poorest have a limited capacity to avail and productively absorb credit. The report prepared by the Division for Social Policy and Development of the UN Department for Economic and Social Affairs, cites studies which show that 'there are limits to the use of credit as an instrument for poverty eradication, including the fact that many people, especially the poorest of the poor, are usually not in a position to undertake an economic activity, partly because they lack business skills, and even the motivation for business'.[20] In a sense, this is an extension of the first debate, since it is argued that it is better to reach the poor who then, by starting enterprises, make place for the poorest to find employment, which was earlier undertaken by the poor. Also, with the success of enterprise, the poor who make progress can also employ the poorest.

Debates such as these can only be resolved if one considers the methods used to identify the 'poorest'. It is absolutely necessary for the same indicators that were used by NGOs/MFIs to identify the target group, which are then used by impact evaluation studies to assess the effect of the programmes on the target group. Often, practitioners and evaluators use different criteria. This is invalid when impact is being accessed.[21] When micro-credit interventions are evaluated for their impact upon poverty, it is necessary to focus upon whether the gap between entitlements and responsibilities has decreased, and for whom, within households and communities. At face value, it can be seen that micro-credit makes an attempt at increasing entitlements of poor households. But since the collective good does not necessarily stand for the individual good and given gender biases within households, it is also necessary to examine whether the individual entitlements of women have increased. This is all the more relevant since women are the

------

[20] Cited in UN IRIN—West Africa: 'UN Report Cautions on Limits of Micro-credit', irin-wa@wa.dha.unon.org.

[21] This problem relates directly to the fourth theme emphasized by the Summit, that is, 'ensuring a positive, measurable impact on the lives of clients and their families'. The impact cannot be measured to be positive or negative if different indicators are used. Different indicators can be used only if the study is investigative and seeks to examine whether the identifying characteristics used by the NGO/MFI are really relevant for capturing the poorest in the area, or if in fact it is only the poor that have been reached. If the examination seeks to test the relevance of the indicators used during identification, then different indicators can be used to assess whether the targeting has been appropriate. For a detailed discussion on issues relating to the collection of data in micro-credit, see Deshmukh-Ranadive (2002a).

vehicles that are supposed to carry these interventions forward. The other side of the argument will be covered only if
the impact evaluation also assesses whether micro-credit
has added to the responsibilities of poor households as collectives and of women as individuals. There could be a
simultaneous increase of both entitlements and responsibilities, in which case an examination is required of the net
effect. Inasmuch as the net effect is positive, poverty levels
will reduce. Similarly, it is important to examine for which
caste, class and ethnic group within the community the
gaps between entitlements and responsibilities have decreased. Often dalits and tribals have the least to benefit
from poverty reduction programmes.

Within the household, while gender forms a category
around which hierarchies are structured, age is also another discriminating factor which accounts for vulnerability. In India, in particular, it is common to find children
from poor families having to work and augment the
household's income. Child poverty is a dimension of poverty
that has received considerable attention. Alongside, it is
found that with an increase in life expectancy in developing countries, as is in India, ageing and its related problems rise to the fore. In poor households, which have the capacity to survive, yet not the capacity to afford non-earning
members, looking after the old becomes a liability. In the
case of both children and the aged, the question of responsibility alters to whether there is some other members
in the household to whom their care can be entrusted as a
responsibility. Socially, this responsibility has been thrust
upon women. However, while interventions can bridge the
gap between responsibilities and entitlements, it must be
examined whether the responsibilities on the shoulders of
children and the old have been reduced so that their human
entitlements of care and nurturing are maintained. In the
lack of adequate systems of social security in India, state
responsibility of the aged is minimal. Likewise, children
are the responsibility of families. In circumstances of poverty, responsibilities within the household shift across
members, and it has been found that crisis causes burdens
to fall upon women and girl children more than on other

members. Paradoxically, interventions that strive to alleviate poverty and augment incomes also increase burdens
upon vulnerable members within families, since these interventions do little to alter gendered divisions of labour
within households.

Women's Empowerment

The second core theme of the Summit was to reach and
empower women. This theme can be further divided into
two goals: of reaching women and of empowering them. The
first goal of reaching women is not as difficult to achieve as
it is to reach the poorest households. Most of the self-help
groups (SHGs) that are formed under current micro-credit
initiatives are those of women. The reasons for targeting
women are themselves subjects for debate. Note has to be
taken of the narrow perception of the core theme, that is,
since women are supposed to be good credit risks, and
women-run enterprises benefit their families, micro-credit
is seen as a tool to empower women. The submissiveness
and pliability of women in relation to repayment schedules
are stated as both valid and suspect reasons. The capacity
of women to start enterprises, to sustain them and to run
SHGs independently without the help of men is also a matter of discussion. There is no doubt about the fact that, given
the current systems of micro-credit, women have access to
credit. However, empowerment is not dependent on mere
access but on control of both the credit and the use to which
that credit is put. And access does not automatically include control.

It is easy to build-in empowerment as a goal of all development initiatives. Empowerment is the most frequently
used term in development dialogue today. It is also the most
nebulous and widely interpreted of concepts. It has simultaneously become a tool for analysis, as also an umbrella
concept to justify almost every conceivable development
intervention. In the World Summit for Social Development
held at Copenhagen in March 1995, empowerment featured

prominently as an objective. The Draft Declaration of the Third Preparatory Committee (New York, 16–27 January 1995) adopted by the heads of states and governments asserted that 'the most productive policies and investments are those which empower people to maximize their capacities, resources and opportunities'. The same document, in Point 23.0, emphasizes that the main objective of development is to empower people, particularly women, to strengthen their capacities. This is to be achieved through the full participation of people in the formulation, implementation and evaluation of decisions determining the functioning and well-being of society. Empowerment is central to the new package of the liberalization discourse, which transfers considerable responsibility of welfare to civil society. While initially, efforts were launched in the name of 'emancipation', today the goal of national and international policies, development programmes and NGO activity seems to have shifted to achieving 'empowerment'. Governmental agencies have also popularized the use of empowerment both as a term and as a goal. The Indian government's country paper for the Copenhagen Summit included a section on 'Empowering the People—Models of Mobilization'. This paper saw the empowerment of people in enabling them to help themselves and removing social, economic, cultural and psychological barriers, which would transform them from being passive recipients of government programmes to being active participants and managers of their own affairs (GOI, 1995). Implicit within this visualization is the strategy of organizing disempowered groups into SHGs, formal associations, cooperatives, etc., so that they can exert collective pressure, articulate their demands and effectively participate in decision-making processes. As Mohanty (2001) states, many scholars and social activists have adopted the use of this term because it is in keeping with the global discourse. NGOs, on the other hand, seem to think that with the adoption of this term, they can counter the criticism leveled against them about accepting prevailing power structures while carrying out development initiatives.

Advocates of micro-credit claim that the very process of forming SHGs is empowering and a critical mass is formed which can be harnessed to pull households out of poverty traps. The flip side of the debate around this issue is that the same critical mass can be usurped by larger political and economic interests to promote their own mandates, by which women become instruments and are further disempowered.[22] Further, empowerment cannot be achieved through the handling of just money since credit by itself does not bind women together enough to unleash a process of empowerment. Other social and development concerns are required to cement groups so that they can metamorphose into vehicles of empowerment. The other issue of debate relating to micro-credit and women's empowerment is that credit can only address practical gender needs and not strategic ones. Hence, one must not be over-ambitious about the goal of empowerment. The process of a micro-credit programme does not directly affect structures within households or attempt to change hierarchies within it. Therefore, membership within an SHG does not automatically carry the dynamics of empowerment into the household even if it has begun within the group. No doubt, women can also get empowered by virtue of membership in a group that is struggling towards a common goal of equity. However, often these processes isolate them from the household and there are increased tensions within the family.

Female SHGs are promoted since it is believed that micro-credit will result in a set of mutually reinforcing 'virtuous spirals' of increasing economic empowerment, improved well-being and social/political/legal empowerment for women. Mayoux (1993) suggests that this dominant view has emerged as the 'confluence' of three rather distinct paradigms' of micro-credit programmes. The first is the financial self-sustainability paradigm preferred by economists. This school of thought advocates that minimalist financial services routed through women will alleviate poverty, benefit families and children. This is the instrumentalist vision that was

---

[22] It has been reported that corporate giants like Hindustan Lever Ltd. is using women from SHGs to help sell their brands of products like shampoos, oils and soaps (email communication from dnrm@ panchayats.org, 28 November 2001).

mentioned earlier. The second paradigm is the poverty alleviation paradigm which sees financial and other services targeted at women as fulfilling women's practical gender needs for income and employment, which would automatically lead the way towards women's empowerment by reducing gender inequality. The third paradigm is the feminist one which sees women's empowerment as an end in itself, and as requiring both processes of internal change as well as organizational changes at the macro level. How does microcredit fit within this paradigm?

According to Mahmud (2003), the weakness of concepts means that the relationships between indicators used to measure empowerment at different dimensions are assumed without causal explanations and without sufficient empirical support. To illustrate this, Mahmud cites Pitt and Khandeker (1995) who found in their study that credit was empowering, since the outcome 'increased income earning time spent in credit-based activities' was assumed to automatically increase women's influence in household decision-making. On the other hand, the study by Goetz and Gupta (1996) found that since male relatives used the loans and women lost direct control over loans, credit in fact was disempowering. Mahmud finds that indicators throw up such paradoxes when they are not grounded in women's lived reality. The primary pivot of gender discrimination is the power hierarchies within which men and women are placed, and within which they experience the same realities differently.

In the context of development, empowerment cannot be *given* to anyone, nor is it a goal that can be reached by an organization or by the state as an institution. It is a process that takes place wherein an inequality moves towards becoming an equality. The inequality that has to alter into equality is the inequality in participation in the various processes of development. These can range from education, health services, housing, livelihoods, employment, remuneration, etc. Empowerment is a process whereby constraints that impede equal participation are reduced so that the inequality starts moving towards becoming equality. In order to understand how constraints can be reduced, we have to move on to the concept of 'spaces'.[23] The stimulus for empowerment as a process to take place comes when something alters in a person's/woman's life that expands spaces. By 'space' is meant that which allows a person the place/freedom/margin to do what s/he intends to do.[24] Every person has an allotment of spaces at a moment in time. This allotment is determined by the domestic and macro environment within which the person lives. Both these environments have the same dimensions as spaces, namely, physical, economic, socio-cultural and political. Spaces determine the person's capacity to act and the ultimate behaviour both within households and outside it. A constriction of spaces amounts to a lack of power to act. It also accounts for fewer alternatives within which behavioural decisions can be taken. Constricted spaces negatively affect *power over, power to, power with* and *power within*. Spaces are also an end for which negotiations take place. Hence, in domestic power dynamics, it is the expansion and contraction of spaces that explain the relative positions of members. Spaces include both tangible and intangible features of categories that are economic, socio-cultural, political and physical.[25]

Physical space constitutes a woman's access to the physical space of her body, of mobility across spaces outside and within her house.[26] Women's ownership, access to, and control of physical space have a significant bearing upon their

---

[23] For a detailed outline of the use of 'spaces' as a concept to capture power and empowerment, see Deshmukh-Ranadive (2002b).

[24] Space is different from capability in the sense that the term 'capability' as used by Amartya Sen and developed by Martha Nussbaum (1995) signifies characteristics within human beings which if deprived, do not allow for a human or a humane existence. Space, on the other hand, is that which allows a person to move, maneouvre and negotiate in developing capabilities.

[25] These dimensions of space are not necessarily exclusive of each other. The purpose of demarcating different kinds of spaces is to facilitate analysis and devise reasonably differentiated categories that can be operationalized in research.

[26] Physical space has been a focus of analysis within feminist geography where behaviour and space are recognized as mutually dependent. One method used is of time geography where everyday routines of women are traced to ascertain the spaces they occupy. The divide between the 'male' public space and 'female' private space is seen as one of the most oppressive aspects of women's lives. See Women and Geography Study Group (1985) and Rose (1993).

position in intra-domestic power dynamics as also outside the domestic unit. Included within the understanding of physical space is women's ownership/access to/control of immovable property such as house, land, commercial space (like a shop), school, place of work, etc. Economic space such as immovable/movable property, assets both tangible and intangible, income, and so on, can allow a woman ownership, access and control of goods and services, which enhance economic independence. Socio-cultural space enhances women's power within the domestic sphere. This space widens when a person's position within kin-based hierarchies is relatively higher than that of others. The placing within families of members is an essential part of the milieu the family is based in. The type of family (nuclear, joint, extended) and kinship structure (unilateral or bilineal) throw up complex determinants of hierarchies. Age, marital status, caste and class are important determinants of socio-cultural space. Political space can be perceived at two levels, private political space and public political space. The first level relates to the political situation that exists within the domestic unit. The conceptualization of this space is different from the socio-cultural space since the latter determines the placement, and political space deals with the dynamics of the working of those placements. Hence, when one is concerned with power dynamics within the domestic domain, it is political space that answers questions on how those dynamics work, while physical, economic and socio-cultural spaces answer questions on why members are so placed. Political space therefore correlates to hierarchical placements of authority and responsibility that are sanctioned by socio-cultural spaces. The second level of political space is related to women's access and control of public office. Political activity, as widely understood, takes place within the public domain and is connected to the administration and governance of society/institutions locally as well as in a larger context. This space is not easy to come by. It is also a function of personality traits like courage, determination and qualities of leadership. The divide between the private and the public is so significant in the lives of women that since political space exists on the other side of the divide, and few bridges exist to assist the crossing, women's access and control of public political space are difficult to come by.

It is not necessary that when spaces expand, they will always result in the process of empowerment. It is important to evaluate the quality of that space. We have to remember that the woman does not live in a vacuum. Since micro-credit intervention does nothing to alter the socio-cultural environment of the household, an expansion of economic space for the woman will not empower her. What actually has to expand is mental space. Mental space is metaphysical in nature and consists of the feeling of freedom that allows a person to think and act. An expansion in this space implies a change in perceptions, which lends a feeling of strength since it precedes action. There is no linear relationship between empowerment and the expansion of spaces. The most important condition for empowerment to take place is an expansion of the person's mental space.

There is, however, no linear relationship between the expansion of physical/economic/socio-cultural/political spaces and that of mental spaces. It has been found that when women operate through collectives the maximum empowerment takes place. The collective allows her to express the injustices she faces as a member of another collective, that is, the household, and society in general. The expansion of mental spaces that allows for action on the part of women is most often facilitated by her membership in a collective that is addressing a similar problem.

The second factor that leads to an expansion of mental spaces is information. Information is a very important source of power as well as an instrument. It is, again, a source and instrument of empowerment. Most often women are oppressed because they are illiterate and do not have access to knowledge. It has been found, however, that education as is formally understood is not a precondition for empowerment to take place. In the first place, the information that is most critical to unleash a process of empowerment is knowledge of the structures of power within which lives are placed. Such knowledge changes self-perception and brings about an awareness of the implications of oppression. Another kind of information that is vital is of rights and duties both as citizens of civic society and also as members within families. This information spans across knowledge about legal machinery as also about human rights and entitlements. Further, information is very important in social mobilization. Groups, like SHGs, in sharing experiences, often gain in strength and solidarity. The intervention of micro-credit by definition imparts information to women. If the facilitating organization takes into account hierarchical structures that contribute towards poverty and disempowerment, then micro-credit interventions can be the catalysts to initiate processes of empowerment.

Just as the individual woman is placed within a domestic environment and has to negotiate her spaces within it, the domestic unit is placed within a larger macro environment shaped by initial physical characteristics,[27] economic opportunities,[28] socio-cultural structures,[29] and political environment.[30] Policies and interventions by state and non-state bodies act upon the macro environment, which in turn alter the domestic environment. Micro-credit succeeds in impacting upon the macro environment. Of all the components, the socio-cultural environment is the most stubborn and difficult to alter, and in consequence, socio-cultural space is difficult to negotiate. The cost of an expansion in this space is often high for an individual woman since it isolates her. That is why collectives and collective action are an effective vehicle to set a process of empowerment into motion. This is exactly the reason that the Self-Employed Women's Association (SEWA) has been heralded as superior to institutions like the Grameen Bank in Bangladesh. The difference between the two is that in the case of SEWA,

---

[27] These depend upon geographical location, soil, climate, landscape, etc.

[28] Offered by the economy, institutions, level of industrialization, state of the rural economy, etc.

[29] Of caste, class, race, religion and inter-group as well as intra-group relations within each category, kinship patterns and gender norms.

[30] Determined by the level, type, quality and transparency of public office. It also depends on the kind of governance that exists in the state. Citizenship and matters related to public life fall within the ambit of political environment.

it is the women who came together first over a series of issues and then built up a series of institutions including the highly successful SEWA bank. In the case of the Bangladesh experience, the Grameen Bank came first and then women were brought together around micro-credit. Therefore, in the former case, the movement preceded the institution and in the second the institution preceded the movement (Samuel, 1999). When the second type of process takes place, in order for it to sustain and ultimately result in empowerment, there has to be more than issues of money to bind members together, which is what has been called the 'credit plus' approach by practitioners (see Fisher and Sriram, 2002). Further, a process of empowerment cannot accelerate unless there is an expansion of socio-cultural space. This is because while an expansion in phycical, economic and political space can lead to an expansion in mental space, with socio-culteral space the logic has to be turned on its head. There has to first be an expansion in mental space for there to be an expansion in socio-cultural space.[31] In order for this to happen, there is need for outside interventions which supplement economic interventions such as micro-credit ones.[32]

---

[31] It may seem as if a conceptualization of power and empowerment in terms of spaces confines empowerment to a static understanding and is in conflict with the actual dynamic nature of its being a process. However, the act of negotiating for more space is the dynamic characteristic of the struggle towards empowerment. Further, in as much as there is action to elbow for more spaces within altered spaces afforded by external stimuli, there cannot be a static understanding of empowerment.

[32] In a project 'Gender Equity in the Family' carried out in the district of Mahbubnagar, Andhra Pradesh, under the Andhra Pradesh District Poverty Initiatives Project (APDPIP), folk theatre has been used to open up the family and household for questioning before entire villages. This project was initiated when it was observed that the formation of micro-credit SHGs aggravate household tensions, since women were becoming economically independent and also held positions of power outside the home by virtue of being in the groups. The theatre performances address issues of gender division of labour in the house, relations between women such as mothers-in-law and daughters-in-law and son preference. The purpose of the project is to alter perceptions within households so that mental spaces expand, which would then lead to an alteration of established hierarchical socio-cultural spaces. See Deshmukh-Ranadive (2003).

The Link

When we attempt to link micro-credit and its impact upon poverty and empowerment, we should look out for the following processes. Poverty of households will have reduced if increases in entitlements are more than increases in responsibilities in such a way that poor households are able to maintain and reproduce themselves in a sustained manner. In other words, the livelihoods generated by micro-credit interventions have to be sustainable over a long period of time so that the poor household can then be free from a cycle of taking repeated loans year after year. Otherwise, the movement out of the vicious circle of poverty will entail a shift into another cycle of formalized indebtedness. In the latter event, the distribution of burdens across members of the household, given existing iniquitous norms, can be expected to fall upon the vulnerable—namely, women and girl children.

Empowerment is more complex to track and trace. There is no doubt about the fact that micro-credit interventions result in a change in the domestic economic environment. At the level of the individual woman, there are changes in physical, economic and public political spaces. Changes in the socio-cultural and private political space are questionable and more unlikely to take place unless there has been concerted effort of the facilitating organization/MFI to deliberately build them into their micro-credit programmes. However, unless a change in these spaces has led to an increase in mental spaces of the women, one cannot talk of empowerment having been set into motion.

Book Outline and Purpose

This book aims at providing insights into the impacts of six NGO and quasi-government interventions in micro-credit, upon poverty alleviation and women's empowerment. The six case studies on social mobilization, micro-credit and women's empowerment are fairly diverse in nature, organizational context, perspective, micro-credit operation and internal functioning (see Table 1.1, also elaborated later).

TABLE 1.1

Profile of Organizations and their Micro-credit Programmes

	SAPAP	Lokadrusti	SML	SSP	ASA	DHAN
Origin of Organization	1996	1988	1992*	1989	1986	1988
Credit	1996	1998	1992	1989	1983	1988
Objective	Poverty reduction	Poverty reduction	Poverty reduction	Women's empowerment	Poverty reduction and dalit empowerment	Poverty reduction
Leadership	Male dalit headed	Male headed	Male headed	Women headed	Male dalit headed	Male headed
Focus	Economic, social, political	Economic, social	Economic	Economic, social, political	Economic, social, political	Economic
Activities	Savings, credit, education, health, watershed, agriculture, Panchayati Raj Institutions (PRIs), violence against women, dalit atrocities	Credit, savings, education, health, watershed, grain bank, violence	Savings, credit, skill development	Savings, credit, networking, disaster, rehabilitation, PRIs, engendering local planning, social issues	Savings, credit, insurance, land rights, housing, dalit atrocities, PRIs, domestic violence	Savings, credit, tank rehabilitation, insurance, skill development, watershed

Target group	Women and men	Women and men	Women	Women	Women and men	Women and men
Rationale for working with women	Anti-poverty**	Male migration, anti-poverty	Efficiency	Anti-poverty, empowerment	Anti-poverty	Anti-poverty, efficiency
Organizational composition	Mixed	Mixed	Mixed	Mainly women	Mixed	Mixed

Notes: *SHARE, the NGO, was initiated in 1992, while SML, the non-bank finance company, was registered in 1999.

**Women considered the poorest amongst the poor.

The book seeks to draw lessons for policy-makers, planners and researchers from the rich diversity in the experiences. Some lessons emerging from the case studies are conceptual in nature, pertaining to women's empowerment and poverty reduction. Others relate to the potential and limitations of micro-credit for women's empowerment and poverty reduction. In addition, the case studies offer useful lessons on what institutional structures and processes facilitate women's empowerment and poverty reduction, and what do not.

In this chapter, our aim has been to provide the context in which micro-credit has assumed importance within development programmes as a tool of poverty alleviation and women's empowerment. We have suggested frameworks for poverty alleviation and empowerment, knitting them together to draw their links with micro-credit. These frameworks and their use in analysis can serve as a basis for designing micro-credit programmes that are more sensitive to the poor and to women. They also facilitate the drawing up of indicators for impact evaluation exercises that are better equipped to capture processes of poverty alleviation and empowerment. The rest of the book demonstrates the impacts of micro-credit projects undertaken in various parts of the country by quasi- and non-governmental organizations.

Murthy et al. (Chapter 2) study the United Nations Development Programme (UNDP)-assisted South Asia Poverty Alleviation Programme (SAPAP) pilot project conducted in three districts of Andhra Pradesh. The Government of Andhra Pradesh (GoAP) decided to emulate the social mobilization approach nurtured in this programme in its major poverty reduction project, namely the World Bank-supported Andhra Pradesh District Poverty Initiatives Project (APDPIP). The GoAP established an independent support organization called the Society for Elimination of Rural Poverty (SERP) to nurture the social mobilization processes demonstrated in SAPAP and to oversee the implementation of the APDPIP. The authors evaluate the impact of this intervention through an examination of SAPAP projects in Mahbubnagar, Kurnool and Ananthapur districts.

In the following chapter (Chapter 3), Anuradha Rajivan presents the interventions of SHARE Micro-finance Limited (SML), a 'for-profit' micro-finance organization currently operating in Andhra Pradesh, with plans to expand to other states as well. The broad objective of the study was to explore the extent to which women's empowerment takes place through the process of formation of women's groups among poor households. These groups have developed as units of micro-credit. Two out of the 13 districts under the SML project were taken up for study.

The fourth chapter by Veena Padia looks at the work of the Development of Humane Action (DHAN) Foundation, which operates its micro-finance programme, the Kalanjiam Community Banking Programme, in Tamil Nadu, Pondicherry, Andhra Pradesh and Karnataka. The *kalanjiam*s or SHGs at the village level have been federated at the cluster and block levels. Of the 20 registered block-level federations, three are urban, one is semi-urban and 16 are rural. Three of these federations—all in Tamil Nadu—have been selected for the study.

In Chapter 5, Soma Kishore Parthasarathy presents a case study of Swayam Shikshan Prayog (SSP), an NGO working in partnership with women's savings and credit groups in the five districts of Latur, Osmanabad, Solapur, Nanded and Amrawati in Maharashtra. SSP has worked towards the promotion of women's savings and credit groups through a two-pronged approach. It seeks to improve livelihoods for women and their families through savings and credit activity and also creates women-centred institutional spaces to address women's strategic needs for agency and negotiation on the other.

Next, Shashi Rajagopalan (Chapter 6) looks at Lokadrusti, an organization based in one of the poorest regions in the country: Khariar in Orissa's Nuapada district. It explores the space available to and used by women in their individual capacities, and as groups engaged in savings and credit.

The penultimate chapter by Kalpana Sankar presents the work of Activists for Social Action (ASA), based at Tiruchirapalli in Tamil Nadu. This study examines what the ASA experience has to say about the role of social mobilization and

micro-finance for poverty reduction and women's empowerment. It also seeks to throw light on the role of economic
empowerment for the overall empowerment of women borrowers. ASA is an MFI based on the Bangladesh Grameen
model of forming SHGs of five members, and federating them
into centres (comprising four SHGs), clusters (comprising
20 centres), branches (comprising five clusters), and franchises (comprising six branches). The micro-finance
programme has been named *Grama Vidiyal*, meaning 'Dawn
of the Rural Poor', and is currently operational in five districts of Tamil Nadu: Tiruchirapalli, Pudukottai, Sivagangai,
Madurai and Dindigul.

In the conclusion (Chapter 8), we situate the six studies
within the frameworks given in the Introduction. The chapter analyses whether micro-credit has proven successful
in alleviating poverty, addressing gender-related poverty and
empowering women. It also highlights strategies that need
to be followed by intervening organizations if the potential
of micro-credit is to be realized. Institutional mechanisms
favourable to poverty alleviation and empowerment are identified.

References

Cantillon, S. and Nolan, B. 2001, 'Poverty within Households: Mea-
suring Gender Differences Using Non-Monetary Indicators', *Feminist Economics*, 7(1): 5–23.
Cassen, R.H., 2002, 'Wellbeing in the 1990s: Towards a Balance Sheet',
Economic and Political Weekly, 37(27): 2789–94.
Deshmukh-Ranadive, Joy, 2001, 'Placing the Household in Perspective. A Framework for Research and Policy', *Asian Journal of Women's
Studies*, 7(1).
———. 2002a, *Database Issues: Women's Access to Credit and Rural Micro-
finance in India*, New Delhi: UN Inter Agency Working Group on
Gender and Development and Human Development Resource Cen-
tre (UNDP).
———. 2002b, *Space for Power, Women's Work and Family Strategies in
South and South-east Asia*, New Delhi: Rainbow Publishers, published in collaboration with the Centre for Women's Development
Studies.
———. 2003, 'Placing Gender Equity in the Family Centrestage: the
Use of *Kala Jatha*', *Economic and Political Weekly*, Review of Women's
Studies, 38(17).

Fisher, Thomas and Sriram, M.S. (eds), 2002, *Beyond Micro-Credit: Putting Development Back into Micro-Finance*, New Delhi: Vistaar Publications.

Goetz, A. and Gupta, R., 1996, 'Who Takes the Credit? Gender, Power and Control over Loan Use in Rural Credit Programs in Bangladesh', *World Development*, 24(1): 45–63.

GOI (Government of India), 1995, *India Country Paper for Copenhagen Summit 1995*, New Delhi: GOI.

Kabeer, N. and Murthy, R.K., 1999, 'Gender, Poverty and Institutional Exclusion: Insights from Integrated Rural Development Programmes (IRDP) and Development of Women and Children in Rural Areas (DWCRA)', in N. Kabeer and R. Subrahmanian (eds), *Institutions, Relations and Outcomes: A Framework and Case Studies for Gender-aware Planning*, New Delhi: Kali for Women.

Mahmud, Simeen, 2003, 'Actually How Empowering is Microcredit?', *Development and Change*, 34(4): 577–605.

Mayoux, L., 1993, 'Gender Inequality and Entrepreneurship: The Indian Silk Industry', *Development Policy Review*, 11(4): 413–26.

Meenakshi, J.V., Ray, Ranjan and Gupta, Souvir, 2000, 'Estimates of Poverty for SC, ST and Female Headed Households', *Economic and Political Weekly*, 29 July.

Mohanty, Manoranjan, 2001, 'On the Concept of Empowerment', in D.K. Singha Roy (ed.), *Social Development and the Empowerment of Marginalised Groups. Perspectives and Strategies*, New Delhi: Sage Publications.

Murthy, R.K. and Rao, N., 1997, *Addressing Poverty: Indian NGOs and their Capacity Enhancement in the 1990s*, New Delhi: Friedrich Ebert Stiftung.

Nussbaum, Martha C., 1995, 'Human Capablities, Female Human Beings', in Martha C. Nussbaum and Jonathan Glover (eds), *Women, Culture, and Development: A Study of Human Capabilities*, Oxford: Clarendon Press.

Pitt, M. and Khandeker, S., 1995, 'Household and Intra-household Impacts of the Grameen Bank and Similar Targeted Credit Programmes in Bangladesh', Paper presented at the workshop on *Credit Programmes for the Poor: Household and Intra-household Impacts and Programme Sustainability*, 19–21 May, Dhaka: World Bank and Bangladesh Institute of Development Studies.

Rose, Gillian, 1993, *Feminism and Geography: The Limits of Geographical Knowledge*, Cambridge: Polity Press in Association with Blackwell Publishers.

Rutherford, Stuart, 2000, *The Poor and their Money*, New Delhi: Oxford University Press.

Samuel, John, 1999, 'The Holy Cow of Micro-credit', *Humanscape*, March.

Sen, Amartya, 1981, *Poverty and Famines: An Essay on Entitlements and Deprivation*, Oxford: Clarendon Press.

Sengupta, Arjun, 2001, 'Right to Development as a Human Right', *Economic and Political Weekly*, 7 July.

60 ✦ Joy Deshmukh-Ranadive and Ranjani K. Murthy

SIDBI (Small Industries Development Bank of India), 2000, *State of the Indian Micro-Finance Industry. Handbook of Micro-Finance*, Vol. 1, SIDBI Micro-Finance Consulting Group, Prepared for a training programme for consultants in micro-finance organized in December 2000, Lucknow.

Stern, Andrew, Stern, Katy, n.d., *Self-Help Group Loans: A Quantitative and Qualitative Study*, Funded by Monsanto Corporation and Washington University.

Women and Geography Study Group, 1985, *Geography and Gender: An Introduction to Feminist Geography*, Leicester, UK: Institute of British Geographers.

Zeller, Manfred, 2000, 'Product Innovation for the Poor: The Role of Microfinance', *Policy Brief* No. 3, in Manohar Sharma (ed). *Microfinance: A Pathway from Poverty*, Washington, DC: International Food Policy Research Institute.

2

Towards Women's Empowerment and Poverty Reduction: Lessons from the Andhra Pradesh South Asia Poverty Alleviation Programme

Ranjani K. Murthy, K. Raju and Amitha Kamath with Research Team*

Introduction

In 1991, the heads of state of the nations of the South Asian Association for Regional Cooperation (SAARC) met in Colombo to deliberate on the actions they could take to attack the abysmal and persistent poverty in their countries. They established the independent South Asian Commission on Poverty Alleviation to study this regional problem and suggest an action plan. The Commission's recommendation led to the 1993 Dhaka Declaration for Eradication of Poverty by 2002, which urged for an empowerment approach to poverty alleviation within which the poor would be

* We would like to acknowledge the contribution of each and every woman who gave her time from her busy schedule. We are also grateful for comments on the first draft from Dr Neera Burra, Assistant Resident Representative, United Nations Development Programme, New Delhi, and the team at the Regional Support Unit, South Asia Poverty Alleviation Programme, Kathmandu.

given support to develop and fully utilize their productive capacities. In 1996, the United Nations Development Programme (UNDP) supported the South Asia Poverty Alleviation Programme (SAPAP).[1] A pilot initiative was launched in three districts of Andhra Pradesh. The project implementation relied on a three-pronged strategy of (a) social mobilization of the poor; (b) skill development; and (c) capital formation. Most of the poor mobilized under the programme were women.

Enthused by the impact of SAPAP, the Government of Andhra Pradesh (GoAP) decided to emulate the social mobilization approach nurtured in the programme onto its major poverty reduction project, namely the World Bank-supported Andhra Pradesh District Poverty Initiatives Project (APDPIP). The GoAP established an independent support organization called the Society for Elimination of Rural Poverty (SERP) to nurture the social mobilization processes demonstrated in SAPAP and to oversee implementation of the APDPIP. Women's empowerment was never an official objective of SAPAP. However, the focus of UNDP's initiative in Andhra Pradesh was on women's empowerment. This study was planned in such a way as to reverse the traditional hierarchical relationship between the 'researcher' and the organization and people being 'researched', thus contributing to institutional learning and development from a gender lens. It was also held that the study should examine SAPAP's impact on not just women's empowerment, but also on poverty reduction and reduction of caste barriers, as the last two elements were integral concerns of SAPAP. In addition, it was expressed that the study should be designed to throw light on current debates on micro-credit, social capital, feminization of poverty and women's empowerment (Box 2.1).

The study examined empowerment at the individual, collective and wider levels through semi-structured interviews (using participatory methods) with individuals, self-help groups (SHGs), village organizations (VOs), and

---

[1] Now absorbed into the Society for Elimination of Rural Poverty.

BOX 2.1

Debates on Micro-credit, Social Capital, Feminization of Poverty and Women's Empowerment

There are three debates centring on micro-credit, social capital, feminization of poverty and women's empowerment. The first debate is on the potential and limitations of micro-credit for women's empowerment, with one set of people holding the position that micro-credit is the panacea for poverty reduction and women's empowerment, and another group arguing that this is far from true—women's labour and time are in fact exploited through such programmes.

The second debate is on the potential and limitations of 'social capital'. One group believes that strengthening social capital— bonding, bridging and linking capital*—can help people emerge from poverty and empower themselves, while another group posits that unless 'physical capital' and 'financial capital' are strengthened, poverty reduction and women's empowerment will be distant goals.

A third debate has centred on whether the focus on gender and poverty deflects attention from the more political agenda of women's empowerment. One position holds that poverty is feminized and that donors and development agencies should focus on the interlinkages between gender, women and poverty. The other position is that evidence on feminization of poverty is weak, and conflating gender issues with poverty takes attention away from the broader agenda of women's empowerment.

Sources: Mayoux, 2001; Murthy and Sankaran, 2001; Woolcock, 2000.
Note: *Bonding social capital refers to social capital arising out of solidarity among members. Bridging social capital refers to capital generated because of groups coming together for common purposes like savings and credit, collective enterprises, and community-based child care. Linking social capital refers to social capital arising out of groups forming links with external institutions like banks, other community and government institutions and social movements (Woolcock, 2000).

mandal-level federations.[2] The impact on poverty and caste discrimination was examined at the village, household and intra-household levels. Comparisons were made between

---

[2] A *mandal* is a sub-district geographical unit unique to Andhra Pradesh. It is both a revenue and development planning unit, but smaller in size than a block.

the current status of members and non-members, as well as members' status before and after group formation. The causality of changes was also ascertained. In a limited way, direct studies of nutritional, health, and education status of members and non-members were carried out by examining the records of schools, *anganwadi* centres and village health sub-centres. Over two months—(August and September 2001), 293 members, 157 non-members, 83 SHGs, 11 VOs, six Mahila Mandal Samakhyas (MMSs), seven auxiliary nurse midwives (ANMs) groups, nine school principals, and nine *anganwadi* workers were met. Semi-structured questions, gender-sensitive participatory methods, focused group discussions and examination of records were the principal methods adopted.

Context

Andhra Pradesh is one of the poorest states in India, with an estimated 30 per cent of its households living in income poverty as per official data.[3] Poverty levels are higher among dalits when compared to members of other communities. If one examines performance vis-à-vis a broader range of human development indices—life expectancy, literacy and per capita income—the absolute value of the Human Development Index (HDI) is only 0.397, which is below the national HDI value (Shiva Kumar, 1995). As in the rest of India, the Gender Development Index (GDI) value here is lower than the HDI value at 0.3888, indicating the persistence of gender inequalities in access to basic needs such as health and education. Poverty is, however, not evenly spread. The coastal districts are better off, while the Telengana and Rayalseema belts are poorer. Mahbubnagar (in the Telengana belt) and Ananthapur and Kurnool (both in the Rayalseema belt) fall under the most backward districts, which is why they were chosen for the implementation of SAPAP.

---

[3] See The World Bank's Project Appraisal Document of the DPIP project.

It is this deep-rooted poverty and its caste- and gender-specific dimensions that the SAPAP project sought to address. As part of the social organization programme, the poor were organized at three levels: hamlet/sub-hamlet level through small homogeneous SHGs, village level through VOs, and the *mandal* level through the MMSs. Over the years, a few occupation- or sector-specific associations also emerged at the village level to address occupational or issue-related problems: labour associations, mining workers' associations, adolescent girls' associations, water users' associations, watershed associations, and so on. By end-March 2001, 5,201 groups were formed in the three districts, covering 936 habitations and 74,777 members, of which 90 per cent were women. Of these 5,201 groups, 3,928 were formed into 536 VOs and 20 *mandal* network organizations (SERP, 2003).

Strong emphasis was placed on training and skill development, since merely forming groups was not enough for building human capacities. To support social mobilization and capacity building, community volunteers (CVs) from the villagers were identified and charged with the responsibility of covering five to six habitations. The third pillar of the SAPAP strategy—capital formation—comprised several interventions. Each SHG was encouraged to start its own small savings and lend this amount to members at rates of interest. In addition, seed capital was injected by the project into individual SHGs and later into VOs and MMSs to increase the capital base of the SHGs.

Methodology and Methods[4]

Empowerment in this study has been seen as a process of 'exposing the oppressive power of existing gender (and social) relations, critically challenging them and creatively

---

[4] It may be useful to distinguish between the methodology and method adopted during the study. Methodology refers to the conceptual framework underlying the strategy, while methods refer to the tools used during the study.

trying to shape different social relations' (Wieringa, 1994). As observed by Williams et al. (1994, cited in Oxaal with Baden, 1997), empowerment can be discussed at three levels: 'power to', 'power with' and 'power within'. 'Power to' refers to the power of individuals to first survive, then control their labour, (family's) resources, body (including freedom from violence), and fertility, and to have a say in decision-making processes within the household and in public. Gender is one variable that has a bearing on the 'power to' dimension of women's empowerment, the others being caste, class, age, headship, marital status, sex of children, and so on. 'Power with' refers to power that derives from people organizing together with a common purpose and understanding to achieve collective goals. In the context of women's and dalit empowerment, 'power with' can be seen as the extent to which women collectives are able to negotiate their gender, caste, class and other interests vis-à-vis institutions of the market (labour market, commodity market, financial market, etc.), the state (government offices, judiciary, gram panchayat, political organizations, etc.), and the community (caste panchayats, social norms on gender and caste, etc.). It also refers to the extent to which collectives are able to influence processes in favour of women and dalits in the wider society. 'Power within' refers to power derived at both individual and collective levels, but involving dimensions such as self-awareness, confidence and assertiveness. In the context of women's and dalit empowerment, it also refers to awareness of strategic gender, caste and class interests.

To ascertain where women were with respect to 'power to' and 'power within' dimensions of empowerment, an individual-level, semi-structured questionnaire was evolved, covering indicators of women's control over their labour, resources, mobility, fertility, sexuality, and awareness of their strategic gender and caste interests. To ascertain dimensions of women's empowerment at collective or 'power with' level, semi-structured questionnaires were designed for holding focused group discussions with SHGs, VOs and MMSs.

Poverty can be discussed at two levels: dimensions and causes. Further, there are gender- and caste-specific aspects to each. An attempt was made to capture the poverty impact at both these levels and also in relation to both gender and caste. In terms of dimensions, poverty can be seen as lack of access to tangible basic needs such as food, clothing, shelter, water, nutrition and health, education, as well as intangible ones such as human dignity and freedom. To effectively capture the impact on gender-specific dimensions of poverty, it is important to go beyond the household to the individual level. The individual member/non-member questionnaire included questions to capture 'access' to basic needs of adult/elderly men, adult/elderly women, boys and girls, in addition to the 'control' aspects of women's empowerment. As there are differences among women and girls on the basis of caste, questions on caste-based equity in access to education, health, water and nutrition were also included. Apart from capturing access to each basic need, an attempt was also made to gauge members' own perceptions on changes in their overall well-being since joining the group.[5] An effort was also made to interview school principals, *anganwadi* workers and ANMs and examine records to ascertain whether education, health and nutrition performance differed between members' and non-members' children of similar economic backgrounds, as well as between members' female and male children.

Looking at the causes, poverty can be seen as an outcome of failure of endowments (land, savings, labour, membership in family/state/community), exchange entitlements (for produce, labour, state/family/community membership), and productivity of assets.[6] Again, these failures operate in gender- and caste-specific ways. Questions on empowerment at the individual level (member/non-member questionnaire) and collective level (SHG/VO/MMS) captured many of these variables automatically. Hence, no set of separate questions was framed to gauge these dimensions.

---

[5] This aspect was explored both through the member/non-member questionnaire, and also the SHG one so as to cross-verify the findings and have a uniform yardstick for comparing improvements of members of different caste and headship backgrounds.

[6] This is an extension of Amartya Sen's entitlement framework. See Murthy and Rao (1997).

The conceptual framework recognized that women are a diverse group and that caste, class, headship, marital status, age, disability and nature of relationship with other village members are important elements of this diversity. An attempt was hence made to examine who is included or excluded from the membership and leadership of groups at various levels and who has access to how much of the loan amounts disbursed. These issues were integrated into the SHG, VO and MMS questionnaires. Among the different aspects of diversity, caste was given particular importance in the context of Andhra Pradesh. Apart from issues of inclusion and exclusion of dalit women, access of dalit women to basic needs and group resources were examined to ascertain whether the group had in any way broken caste hierarchies within and outside villages.

Two criteria shaped the sample size: that it should allow for the generalization of results, and that it should be manageable within the time frame. The main criterion for selection of members was that the members selected in each district should represent caste, age, economic, marital and headship profiles of members in the particular district. Yet another criterion was that the proportion of members with access to non-internal loans selected should roughly match their representation in the district. Comparability with population was again the principle for selection of SHGs. While selecting VOs and MMSs, an attempt was made to roughly capture experiences in different geopolitical zones of the district, experiences of organizations dominated by different caste groups and those of different grades.[7]

---

[7] A grading system of SHGs was evolved by SAPAP that assessed groups on the basis of financial performance and socio-economic impact. A few gender indicators were also included. Based on this system, groups were classified into four categories: A, B, C and D, with Grade A at one end indicating groups performing excellently, and Grade D at the other indicating groups not performing well or defunct. Most SAPAP groups fell under the categories of A or B; hence, one finds more of them in the sample selected for the study. The proportion and number of C and D groups in the sample is too small, and hence comparisons of performance across grades in this study is restricted to (and between) A and B grade groups.

A combination of semi-structured interviews and participatory methods was used as part of the study. Care was taken to ensure that the interviews were conducted in a dialogue mode with the flow of conversation determining the sequence of questions, rather than the sequence of questions in the questionnaire determining the flow. This dialogue was interspersed with the participatory methods, such as a decision-making matrix, gender division of labour, resources mapping, body mapping, mobility mapping, happiness mapping, caste discrimination mapping, *chapati* diagramming (for capturing institutional access), and wealth ranking (for capturing perceptions on poverty impact).

Impact of SAPAP on Poverty Levels

Targeting and Coverage

The first question that comes to mind during discussions on poverty is whether the poor have been reached, and who among the poor have been reached and who have not. Findings suggest that the project has reached out to women from marginalized sections. At the time of group formation, 72 per cent of members were very poor or poor, 38 per cent did not own land, 33 per cent were dalits, 9 per cent were tribals, 11 per cent were Muslims, and 25 per cent were women heading their households. The proportion of members belonging to these categories was higher than their representation in the population in the three districts. In terms of coverage, data from 11 VOs suggested that 79 per cent of the Scheduled Tribes (STs), 47 per cent of the Muslims and 42 per cent of the dalits in the villages covered by the VOs have joined the SHGs. The coverage of backward castes (BCs) and other Hindus (upper-caste groups) is significantly lower at 28 and 19 per cent, respectively, revealing the pro-poor focus and bias of the project.

There is under-representation of women aged below 25 years and of differentially-abled women; this constitutes an area for improvement within the project. Women under 25 years (18–25) constitute 13 per cent[8] of the members, and differentially-abled women constitute 3 per cent—perhaps lower than their representation in the population. The study also supports findings from another study (IFAD, 1999) in that it is difficult for SHGs involved in savings and credit to reach out to elderly poor women (above 55 years) as they have little income from which to save. They constitute only 4 per cent of the members. On the other hand, since they constitute a larger proportion of the population, it seems that they need effective social security measures. Of the poor women who earlier migrated for a season and have joined the groups, a majority has stopped migrating. In contrast, there is evidence that those who migrate for over six to eight months have not joined the groups. To reach them, it may be necessary to include special programmes for wage employment, land allotment, and non-farm employment programmes.

Impact on Generic Dimensions of Poverty

Members of SHGs have better access than non-members with respect to almost every basic need: food, nutrition, water,[9] fuel, electricity, housing, education and health. Consequently, infant deaths, premature child deaths and premature adult deaths[10] are lower among member

---

[8] Data from 83 SHGs gathered in the study. The same data has been used for computing the proportion of elderly members.

[9] The pattern with respect to access to water is mixed. The access of members to safe water and within 0.25 km is slightly lower (92.8 and 66.5 per cent, respectively) than that of non-members (94.8 and 68.2 per cent, respectively). However, a lower percentage of women members reported experiencing water scarcity as compared to non-members (52.9 and 58.6 per cent, respectively).

[10] These terms are not to be confused with infant and child mortality rates or death rates that are calculated from birth and death registers. The figures on infant deaths, for example, have been calculated on the basis of data from the members and non-members surveyed on

households when compared to non-member households. Further, members reported that this access had improved in comparison to the situation five years ago. Household food security has improved since group formation. Faced with food shortage, fewer households adopt negative strategies such as cutting down on consumption of essentials.[11] Members also report that, to a significant extent,[12] this improvement is due to the project interventions: either due to increase in income, or direct interventions by the SHGs and VOs in the contexts of accessing water, gas, electricity and credit. As both members and non-members interviewed were from similar socio-economic backgrounds, better access of members to basic needs cannot be attributed to class differences. An indirect indicator of the poverty impact is the greater reduction in seasonal migration among members compared to non-members and reduction in the proportion of members who reported still having assets pledged with moneylenders.

While poverty, in terms of inadequate access to basic needs, has reduced significantly, it still persists in other dimensions. Poverty manifests itself seasonally: 26 per cent of member households face food shortage during lean months of the year (varies with occupation), of whom 29 per cent are food insecure for more than three months a year; 53 per cent face water scarcity during summer, and have to travel long distances during this period to fetch water; and around 8 per cent do not have access to safe water throughout the year.

---

proportion of infants born after SHG formation (members) or in the last five years (non-members) who died within the first year of their birth.

[11] Nine per cent of the member households reported that they cut down food consumption now compared to 29 per cent before group formation. The comparative (current) figure for non-members is 27 per cent.

[12] The extent to which improvement can be attributed to group activities varies with the basic need. Increase in food security and child enrolment is largely due to group efforts (72.6 and 88 per cent, respectively), while improvements in electricity and the distance at which water is available is only partly due to group activities (11 and 37 per cent, respectively).

Subjective Perceptions of the Poor on Poverty Impact[13]

Just as an outsider's assessment is important, women members' own perceptions of improvement in their condition of poverty is equally important. The wealth-ranking exercise carried out with 83 SHGs suggests that the women themselves perceive a substantial reduction in member households' poverty compared to their condition before group formation. Also, 69 per cent of the members reported that their poverty had reduced since the time of joining the group. A majority attributed this to the activities initiated through the group loan. Nineteen per cent, however, reported a decline in their condition. Half of those who reported a decline attributed it to the failure of effective group interventions and the rest to other reasons such as death of husband, death of animal, migration of an earning member, expenses incurred on the marriage of daughters (dowry), and sickness in the family. Twelve per cent reported no change in their poverty status. Significantly, while 48 per cent of the members were very poor before group formation, the proportion after group formation was only 18 per cent. They had graduated to other categories: either poor or moderately better off.[14]

Impact on Gender-specific Dimensions of Poverty

A review of the gender differentials in access of members and non-members to different basic needs shows that with

---

[13] The yardstick used by the members to classify the poverty levels of member households included both dimensions and causes of poverty: number of meals consumed in a day, number of new clothes bought, ownership of jewels, literacy and education levels, ratio of workers to dependents, ownership of land/irrigated land, source of occupation, amount of indebtedness, ownership, nature and size of house, etc. A few aspects fell into neither dimensions nor causes of poverty in the typical sense, such as number of daughters compared to sons, but reflected the social reality of gender discrimination in society.

[14] The term 'moderately better off' refers to those households that are able to meet basic needs round the year, but do not have as high a level of savings or assets as the wealthy people in the village.

respect to food, nutrition, clothing, education and access to institutional delivery, the differentials are lower among members than non-members. Gender disparities among member households with respect to mortality and access to food are lower compared to non-members. A greater proportion of members, compared to non-members, reported a decline in gender disparities in the last five years.

The difference between the extent of gender disparities in member and non-member households was not uniform with respect to all basic needs. Gender disparities were much lower among members with respect to nutrition, child/adult premature death, and ability of women to sign. There is, however, little difference in the extent of gender bias with respect to norms on eating, male preference in distribution of food, and gender bias in access to clothing.

A point of concern is that though gender disparities are lower among members than non-members, they do persist. In 90 per cent of the member households, wherein different family members do not eat together, women and girls eat last.[15] In 46 per cent of member households, all members do not have equal access to special food, and gender discrimination is prevalent. A slightly greater proportion of girls and women report not having purchased any new set of clothes in the previous year (both 8 per cent) when compared to boys and men (7 and 6 per cent, respectively).

Impact on Causes of Poverty

If one examines the causes of poverty, the project has made a significant impact on the causes of *household* poverty: on ownership of productive assets, diversification of skills and enterprises, relations of employment[16] and returns to labour power and produce. Though 38 per cent of the members continued to come from landless households, the

---

[15] This male privilege seems to decline with age. No preference seems to be given to elderly men, vis-à-vis elderly women.
[16] Whether they are wage labourers, bonded labourers, own account workers, or unpaid family labourers.

number would have been higher if not for the project's interventions. The greatest differences between members and non-members' access to means to overcome poverty were in the area of access to movable productive assets: livestock and equipment, diversification of sources of livelihood (men and women), and access of women members to employment. The least difference was in the area of acquisition of land, access to just wages (both men and women), nature of work that women in particular did, and income from activities that men and women undertook. A point of concern is the higher leakage reported on alcohol consumption by member households as compared to non-member households.

Gender-specific Causes of Poverty

The differences between members and non-members were studied with respect to the following parameters: independent access to means of overcoming poverty, productive assets they have control over, adequate sources of own livelihoods, employment at just wages, and adequate income and control over their own and husband's income. Results showed that access and control is better with members than with non-members. Further, the proportion of women members reporting an increase in sources of livelihood *managed by them* and an improvement in nature and quantum of employment was greater than the proportion reporting a decline. The reverse was true in the case of non-members. The shift away from stagnant agriculture into service and trade was also higher in the case of women members compared to non-members. The *difference* between members' and non-members' independent means to overcome poverty was highest with respect to the following causal variables: perceived rights over livestock; followed by women's legal ownership of land acquired through the group and their ability to have a say over the use of husband's income. The least difference was noted with respect to wages, number of sources of livelihood, and number of days for which employment is available for women.

In *absolute terms*, the picture is different. Gender disparities continue to persist with respect to access to each and
every means of overcoming poverty, other than the number
of days of employment. The worst gender disparity can be
found with respect to legal and normative ownership[17] of
productive and immovable assets (not acquired through the
group), wage differentials (women's wages are 56 per cent
that of men), and consequent income differences.[18] Coupled
with the decline in their husbands' access to employment,
the burden of earning for the family seems to be shifting on
to women. In contrast to the situation five years ago, women
members now work for a slightly more number of days than
men, and in conditions that need to be improved. Further,
the social relations of women's employment have not
changed significantly (62 per cent report working in part
bondage) and continue to be exploitative. Another concern
is that, about half the women reported that they did not have
full or major control over the income they earned. That is,
they handed over more than 75 per cent of their incomes to
their husbands or parents-in-law.

Caste, Class, Headship, Religion and Impact of Poverty

Caste   The access of different community groups to basic
           needs is not uniform. Access of dalit members to
basic needs is one of the lowest (except to toilets and gas),
and access of upper castes and Lambanis is among the highest, with access of other communities falling in between.[19]
The lower access of dalits can be attributed to lower levels of
land ownership, higher levels of income poverty, and prevalence of caste-based discrimination. The proportion of dalit

---

[17] Whether they feel that they have the powers to dispose of it as per
their choice.
[18] The average monthly income earned by women from the activity
they managed was Rs 139, while men reported earning Rs 223 on an
average.
[19] As the representation of upper castes and Lambanis in the representative sample is low (there being fewer SHG members from these
communities), a larger sample size is required to arrive at a firm conclusion.

member households facing food and water shortage was higher than that of member households from other communities (other than STs). More dalit member households lived in rented houses (along with Muslims) and without access to electricity when compared to members of other communities. They had lower access to drainage (along with STs and Muslims) than other communities. A greater number of dalit women delivered babies without support from trained personnel when compared to women members of any other community. The number of infant, child and premature deaths was the second highest in this community (following Muslims). A significant 27 per cent of dalit women felt that they and their family members experienced caste-based discrimination by health personnel. Also, 32 per cent reported that they had to bear with snide comments when they wore new clothes (even from fellow SHG/VO members). Surprisingly, the extent of ownership of toilet and gas was second highest (following Muslims) in dalit houses. This perhaps reflects a combination of the following factors: greater subsidy for dalits in this context and the fact that the grounds wherein women have to go to defecate are located far away or women's greater autonomy to decide household priorities. In general, poverty (income and human) was higher and gender disparities lower amongt dalits, while the reverse was true in the case of upper-caste and Lambani women, with other caste groups falling in between the extremes.

Class　As mentioned, one of the strengths of the project is its effective targeting of the poor. The project has also made a quantum impact on the access of poor women members to credit, as a majority of them had not accessed loans earlier. However, like in many other micro-credit-based projects, the poorest members who have joined groups have not been able to access as much number and quantum of loans as the poor, moderately off, and better off members, as illustrated in Table 2.1 (IFAD, 1999).

Another concern is that the proportion of overdue loans to loan taken was the second highest (48 per cent) among the very poor, revealing their poor ability to absorb credit. The pattern of lesser absorption capacity of the very poor

TABLE 2.1
Access to Loans across Economic Status of Members

Category of members	Average number of loans	Average loan amount (rupees)
Very poor	5	10,988
Poor	12	15,991
Moderate	9	21,414
Better off	6	12,200

may explain the fact that a majority of the very poor have managed to climb a step higher, to the 'poor' category, but have not been able to overcome poverty.

Religion Muslim households and women have greater private access to most gender-specific needs[20] and non-gender-specific basic needs.[21] In contrast, this is not true of publicly provisioned ones. The key question here is, whether greater access to gender-specific basic needs (toilet, gas, tap water) is due to greater control of women over household income or whether it reflects restrictions on women's mobility.[22] Yet another possibility is the lower amount of leakage of income on alcohol within this religious group when compared to other communities. Food shortage is the least in Muslim households as per information reported by Muslim members. As many as 74 per cent of Muslim women members reported that their household had access to tap water, when compared to the average of 48 per cent. Similarly, the percentage that reported having access to gas was again the highest (18.5 per cent). Muslim women had maximum access to toilets when compared to women from other communities, though it is far from adequate in itself. They had the highest access to electricity

---

[20] These are needs, the absence of which affects women more than men.
[21] These are needs, the absence of which affects men and women equally.
[22] The greater access cannot be attributed to the greater prosperity of Muslim households. They have lesser access to land and income levels are lower than those of upper-caste households.

(89 per cent) as well. However, they had the least access to their own house (78 per cent) and second least access to drainage (14.8 per cent). The former could be attributed to the absence of government housing programmes for Muslims, and the latter to lower attention by government to strengthening infrastructure in Muslim colonies. Higher infant and child deaths, despite better access to food, point to the possibility of lower access to health care or poor health-seeking behaviour.

Headship There is evidence that with respect to absolute levels of income poverty, MHHs (male-headed households) perform better than WHHs (women-headed households) and have seen greater improvement. This is not surprising since although WHHs had greater access to loans (in terms of numbers) when compared to women from MHHs, the quantum of loan they could access or absorb was lower (in particular, by widows and destitutes).[23] However, in MHHs, a strong difference exists between women's access to gender-specific basic needs and women's non-gender-specific ones: food, electricity and housing. The project has had greater impact on the latter than the former. Similarly, gender disparities among children in terms of access to food, nutrition and education are also higher in MHHs than in WHHs, debunking the popular theory that women are women's worst enemies. It was reported by 77 per cent of the MHHs that they were able to access three meals round the year, when compared to 66 per cent in the case of WHHs. Gender disparities in food distribution, special food, and clothing were higher in MHHs than in WHHs. This is starkly reflected in the fact that in WHHs there was no female infant death (notwithstanding the biological disadvantage prevalent in male infants) while in the case of MHHs, 43 per cent of infant deaths were those of females. Similarly, 29 per cent of child premature deaths in WHHs

---

[23] In terms of numbers, younger women (below 25 years) appear to have lesser access to loans than older women. However, in terms of average quantum of loan they record the highest and *women above 55 years are able to absorb the least*. The quantum of overdue is also the highest among the elderly age group.

were those of female children, wherein the comparative figure in the case of MHHs was 57 per cent.

Impact on Women's Empowerment

Impact on Power of Individual Women to Exercise Control over their Lives

The power of individual women members (and their female foetuses/infants/ children) to first survive and then have control over their labour, mobility, resources, repro-duction, body and decision-making processes has indeed improved since group formation. The degree of power exercised by members on these issues is significantly higher than that of non-members. Details on power of women over each aspect of their life are elaborated first, followed by overall observations on where maximum difference between member and non-member performance is discernible, and where it is not.

Power to Survive

The power to survive is a key fundamental right of people. It is also one of the articles in the Child Rights Convention, as well as an element of the Convention on the Elimination of All Forms of Discrimination against Women (CEDAW). Here, we shall examine the right of female foetuses, infants, children and women to survive. Of those members who went in for induced abortion (6 per cent), a lower proportion went in for scanning when compared to non-members. None reported sex-selective abortion as the reason for undergoing scanning, but this is a matter worth investigating, as a significant son preference seems to prevail.[24] The fact that a lower proportion of members than non-members went in for scanning before abortion indicates the possibility that the practice of female foeticide may be lower among members. This view is also supported by the evidence on infant deaths. A higher proportion of female infant deaths to total infant deaths was reported among non-members than members. The same pattern held true for female child/adult

---
[24] See the section on 'power within'.

premature deaths among members and non-members.[25] Though no data was gathered on death related to pregnancy, the data on abortions is an indirect indicator, where 35 per cent of abortions took place in the sixth month or after among members, when compared to 45 per cent in the case of non-members. Abortions after six months pose high risk for pregnant women. While overall female foetuses, infants and children in member households may have a greater chance to survive than non-members, it is a point of concern that *all the members who knew the sex of the aborted foetus reported that it was a female one.* As the sample size of members who went in for abortion is small, this may be studied in greater depth. The fact that 35 per cent of the abortions took place in the sixth month or afterwards is also a point of concern as it poses many risks for the mothers. The greater proportion of women in the age group of 36–45 years who went in for scanning before abortion reported that the foetus was female.

Women's Control over their Labour/ Access to Family Labour

An indicator of women's control over their labour is the degree to which they have access to the labour of their husbands for the activities that they (women) manage (for example, livestock), compared to the degree to which the husbands have access to women's labour for the activities that the men manage (for example, agriculture). Women members report greater access to their husband's labour than non-members, though it is lower than the access of husbands to their wives' labour. Another indicator of women's control over their labour is the degree to which they take up non-traditional tasks (for example, marketing) and enterprises (for example, cycle shop, carpentry, ice-cream vending, clothes shop, etc.). Again, the proportion of women

---

[25] Given the biological advantage of females to males at birth, female infant and child mortality should be lower than male infant and child mortality.

members reporting that they have started carrying out non-traditional tasks and enterprises vis-à-vis the activities they were already doing is higher than in the case of non-members. More women members (53 per cent) than non-members (21 per cent) reported that when they went to meetings and banks, their husbands did the housework and took care of the children.

An area of concern is the possibility that members draw upon their children's labour much more than non-members do. While 56 per cent of the members reported using female children's labour and 39 per cent reported using male children's labour (predominantly in non-school hours), the proportion of non-members reporting the same was 45 and 27 per cent, respectively. While husbands of members reported using female and male children in non-school hours to almost the same extent (16.5 and 15.5 per cent, respectively), women members reported using female child labour much more than male child labour. Member dependency on children's labour during off-school hours can be attributed to the fact that as yet, men do not routinely help out in domestic work or child care. Only 27 per cent of them reported that their husbands did housework and provided child care support as a routine. This was very similar to the figure reported by non-members (26 per cent).

The degree to which women and men have access to the labour of family members and have broken norms on the gendered division of labour varies with community, age and headship. Dalit women had the greatest access to husbands' labour and BC men had the greatest access to their wives' labour. Muslim women and men had the least access to each other's labour, pointing to possible strong division of enterprises themselves. Muslim women, however, had the maximum access to their children's labour, pointing to the possibility that if women cannot draw help from their husbands, then they draw upon the labour of children in non-school hours. The same was true of women in WHHs, when compared to women in MHHs. The trend of women entering new domains was the highest among Muslim women and the least among dalits. However, it is quite possible that the greater proportion of dalit women was already engaged in marketing and purchasing activities before joining SHGs. The trend of men helping out women routinely in reproductive tasks was least among Muslims. Hence, it is not surprising that Muslim women reported the maximum increase in their workload.

Women's Access to and Control over Resources

With respect to women's access to and control over other resources, savings were one resource to which members had significant access.[26] While 79 per cent of members reported savings as a household asset created in the last five years, only 4 per cent of non-members did so. While all members with savings reported that savings were legally theirs as they were in their name, the proportion was lower in the case of non-members who had savings (83 per cent). Further, while 78 per cent of members with savings felt that they had powers to dispose of savings on their own, only 50 per cent of non-members felt so. Another key asset for women was jewellery. Though jewellery is a non-productive asset, women perceive it as their own to a greater extent than land and immovable assets. Apart from redeeming jewellery pledged in the past,[27] 14 per cent of members reported having purchased jewellery in the last five years when compared to 5 per cent of non-members. Also, 91 per cent of the members expressed that they collected receipts in their own names when they purchased jewellery; hence, it was quasi-legally their own. In contrast, only 57 per cent of non-members reported such ownership.

----

[26] Data from SC-exclusive group, BC-exclusive group, other caste (OC)-exclusive group, BC/OC-mixed group, and dalit-mixed group suggest that the average saving per member was maximum among upper-caste-exclusive group (Rs 2,190) followed by Muslim-exclusive groups (Rs 1,868). The average saving per member was least among BC groups (Rs 1,329).

[27] Sixty per cent of those who had mortgaged an asset had pledged jewellery. Against this, 25 per cent of those who had redeemed an asset stated that jewellery was redeemed. Thus, jewellery may be accorded lower priority (compared to land) while deciding which asset should be redeemed.

Also, 67 per cent of members reported that they had the powers to dispose of their jewellery independently, while none of the non-members reported having such powers. The pattern with respect to utensils was also similar, though very few members reported utensils as new assets created through the programme.

An area of concern is that a member's control over immovable assets created through the programme appears to be lower than that over movable ones. Women's legal or/ and perceived ownership of land and houses, created through the programme, is for example lower than their ownership of savings, jewellery, or utensils. Often, immovable assets owned by poor people are more expensive and valuable than the movable ones they own. Land, in particular, is a key productive asset and a source of livelihood. Yet another issue is that women's actual power to dispose of many assets or decide on their use is lower than their legal ownership of the same.

Other than livestock and shops, Muslim women members reported the maximum asset creation for their household through joining the group (though when they joined the group, most Muslim households did not own land). This may be due to the fact that there is lower leakage of men's income into alcohol, as also that none of the Muslim women consume alcohol in contrast to women from dalit, BC and ST communities who do. A point of concern is that dalit women, who are the poorest, reported the least amount of acquisition of immovable assets.[28] Acquisition of immovable assets was higher among women in MHHs than women in WHHs, while no particular pattern was found with respect to acquisition of movable ones. The disadvantage of dalits and WHHs in acquiring immovable assets can be linked to the low wages and income earned by dalits and women when compared to upper castes and men from their livelihood sources. With a few exceptions, women members above 45 years seemed to have acquired fewer assets compared to women from other age groups. Thus, religion, caste, age and

---

[28] There was no community-specific pattern with respect to ownership of movable assets.

headship have important bearing on the acquisition of immovable assets. The power of women to independently dispose of assets that they legally own was, however, higher among elderly women and women in WHHs. No specific pattern was found with respect to caste or religion on powers to dispose of movable assets but with respect to immovable assets, Muslim women appear to have slightly greater powers to dispose of assets when compared to women from other communities (see Box 2.2 for an overview of the relation between access to loan and control of assets).

Women's Freedom to Move and Interact

Freedom to move and interact is another element of empowerment. It determines access to information, markets, and resources. Restrictions on women's movement also clearly impinge on their human rights. A significantly (66 per cent) greater proportion of members than non-members reported visiting new places in the last five years. The new places visited by members were the MMS office (97 per cent), banks (79 per cent), the *mandal* development office (67 per cent), the *mandal* revenue office (65 per cent), the panchayat (37 per cent), the UNDP district office (28 per cent), the Collector's office (26 per cent), and the government block office (21 per cent). The proportion of non-members who reported going to these places was lower, except in the case of the panchayat and block offices.

More Muslim and BC women reported having visited new places than dalits, while a greater proportion of dalit women reported travelling without husbands. The fact that fewer dalit women report visiting new places perhaps indicates that either dalit women are very busy eking out livelihoods, or they have visited some of these places earlier; rather than indicating restrictions on their mobility. More women in WHHs reported expanded mobility than women in MHHs, pointing to the possibility of greater restrictions on women's mobility in MHHs. A lower proportion of women (under 25 years) reported expanded mobility compared to older women

BOX 2.2

Does Access to Loan Lead to Control?

Even if the loan is partly for an activity managed by men, the key question is whether women are taking the decisions on whether to take a loan, its purpose, its amount, repayment of loan, and how the profits should be used. Such an analysis strongly suggests that less than 25 per cent of men take the decision by themselves on these areas. Loan-related decisions are either taken jointly or exclusively by members (around 37 per cent). Thus, the fact that agriculture-related loans constitute a significant proportion of the loans may be partly due to women's prioritization of food security* and partly due to male control over credit. On the whole, it can be concluded that most members are not mere puppets channelling loans to men, but play significant roles in decision-making on credit, albeit within the parameters of the gender division of management of livelihoods.

Who bears the burden of repayment and savings?

A significant 55 per cent of the members stated that they repaid loans taken from the group from income generated through the activity or household income, and another 21 per cent by cutting down consumption of luxuries (*paan*, tobacco). However, 11 per cent reported that they cut down on family consumption for repaying loans, and 6 per cent stated that they borrowed from outside to repay loans. The rest did not state clear reasons.

During the months when work is available, all group members save out of their own income. However, during the lean season, only 64 per cent stated that they saved out of their own or household income. Seventeen per cent reported cutting down consumption of luxuries to save with the group. However, 25 per cent reported that they adopted negative strategies to save: cutting down own consumption (15 per cent), borrowing from others (3 per cent), or migrating (7 per cent).

Note: *As it contributes directly, and to a greater extent, to family food security than other activities.

in SHGs. The need to take care of young infants might be a key factor in this regard.

Another indicator of women's mobility is their ability and freedom to travel without male escorts. With respect to all the offices listed earlier, more members than non-members reported travelling without their husbands or other men. Yet another dimension of mobility is the mode of travel. A slightly greater proportion of members reported learning to drive a new vehicle than non-members. Members, however, have lower access to vehicles than their husbands. Another aspect of women's mobility is whether they have the freedom to move during all times. Almost an equal percentage of members and non-members reported that there are restrictions placed on their movement during menstruation (55 per cent). However, 38 per cent of members reported a reduction in such restrictions in contrast to 9 per cent in the case of non-members. Restrictions on entering the kitchen (21 per cent) were much less than those on visiting temples (80 per cent) or sacred groves (87 per cent), showing the difficulty in breaking gender and religious norms. Restrictions on entering the kitchen during menstruation were lower among dalit women, but higher with respect to visiting sacred groves or temples. As expected, such restrictions were higher among women in MHHs than women in WHHs. No age-specific pattern was discernible.

The freedom to interact and make friends outside the family is a basic human right. Friends can be a social resource in times of material and emotional crises. Eighty-three per cent of the members reported making new friends in the last five years, in contrast to 26 per cent in the case of non-members. Of the members with new friends, 92 per cent mentioned that they had friends from other caste SHGs, in contrast to 75 per cent in the case of non-members. Caste- and religion-based norms are slowly being broken. Forty-three per cent reported that among their new friends were men too, in contrast to 30 per cent in the case of non-members. Thus, norms and attitudes on caste and gender are slowly changing, and to a greater extent in members than in non-members. However, the fact that interaction with men is still limited is a concern, as most large traders are men and building friendships with such men can lead to better returns in the commodity market. Another issue is the fact that the proportion of dalit women making new friends and making friends from other communities is lower than the average, pointing to the heavy workload of dalit women as well as the fact that while caste-based norms are breaking down, they are far from absent. It is Muslim women who seem to have found the maximum increase in friendships and contacts outside the community after joining a group. It is also the younger women (under 25 years) who, despite their heavy workloads, are investing more time in making friends, and that too outside the community.

Women's Access to Leadership Positions

The SHGs, VOs and MMSs have themselves expanded avenues for women to assume leadership positions. Some SHGs have two leaders (without designation) while others have leaders with designations such as president, secretary and treasurer. Two key criteria cited for selection of leaders are the ability to function democratically and the leadership quality. Each group is supposed to rotate its leaders periodically. In practice, this system has been institutionalized in 66 per cent of the SHGs. Twenty-eight per cent of the members have at one time or the other assumed leadership positions within their groups. A positive aspect is that the proportion of dalit and Muslim women who have assumed leadership positions is higher than their representation as members. Sixty-seven per cent of the leaders are from either poor or very poor backgrounds, compared to the fact that 59 per cent of the members currently[29] fall under these two categories. However, the representation of the very poor alone in leadership positions (15 per cent) is slightly lower than in the membership population (18 per cent). Tribal members are found less as leaders (4 per cent) than as members (9 per cent). Though dalit members are slightly over-represented in leadership positions, there are indications that this may be due to the fact that dalit-exclusive SHGs appoint more leaders per group than the fact that they are elected into leadership positions in mixed

---

[29] The proportion was higher (72 per cent) at the time of group formation.

SHGs. In 64 per cent of the mixed SHGs comprising dalits and non-dalits, no dalit is found in a leadership position.

It is encouraging that leadership positions of VOs and MMSs are held exclusively by women. Like in SHGs, the proportion of dalits as leaders of VOs, particularly as presidents and treasurers, is around double their membership in SHGs covered by the VOs. However, unlike in SHGs, Muslim women are found less in leadership positions of VOs than their representation as members, probably due to restrictions on their mobility and interaction outside the village. Similar to the leadership pattern in SHGs, ST women rarely assume leadership positions (less than their representation as members). BC women are under-represented as presidents, but are slightly over-represented in other leadership positions. OC women are, surprisingly, over-represented in both positions. A similar pattern is observed with respect to MMS leadership.

A significant proportion of presidents (56 per cent) and other leaders of VOs are in the 26–35-year age group, neither too young nor too old to take on such responsibilities. None of the presidents and other VO leaders studied comes from well-off sections, with 78 per cent falling below the poverty line. It is however a point of concern that single women are found less in leadership positions of VOs when compared to their representation in the population. This could be due to their heavy workload. A similar pattern was found at the MMS level (with the exception of one MMS), except that the very poor seem under-represented in MMS leadership.

A point of concern is that only a small proportion of VO staff (other than community health assistants and health workers) are women. Similarly, the bookkeepers appointed directly by SHGs were also predominantly male. On the positive side, the proportion of dalits and poor among the VO staff was commendable. Seventy-five per cent of VNAs (veterinary assistants) attached to VOs, for example, were dalits and belonged to households below the poverty line. A similar gender composition was found with respect to five of the six MMSs studied, pointing to the need for bringing in more women into staff positions. That it is possible to increase the proportion of women staff is indicated by the example of one MMS, where women constitute 60 per cent of the staff.

With respect to accessing political spaces outside the SHGs, 87 per cent of the members had voter identity cards against 80 per cent in the case of non-members. The freedom to independently exercise their votes was expressed by 60 per cent of the members as against 37 per cent of the non-members. It is estimated that in the recent elections, women members contested between 20 and 25 per cent of reserved seats in gram panchayats for women.[30] In fact, in one district, women contested 54 out of 60 seats in six gram panchayats, and won around 18 per cent. An area for strengthening is women's access to leadership positions in caste panchayats.[31] Though SHGs are occasionally invited for meetings, panchayat leadership is in the hands of men.

Women's Control over Reproduction

A more subtle dimension of the empowerment is the power of women to make reproductive choices with respect to the number of children,[32] spacing between children, usage of contraceptives, nature of contraceptives, decision to abort, and space of delivery. In all these respects, it was found that women members had a greater say than non-members. The greatest gap between the reproductive decision-making powers of members and non-members pertained to abortion. Fifty-one per cent of members reported that they took the

---

[30] As per the 73rd Constitutional Amendment passed in 1993, 33 per cent of the seats to local self-governance institutions at the village, *taluka*, and district levels are to be reserved for women. In Andhra Pradesh, elections got over towards the end of the study and exact figures are being collected by each district. Data was available for one district.

[31] Unlike gram panchayats, which are statutory and not caste-specific, caste panchayats are non-statutory and specific to each caste group. They are traditional institutions, having existed for hundreds of years.

[32] Though whether to have children is also an important area of decision-making, this was not examined as it was felt that it was premature to examine this issue.

decision for or against abortion, while only 30 per cent of non-members reported such choice. Such a gap in reproductive decision-making can be attributed to the confidence women have gained after joining the group, as well as the greater cash contribution of women to the family income. Of the SHG members, 61 per cent reported improvement in reproductive decision-making in the past five years when compared to 25 per cent in the case of non-members. The greater reproductive choice is also reflected in better couple protection rates. Among SHG members, 87 per cent pointed out that they or their husbands adopted contraceptive methods, as against 72 per cent in the case of non-members.

Though reproductive decision-making of members is higher than in non-members, most reproductive decisions in member families' are taken largely by husbands and to a lesser extent by mothers-in-law or/and fathers-in-law. Women in WHHs (including households where the husband is sick or has migrated) had greater decision-making power on this issue than women in MHHs. Compared to women in other age categories, women below 25 years reported greater powers to decide on spacing, contraception, abortion, and place of delivery, but not on how many children to have.

Women's Control over their Bodies

Women's control over their bodies is the dimension of women's empowerment which is the most difficult to achieve. The key issues include women's ability to live lives free of violence at home, at the workplace, and in the broader public space.[33] The percentage of members reporting domestic violence (45 per cent) was significantly lower than

---

[33] Yet another issue is women's ability to negotiate fulfilment of their sexual needs, and resist any form of marital rape. These two issues were left out as they were highly sensitive in nature, and it was felt that they could be best addressed through in-depth case studies than large-scale studies.

the percentage of non-members reporting such incidence (74 per cent). Further, when compared to the situation five years ago, 18 per cent of the members reported less violence as against 5 per cent in the case of non-members. In the case of members, the incidence of mental abuse was highest (16 per cent) followed by wife beating (13 per cent) and physical violence following drunken behaviour (13 per cent). Other forms of violence reported were suspicion, dowry harassment, and girl child abuse. The forms of domestic violence among non-members were similar, but the incidence of wife beating (29 per cent) and suspicion was significantly higher (9 per cent). Among both members and non-members and with respect to all forms of violence, husbands were the main perpetrators of domestic violence, and not parents-in-law as the popular assumption goes.

The proportion of women reporting domestic violence even now was highest among Muslims (78 per cent) and the least among BCs (15 per cent). The maximum decline in domestic violence since group formation has taken place among BCs (19 percentage points) and the least among dalits (0 per cent). Almost all forms of violence were reported in all communities, other than girl child abuse that was not reported among Muslims and BCs. The proportion of women in MHHs reporting domestic violence was significantly higher than in WHHs (75 per cent). As is to be expected, all forms of violence were lower among WHHs, other than dowry harassment (which was more or less similar) and suspicion by family members (which was higher). Domestic violence declined with the age of women. Suspicion, girl child abuse, and dowry harassment were absent by the time women were 45. Wife beating, dowry harassment, and suspicion were highest in the case of women under 25 years, but none of the women in this age group reported girl child abuse. Women less than 25 years reported the least decline in violence in the last five years.

Significant differences in incidences of violence at the workplace were found between members and non-members. Twenty-nine per cent of members reported facing some form of violence at workplace against 62 per cent of non-members. Violence at the workplace had declined by 30 per cent after members joined SAPAP SHGs, in contrast to 7 per cent in the case of non-members. Seventeen per cent of members reported obscene comments, 6 per cent reported caste-based comments, 5 per cent reported sexual harassment at workplace and some reported other forms of violence. Similar pattern was noted in the case of non-members. The proportion of women reporting violence at workplace was least among BCs and highest among dalits. Such incidence was higher among women in WHH (47 per cent) and women of two age groups: those less than 25 years (86 per cent) and those above 45 years (84 per cent). That the situation of dalit women may have been worse some years back is indicated by the fact that they reported the maximum decline in violence at the workplace. Women below 25 years did not report any decrease in violence at the workplace in the last five years.

An area of concern is the fact that 34 per cent of dalit members reported caste-based violence in public, against 23 per cent in the case of dalit non-members. At the same time, 64 per cent of dalit members reported a decline in caste-based violence as against 25 per cent in the case of non-members. This data suggests that the increase in caste-based violence cannot be ascribed to a backlash to the growing organization of dalits, but may reflect the possibility that members are more confident about reporting such violence. This aspect needs to be examined in greater detail.

Empowerment at the Individual Level

While women's control over all aspects of their lives has improved, there are differences regarding aspects of their lives over which they have greater control. On the whole, women seem to have greater control over their savings and jewellery, mobility, friendships, ability to invite or visit their parents when they want, and decide whom they want to vote for. A majority of them said that they did not face violence at the workplace. Women have started entering the male domain of leadership in local self-governance institutions. On the other hand, they have lesser control over their reproductive work, nature/social relations of productive work they do, immovable property of the household and reproductive rights. A significant proportion continues to experience violence at home. Also, women occupy few staff positions in VOs and MMSs.

The maximum difference (the difference being 45 percentage points or higher) between members and non-members' performance with respect to individual empowerment can be seen in the following variables: mobility, happiness, access to friends outside their family, access to savings in their own name, extent to which they have started embarking on non-traditional tasks and enterprises, extent to which their workplace is free of violence, and perhaps the extent of their participation in local self-governance institutions. The least difference (10 percentage points or lower) can be observed with respect to the following variables: extent of women's access to husband's labour (productive and reproductive), ability to control alcohol consumption on the part of their husbands, rights to land and house, and control over wage levels/gender differentials in wages.

Empowerment at the Collective Level: 'Power With'

This section examines the collective power of women members to negotiate their gender, caste, class and other interests with respect to institutions of the market, the state and the community. It also examines how women collectively intervened to address gender imbalances within the family. Interventions by SHGs—the first layer of the collective—are first examined, followed by an analysis of interventions by VOs and MMSs—the second and third layers respectively. Caselets of positive intervention, mainly from one district (those from other districts are yet to be documented systematically) are illustrated in Boxes 2.3 to 2.7.

Collective Interventions in Family

There has been no hesitation on the part of SHGs to collectively intervene in the family. Seventy-one per cent of the SHGs reported having motivated some of the member families to send female children to school and 16 per cent extended support to widows to get married. Fifty-one per cent of the SHGs reported having intervened in members' families to prevent child marriages, 18 per cent to prevent dowry harassment, 17 per cent to prevent temple prostitution, 31 per cent to prevent male alcoholism, and 16 per cent to prevent sex-selective abortion. Although it is commonly believed that domestic violence, particularly wife beating, is a private affair and socially acceptable, there is an encouraging finding: 17 per cent of the SHGs reported that they intervened collectively in instances of domestic violence against women. Such examples have recently been documented and disseminated among SHGs. Such a move is important as domestic violence is high. Interestingly, dalit-exclusive SHGs appear to intervene more to promote gender-just practices within the family, than either BC-exclusive SHGs or dalit-mixed and other mixed SHGs.

VOs and MMSs have also intervened in similar ways in families. A unique experiment on the part of the Orrakkal MMS in Kurnool district has been to bring together single women in a block on to one platform to fight for their property, maintenance, residence, and other rights within the family, as well as to ward off any exploitation from the community (Box 2.3). One MMS has also provided karate training to interested members and their female children to enable them to protect themselves in instances of violence within the family and the wider community.

Collective Interventions at the Community Level

Two issues are examined here: how far SHGs, VOs and MMSs have been able to challenge anti-women and anti-dalit social practices, and how far they have been able to link with other non-governmental, community-level organizations.

BOX 2.3

**Single Women's Group: Negotiating Identity and
Interests in Family and Community**

The idea of a single women's* group emerged out of discussions
of single members of different SHGs in a village of Orrakkal
block in Kurnool district. The women felt that single women
experience certain unique problems arising out of not only their
gender but also their single identity. If they are widows, they are
often denied rights to their husbands' properties. In extreme
cases, they are thrown out of their marital homes. While widower remarriage is socially accepted, widow remarriage is not.
Deserted and divorced women often find it difficult to get maintenance. Differentially abled women stand small chances of getting married and remain vulnerable to exploitation, sexually and
otherwise.

Single women members of that particular village met separately. They not only started gaining confidence out of their
collective identity but also gave each other mutual support when
harassed. Slowly, single women members of SHGs from other
villages also joined in, as well as single non-members. This led
to the formation of a group called *Jeevan Rekha* (lifeline) open to
widows, destitute, deserted, divorced and never married adult
women (including the handicapped). It now comprises 220
members. Over the last three years, the group has succeeded in
helping four members access husbands' properties, 10 members
purchase land, 12 members construct houses, and two members
get remarried. If necessary, counselling services are provided to
single women at the MMS.

Note: *The term single women refers not just to never married
women, but also to widows, and divorced and separated women.

Child marriage and dowry are strong social norms in large
parts of the project area. Social norms also restrict the education of female children. Widow remarriage is widely looked
down upon. The *devadasi* system, under which predominantly dalit women are considered married to gods and
goddesses but are sexually exploited by the upper castes,[34]

---

[34] This system is known by a variety of names: *Jogini* (Mahbubnagar),
Parvati Parameshwar (Kurnool), *basavi* (Ananthpur). Under this system,
some dalit girls (normally from poor households) are married though
an official ceremony to Goddess Yellamma as soon as they attain

is prevalent in small pockets in all the three districts. Female foeticide is practised in parts of rural areas, especially those near towns. Several SHGs reported playing an active part in addressing such issues, more so than with respect to domestic violence. Regarding social issues, 54 per cent of the SHGs reported launching campaigns to promote female child education, 31 per cent against child marriages, 20 per cent against the practice of untouchability, 19 per cent against harmful superstitious beliefs, 7 per cent each against giving and taking dowry and the *jogini* system, and 6 per cent against female foeticide. Further, 7 per cent of the SHGs reported promoting widow remarriages. The fact that the campaign against dowry is one of the weakest can be attributed to the widespread negative economic implications for members with only sons or more sons to combat dowry. Dalit-exclusive SHGs took greater part in such social campaigns than BC-exclusive or mixed-caste SHGs. This can be attributed to the fact that dalit women and members of their community stand to lose the most by some of the practices. It could also be attributed to the greater autonomy that dalit women enjoy within their families.

Apart from waging campaigns against untouchability, 17 per cent of the SHGs reported that they took up cases of specific caste atrocities in the village. The percentage of SHGs taking on caste issues appear to be higher in the case of dalit-exclusive SHGs (22 per cent) and BC–SC mixed SHGs (40 per cent). Caste-based discrimination in tea stalls (where dalits are served in glass tumblers, while others are served in stainless steel tumblers) and at the workplace were among the issues taken up by the SHGs. Significantly, younger SHGs that have been operational for less than three years, seem more active in taking on caste-related issues than the older SHGs. This may be because the proportion of

---

puberty. Subsequently, they are not allowed to marry a man, and are expected to extend sexual favours to their patrons. Normally, an upper caste man, who is already married, comes forward as a patron, and may even father a child through the *devadasi*. The child, however, does not have inheritance rights. There is also no binding that the patron supports the *devadasi* in her old age. Though legally banned now, this system still continues in some parts of India.

BOX 2.4

Taking Legal Action for Atrocity against a Dalit Woman: Example from Mahbubnagar

Kistamma, a 35-year-old dalit woman, lives alone with her children in Peddarapaly village of Mahbubnagar district since her husband migrated to Hyderabad to earn a living. One day, as she was returning home from her workplace, a man from a backward caste assaulted and gagged her, and brutally raped her on a heap of stones. She could hardly speak as her tongue was also damaged. She complained to the village elders, who fined the culprit Rs 1,500 and let him go. On hearing of the case, the Women's Rights Protection Committees of five MMSs appointed a team to investigate the matter. The team met the village elders and the woman and convinced them that the fine imposed did not mete out any justice, and that the right thing to do was to report the matter to the police. Kistamma was then taken to meet the District Collector, who asked her to admit herself to the government hospital for medical examination, and then file a case. As she was in no shape to travel 7 km to the hospital, she was seated on a chair and lifted into a jeep and brought to the district headquarters. A case was booked for rape and atrocity on an SC woman under SC/ST Atrocities Act. The culprit was arrested and remanded to judicial custody.

dalits in younger SHGs is higher than in the older SHGs. While 17 per cent of the SHGs reported having addressed caste-related issues, only 1 per cent reported that caste panchayats or village leaders invited them to mediate in the case of caste conflicts in the village. Significantly, the caste panchayat seems to be calling them more to resolve marital problems rather than caste-related problems.

VOs and MMSs have also intervened against caste discrimination. Some of them have gone beyond collective action to using legal redress to address caste-based (often interlocked with gender) exploitation. The MMS of Mahbubnagar has, for example, booked cases under SC/ST atrocities act for violence against dalits. However, like in the case of SHGs, VOs and MMSs are yet to be recognized by caste panchayats and asked to intervene in instances of caste conflicts in the village. This may happen as the project matures.

Almost all the SHGs, VOs and MMSs reported having established some linkage or the other with other local institutions. Above 50 per cent of the SHGs reported having established linkages with MMSs, mother's groups, and village education groups.[35] Between 30 and 49 per cent of the groups mentioned that they had established contacts with forest protection groups, DWCRA groups, caste panchayats and district committees. It is necessary for linkages to be built with unions of informal sector workers, social movements, NGOs active on gender issues and women lawyers. Linkages were weaker with groups perceived to be in the male domain, such as watershed groups. A greater proportion of dalit-exclusive SHGs institutions, rather than BC-exclusive SHGs or either kind of mixed-caste SHGs, had established linkages with other community groups. It does appear that, other than in one district,[36] linkages between VOs and MMSs and village-level community organizations are weaker than those of SHGs. This is because SHGs are more visible as they meet more frequently and have been functioning for a longer period than VOs and MMSs. With respect to organizations outside the village, this trend is not true. MMSs in particular seem to have better linkages than SHGs, with women lawyers, NGOs in the district, social movements, unions and All India Democratic Women's Association (women's wing of Communist Party of India [Marxist]).

Collective Interventions in Market Organizations

Fifty-nine per cent of SHGs reported having intervened *directly* in some kind of market organization: labour, commodity, financial, and—*interestingly*—the arrack market. The

---

[35] Mother's groups are formed by *anganwadi* centres (nutritional and child care centres) for educating mothers with children in the 0–3 age group on nutritional improvement of self and children. Village education groups are attached to schools to improve school enrolment as well as monitor the functioning of schools.
[36] In that district, the MMS was formed first and initiated the VO and several SHGs.

most common intervention was in the financial market: 42 per cent of the SHGs stated they had negotiated bank loans for the group or its members. Another 3 per cent reported that they negotiated with moneylenders for redemption of loan or asset of members. The next common intervention was in the arrack market: 26 per cent of the SHGs reported that they closed the arrack shop in their village. This is indeed an impressive achievement considering that arrack trade is closely linked with the police and political nexus. Labour market was the third important area where the group had intervened: 16 per cent reported that they organized themselves along with other SHGs in the village to demand higher wages, 8 per cent to demand wages equal to men's, and 10 per cent to demand better working conditions. Twenty-six per cent of the SHGs reported that they had freed a woman member or a member of her family from bondage. The proportion was particularly high in the case of dalit-exclusive SHGs.

SHG interventions in the commodity market were at a more nascent stage: 8 per cent of the SHGs reported having established storage godowns so that members would not need to sell immediately after harvest, while at the same time ensuring minimal storage losses; 7 per cent of the SHGs reported that along with other SHGs they had formed marketing societies, and engaged in bulk marketing to reduce transportation costs and to bargain for a better price; 6 per cent reported that they had started collective purchasing of raw materials such as seeds and fertilizers to reduce input costs; 4 per cent reported setting up bulk spaces for drying fish, as the market for fresh fish is riskier and limited; and 25 per cent of the SHGs expressed that they experienced constraints in intervening in commodity market institutions. Apart from lack of capital, resistance from upper-caste landlords and employers was reported as a constraint.

VOs and MMSs seem to have intervened in more innovative ways in the financial, labour and commodity markets than SHGs. Most MMSs have borrowed from the government of Andhra Pradesh (District Rural Development Agency [DRDA], Scheduled Caste Corporation), UNDP and NGOs (BASICS and Friends of Women's World Banking [FWWB]) to on-lend to VOs,

and through them to SHGs.[37] Realizing the need for an independent financial base, one MMS has initiated a women's
bank to meet large credit needs of members (Box 2.5).

Though wage struggles are still at a nascent stage at the
VO and MMS levels as well, an innovative experiment on
the part of one MMS to support women's participation in the
labour market has been the setting up of *ammavadis* or

BOX 2.5

Mahila Bank: Collective Intervention in the Financial Market

The Mahila Bank was born because women members of SHGs in
Kurnool district realized that despite four years of savings they
could not avail loans larger than Rs 4,000–5,000. Commercial
banks would not lend to women readily, as most of them did not
have collateral such as land or house to offer. If such need ever
arose, they would have to go back to the moneylenders. The VOs
placed this problem in front of the MMS which then approached
the SAPAP Project Officer. The matter then went to the District
Collector who mooted the idea of a Mahila Bank, as he had seen
it successfully working in Sri Lanka. The VOs then returned to
their village and started brainstorming on the bank structure.
Within weeks, a large MMS meeting was held; SAPAP staff, the
District Collector, and other government officials were invited.
Various possibilities on structures and legal requirements of
setting up a woman's own bank were discussed. The VOs decided that every group should pool in Rs 5,000 to the bank
funds. The total amount came to Rs 550,000, which was subsequently increased to Rs 2.45 million through a grant from the
DRDA. All VO presidents were made board members of the Bank
and concrete rules and conditions on transactions were framed.
Today, the Mahila Bank's capital has expanded to Rs 4.5 million through interest, and it has lent to 20 VOs. In contrast to
commercial banks, the Mahila Bank does not ask for collateral
for loans, and hence women are more easily able to access loans.

Source: SERP, 2003: 40–41.

---

[37] Data from 11 VOs suggests that there is no caste bias in access of
different caste SHGs (dalit-exclusive, BC-exclusive, ST-exclusive) to
loans from VOs. Forty per cent of the VOs mentioned that preference
was given to SC-exclusive groups while lending, as the members were
poorer. Whether there is a bias against ST-exclusive groups needs to
be explored with a larger sample, while at the same time noting that
they are not the poorest—economically.

crèches that are open from morning to late in the evening. The idea of *ammavadi* centres originated since government-run *anganwadi* centres close by 2 p.m., after which it is difficult for poor women with young children to work. If economic circumstances demand that they work beyond these hours, they are forced to pull their elder daughters out of school to look after the younger ones. The *ammavadi* centres run with the financial contribution of parents, through which a person is paid to look after the centre. Currently, 35 such centres are in operation in three *mandal*s of Kurnool. Another intervention in the labour market on the part of MMSs has been to strengthen the skill base of members by providing training for tailoring, embroidery, knitting and word processing (on computers).

A greater proportion of VOs (than SHGs) reported having established godowns, milk collection and marketing centres,[38] and agricultural market societies and engaging in bulk procurement of raw materials; 12.5 per cent of VOs had purchased vehicles for cutting down transportation costs—an intervention that would have been difficult at the SHG level. An innovative activity on the part of VOs (12.5 per cent) and MMSs (33 per cent) to cut down consumption costs is bulk purchase of provisions. Three of the six MMSs studied have initiated collective enterprises like collection and sale of *neem* fruit and mango kernels, handicrafts, garment-making, running a computer centre, etc. Nevertheless, like in the case of SHGs, the interventions of VOs and MMSs in the commodity market were significantly weaker than in the financial market.

The interventions of SHGs, VOs and MMSs seem to have had a significant impact on the wider financial market but only a small dent on the labour market. Fifty-three per cent of the SHGs reported that the number of moneylenders in the village had declined after group formation, and 41 per cent reported that the interest rate charged by the money-lenders who continued operating had reduced. Significantly, in a majority of instances, the interest rate dropped by over

---

[38] One MMS has initiated 15 milk collection and marketing societies, with computerized testing facilities.

25 per cent, and in the case of 38 per cent of SHGs (which reported a decline) it dropped by over 50 per cent. Thirty-eight per cent of the SHGs reported that the wage struggles they undertook for members, as well as the rise in wages resulting out of increase in employment opportunities through loan activities of the group, had led to a general rise in wages in the village. Half of those who reported such wage increase pointed that the benefits accrued only to women, while the remaining stated that both men and women benefited. The wage increase was however reported to be only 25 per cent for women.

Collective Interventions vis-à-vis the State and Statutory Local Bodies

A high 95 per cent of the group members exercised their vote during last panchayat elections. Of the 83 SHGs, 19 per cent reported that they had discussed in the group the pros and cons of voting for different candidates. A higher proportion of VOs (36 per cent) and MMS (60 per cent) reported discussing the merits of different candidates. Around 15 per cent of the members reported that they abided by the decisions taken in these fora. Thus, groups at various levels have started to play a role in shaping the political decision-making of women members.

Equally important, between 25 and 33 per cent of SHGs, VOs and MMSs reported that they are invited by the gram panchayat to take part in gram sabha meetings. Around 20 per cent of members reported attending the gram sabha meeting held recently.[39] Most SHGs that attend gram sabha meetings hold prior meetings to discuss what issues to place before the gram sabha. The percentage of VOs and MMSs that reported convening such a preparatory meeting was lower. This could perhaps be attributed to the fact that SHGs meet weekly in contrast to VOs and MMSs which meet less frequently. Further, the MMSs' area does not exactly match

---

[39] One MMS reported that the gram sabha was not held due to factional politics.

that of the gram sabha. An issue of concern is that none of the MMSs reported being invited to *mandal* panchayat meetings as special invitees.

By far, basic needs figured prominently in the list of issues (access to drinking water, drainage, road, electricity, improvement of schools, and public distribution system [PDS]) placed by SHGs, VOs and MMSs before the gram sabha. Thirteen per cent of the SHGs, which attended gram sabha meetings, however mentioned that they took up issues of domestic violence that could not be resolved at the SHG or VO level to gram sabha meetings. The participation of dalit-exclusive and dalit-mixed groups in gram sabha meetings was higher than that of BC and BC-mixed SHGs. Participation of 'A' grade (functioning excellently) SHGs and (surprisingly) SHGs operational for less than five years was higher than the SHGs in the six to seven year 'age' group. None of the SHGs, VOs or MMSs has yet played any role in making the gram panchayat more accountable to the gram sabha by ensuring transparency of its budget allocation and expenditures.

It is estimated that in the elections held towards the latter half of 2001, women members contested between 20–25 per cent of reserved seats for women. In Kurnool district, 54 women members contested elections from six gram panchayats. They contested both general seats and seats reserved for women. Though only 10 of them (18 per cent) won the elections, the very process of contesting empowered the concerned women as well as the MMSs, which selected them. The women also showed that there are nonviolent, non-corrupt and non-party-based ways of contesting elections (Box 2.6). Significantly, almost all the women who contested elections in these six gram panchayats were members of SHGs.

Moving on to collective interventions vis-à-vis government organizations, linkages with local government institutions seem stronger than with non-governmental local institutions. Above 75 per cent of the SHGs reported collaborating in some form or the other with (in the order of importance) schools, health sub-centres, *anganwadi* centres, the block development office, and literacy programmes

BOX 2.6

**Claiming Political Space and Redefining Political Processes:
The Case of Elections in Kurnool District**

Kurnool district is particularly noted for its factional politics
(both caste-based and otherwise). Gram panchayat elections are
often used as sites for demonstrating power by different factions.
Murders and violence are not uncommon during elections. When
one of the MMSs decided to field 54 women candidates to contest
for seats in the the gram panchayat, the decision directly cut
into the base of these factions. In fact, different factional leaders
approached the MMS leaders and tried to buy them out of the
idea. However, the MMS did not buckle under the pressure as
its main purpose was to clean the political environment, place
gender concerns firmly on the gram panchayat's agenda, and
make the gram sabha accountable to poor women. When the
effort to buy them off failed, the candidates and the SAPAP Project
Officer were threatened over telephone. Nevertheless none of
them detracted, and campaigned without distributing liquor or
money, without making false promises, and without downplaying
the opposing candidate. Women candidates did not affiliate
themselves with any particular political party. Though only 18
per cent of the contesting candidates won, they claimed and
redefined political space. In some instances, husbands supported
the women candidates, and through women's participation in
elections, powers within the family also got redefined.

---

of the government. Between 50 and 74 per cent of the SHGs
reported having contacts with the PDS, health camps and
animal husbandry department, and 25–49 per cent with the
police, revenue department, agricultural credit society, milk
producer's cooperative society and agricultural department.
Linkages were weakest with banks, DWCRA markets, the
sericulture department and legal aid cells. One pattern that
seems to emerge is that linkages are stronger with those
government institutions working on issues considered to
be the woman's task (child care, education), as well as those
associated with women-managed activities (livestock), and
weaker with those considered men's task (marketing) as
well men-managed activities (agriculture). In terms of psychological distance, most village-based organizations
providing basic services were considered more approachable

(other than village health sub-centres).[40] Organizations
based outside the village run by officials were considered
less approachable. The block development office (BDO), district administration, agriculture, animal husbandry, sericulture department, police and legal aid board figured in
the latter list. Consistent with the pattern observed throughout, the linkages of dalit-exclusive and dalit-mixed SHGs
was higher than BC-exclusive and BC–OC-mixed SHGs. 'A'
grade SHGs seem to perform better than 'B' grade ones (functioning well, but not excellently) in this respect.

The pattern of institutional linkage at the VO and MMS
level was similar in most ways to the pattern of linkages of
SHGs. The main point of difference was that unlike SHGs,
over 90 per cent of the VOs and MMSs had established linkages with banks. The linkage of VOs and MMSs with the
police and district administration was good (over 55 per cent)
and much stronger than at the SHG level. Thus, organizations at higher levels are important for macro linkages.
Linkages of VOs and MMSs however need to be strengthened with DWCRA markets, sericulture and agricultural
departments, and legal aid cells. As is to be expected with
respect to village-level government organizations (schools,
health centres, etc.), SHGs and VOs seem to have stronger
linkages than the MMSs.

Impact on Strategic Gender Awareness:
The 'Power Within'

An indicator of the *power within* at the individual level is the
ability of women to challenge gender-related attitudes and
social norms in their own personal lives. Son preference is

---

[40] This can perhaps be attributed to the fact that a lower proportion of
staff of sub-centres was made up of members or leaders of groups,
when compared to *anganwadi* centres. Sixty-six per cent of *anganwadi*
workers were members or leaders of SHGs, in contrast to 0 per cent
in the case of ANMs. Hundred per cent of *dais* in *anganwadi* centres
were members of SHGs, when compared to 43 per cent in the case of
sub-centres. A greater proportion of *anganwadi* workers reside in the
village when compared to ANMs. The ANMs of course are better off
than *anganwadi* workers.

very high in India, and one key question that was posed before members and non-members was whether they would like to have a son or a daughter, if they had a chance to choose the sex of their child in their next birth (a hypothetical question related to the popular belief in rebirth among Hindus in India). Thirty per cent of members reported son preference in contrast to 36 per cent in the case of non-members. The rest of the members either had no preference (51 per cent) or preferred to have a female child (19 per cent). However, women members were yet to break the social norms governing the freedom given to adolescent children. It was found that only 19 per cent of members allowed the same freedom to adolescent daughters as sons, but it was nevertheless higher than the figure for non-members, at 11 per cent. This may only partly reflect women's attitudes on gender-based access to freedom, as the reality of violence against adolescent girls in public also has a role to play. Son preference was lower and freedom given to adolescent girls was higher among dalit and Muslim members than among BC members. Women members heading households seemed more gender-sensitive in these two respects than women members of MHH. No age-specific pattern was noted.

Another indicator of women's empowerment was reflected in the changed perceptions of others about women's confidence, assertiveness and independence. All the husbands questioned reported that their wives were more independent now than before joining the group five years ago. Only 21 per cent of husbands of non-members who were met reported such a change; 6 per cent of children of members reported greater independence on the part of mothers, in contrast to 0 per cent in the case of non-members; and 12 per cent of children felt that they were more assertive within the family, in contrast to 0 per cent in the case of non-members. All the husbands and children questioned were happy with these changes.

At the collective level, it is important to observe the perception of the group with respect to its own objectives and to the needs of its members. Of the 83 SHGs, 11 VOs and 6 MMSs studied, a majority were able to articulate gender-specific goals. That is, the goals were not just articulated

BOX 2.7

Prabhavatamma: Challenging Gender and Social Norms in Her Life

Prabhavatamma, a dalit woman, is now the president of the VO in Puricherla. She was married at the age of 12 into a poor, landless family. During the first 10 years of her marriage, she suffered considerable physical and mental harassment from her parents-in-law, as she was unable to bear children. After that, her status improved slightly as she bore six children in quick succession. As soon as her children were old enough to work, they were sent off to labour in bondage with a landlord to clear off past family debts. Her oldest daughter was married off when she was 12, but returned within a year, as she was ill-treated by her husband. The caste panchayat decided that the daughter should return to her husband, but Prabhavatamma paid a fine of Rs 2,000 to the panchayat and kept her daughter with her even against her own husband's wishes. Around the same time, SHGs were started under the SAPAP programme and Prabhavatamma joined one of them. Through the group, she came to understand the importance of educating female children. She decided to enrol two of her younger daughters in Bhavita, a child labour school, against the wishes of her husband's family and community members. Today, other women members follow her example. Recently, she got her older daughter remarried, breaking many social norms. In recognition of her abilities and confidence, she was nominated president of the VO. She has initiated a water harvesting scheme benefiting 200 villagers.

with respect to generic categories such as (improvement of) poor people or households, but with respect to women and girls in particular.[41] Among various gender-specific objectives listed by the SHGs were development of health and education of female children (58 SHGs), poverty reduction of women (52 SHGs), women's economic empowerment (45 SHGs), women's social empowerment (40 SHGs), women's political empowerment (27 SHGs), and women's all-round empowerment (20 SHGs). Issues of women's empowerment and poverty reduction were seen as equally important goals.

---

[41] However, given the context of poverty, it was not surprising that a greater number of groups stated non-gender-specific goals such as to increase poor people's savings (70), poor people's access of poor to loan (69), and reduction of poverty in poor families (68).

Equally, the specific disadvantages faced by female children were recognized. However, eradication of caste-specific barriers facing dalit women did not particularly figure as an official objective other than in the case of dalit SHGs. Addressing specific disadvantages faced by WHHs, elderly women and women with differential abilities were yet to figure in the list of objectives. No specific pattern was seen on the ability of SHGs of different caste compositions, grades and ages to articulate gender-specific goals.

Another indicator of the strategic[42] awareness with respect to class, caste and gender is the ability of the SHG, VO or MMS to identify not just common village problems but also class-, caste- and gender-specific problems of group members. Ill-health and lack of health facilities figured as the most pressing problems articulated by SHGs. A second set of key problems reported by the SHGs clearly indicated members' ability to articulate caste and class concerns: caste oppression, exploitative working hours, low wages, low price for produce, and indebtedness. Other common village issues identified by the SHGs were access to drinking water, roads, burial grounds, transport, quality schools and well-managed *balwadi* centres, as well as dealing with widespread alcoholism and superstitious beliefs. A positive feature is that child care and drinking water were not just seen as gender-specific problems, but as common problems pertaining to both men and women. Moving on to articulation of gender-specific issues, a surprisingly high proportion of needs (80 per cent) identified by SHG members related to the position of women in general, rather than to the day-to-day problems faced by them. In order of importance, these include domestic violence, reproductive rights and health of women, equal wages for work of equal value, housing rights of women, political participation of women, violence at the workplace, land rights of women, and maintenance for women. Reproductive health figured as the single most important practical need of women. A greater proportion of dalit-exclusive SHGs and mixed SHGs with dalit

---

[42] Strategic awareness refers to the ability to identify interests arising out of one's position in hierarchical social relations on the basis of caste, class and gender.

members were able to articulate caste and class concerns that pertained to their position (untouchability) rather than condition (low levels of literacy) in society. Though not a reflection of strategic awareness, but of strategic ability, it may be worth commenting on two gender-specific issues more SHGs reported not being able to address: domestic violence and reproductive rights and health of women.

Key Lessons

The study suggests that the SAPAP pilot project in AP has immensely strengthened the struggles of poor women members in its project area against poverty and gender- and caste-based discrimination. It has also performed better than the main programme of the GoAP for women's empowerment and poverty reduction: the Development of Women and Children in Rural Areas (DWCRA).[43] At the same time, the study points to the need for additional strategies to address gender-specific dimensions and causes of poverty, as well as for strengthening the process of women's empowerment. Together, the achievements of SAPAP and the challenges it

---

[43] A similar study was carried out of the DWCRA programme in Andhra Pradesh, using the same methodology. SAPAP's superior performance over DWCRA in poverty reduction is reflected in (a) better access of members and their family to food, clothing and shelter, leading to lesser mortality of infants and children; (b) lesser dependency of member households on moneylenders; and (c) greater reduction in household poverty as per self-assessment (wealth-ranking method). Gender disparities in access to basic needs were also lower in SAPAP member households. With respect to most empowerment variables, SAPAP performed better. SAPAP members exercised greater control over their labour, mobility, income, other resources, and household decision-making when compared to DWCRA members. At a collective level, SAPAP members intervened more in instances of caste atrocities, and engaged more with financial and commodity markets. SAPAP members gave greater freedom to their adolescent girls. However, members of DWCRA reported greater control over reproduction than SAPAP members (perhaps because of greater contacts with health personnel). DWCRA groups were better at mobilizing government programmes and engaging in the labour market, as well as establishing contact with caste panchayats. There was no major difference in incidence of domestic violence between SAPAP and DWCRA member households (Murthy et al., 2002).

faces point to several lessons on micro-credit, poverty reduction and women's empowerment.

Globally there is a debate on whether micro-credit can
really address poverty and/or women's empowerment, with
one group holding that micro-credit is the answer to both
problems, and another group arguing that this is far from
true and in fact women are exploited through participation
in such programmes. The study points to the fact that both
positions are not really correct, and the reality is some-
where in between. It is definitely possible for group-based
micro-credit interventions to reach the poor (including the
landless, dalits and WHHs), expand their access to resources,
and reduce their poverty, provided adequate investment is
made in social mobilization, capital formation and capacity
building. However, some groups like the elderly, poor households and chronic distress migrant households often fall
outside the ambit of such programmes. To reach them, it is
necessary to combine micro-credit with welfare programmes
for the elderly and strategies to expand wage employment
and land rights for chronic migrants. The latter set of added
interventions as well as collective interventions in labour
and commodity markets may also be necessary to make a
significant dent on poverty of the poorest members who have
joined groups. Equally, there is a need for planned interventions to address gender-specific causes of poverty within
interventions (land and housing rights, dowry, equal wages,
gender disparities in access to basic needs) and sensitize
men to play greater roles in reproductive work. By creating
space for women (and dalits) to come together, an empowering space is created on its own by group-based micro-credit
programmes. In particular, mobility, confidence and independent access to savings and credit are automatically expanded. However, there are limits to how far automatic momentum can both address gender-specific causes of poverty
and lead to changes in women's control over their bodies,
reproduction and political spaces. Specific strategies are
required on these issues.

There are again polarized debates on whether a focus on
gender and poverty agenda deflects attention from the more
political agenda of women's empowerment. One position holds
that poverty is feminized, and that development agencies

should focus on the interlinkage between gender, women and poverty. The other position is that evidence on feminization of poverty is weak, and conflating gender issues with poverty takes attention away from the broader agenda of women's empowerment. The study supports the view that poverty is indeed feminized in India. WHHs form a greater proportion of poor when compared to MHHs (other than perhaps single men households, which are very few in proportion). Poor women and girls face poverty more intensely and in gender-specific ways and face greater hurdles in overcoming poverty. The study also shows that gender-specific dimensions and causes of poverty cannot be addressed without empowering women. Even to ensure that increased household income expands women's access to gender-intensified needs such as gas and toilets requires an element of empowerment. Nevertheless, a gender and poverty agenda alone cannot address the entire range of ways by which women are disempowered. In particular, strategies are required to address domestic violence, promote women's reproductive rights, strengthen women's participation in local bodies and sensitize men. Thus a gender and poverty agenda does not deflect attention from the agenda of women's empowerment, but at the same time women's empowerment requires a broader range of interventions than those required to address gender-specific dimensions and causes of poverty.

The study highlights the fact that women's empowerment and sustained impact on gender-specific dimensions and causes of poverty cannot be achieved without sensitizing men on gender issues. In particular, there is a need to sensitize male relatives about their responsibility for domestic work and child care. It is necessary also to challenge dominant notions of masculinity that lead to domestic violence and leakage on alcohol consumption. Men should be encouraged to share in the productive work burden of women members without taking over the latter's enterprise. Otherwise, women and children's access to rest and health, and the household's ability to invest in the education of school-going children gets adversely affected. Sensitization of men in MHHs, men from BCs and upper-caste households and Lambani men seems particularly important. Male community leaders also need to be reached through such efforts. The study also supports the lesson that not all tribal communities are automatically egalitarian, and there is a need to study gender relations in each community in the project area before intervening.

Apart from dalit empowerment in general, a caste equity perspective has to be institutionalized for effective poverty reduction and women's empowerment. The study supports the view that as a majority of dalits are poor and a significant proportion of the poor are dalits, it is central that poverty reduction strategies target them. The study also points out that like gender-specific dimensions, there are caste-specific dimensions to poverty. Whether improved household incomes for dalits lead to similar access to basic needs such as nutrition, education and health depends on whether caste biases in different institutions have been eliminated. Such interventions have to be consciously woven. The study shows that changes in gender-related attitudes cannot be brought about with changes in caste-related values. Women who were set back in challenging gender norms in their own lives were from the upper castes and BCs, and these were also those that were inadequate in challenging caste hierarchies. Women's empowerment cannot be achieved by making women aware of one kind of hierarchy and not the other. There is a need to design strategies for opening such windows of questioning for women, especially for those from privileged social groups.

The study highlights that while strengthening social capital of poor women by forming SHGs is indeed an important strategy for poverty reduction and women's empowerment, it is not adequate to merely strengthen bonding social capital among members. Bridging social capital, linking social capital and—a third category—claim-making social capital (vis-à-vis family, labour, commodity and financial markets, government, and panchayats and thereby widening the resource and power base of members) needs to be strengthened.[44] Groups at different levels serve different purposes.

---

[44] Claim-making social capital is an extension of the social capital concept by the authors to refer to the process of using collective power to challenge hierarchies, norms and resource allocation patterns of societal institutions.

The sense of bonding is highest at the SHG level, while groups' ability to organize community-based services, link with other organizations and make demands on institutions is higher at the MMS level, VOs falling in between. Federations are hence central for poverty reduction and women's empowerment.

The study also offers insights into the comparative advantage of group-based micro-credit programmes over lending by commercial banks in meeting credit needs of poor. While thrift and savings SHGs tend to meet the credit needs of poor women better than commercial banks and private moneylenders, they cannot automatically be assumed to function in a pro-poor manner. It is important to have rules to give first priority to the poorest in giving loans and ensuring equity in access to number and amount of loans. Rules are also required on pro-poor savings and repayment practices. There is a need to monitor whether members borrow with interest or cut down their consumption to save during lean seasons or/and repay the group loan.

In the past, government agencies and NGOs have emphasized either capital formation (for example, IRDP) or social mobilization/capacity building (early stages of Mahila Samakhya) as strategies for reducing women's poverty and empowering women. The study points to the fact that all three strategies are equally important and need to be combined.[45] For the three strategies to really work effectively, the role of the state in implementing welfare programmes and service delivery is crucial. In contrast to the popular opinion that the state should cut back its role, state services in the area of child care, drinking water provision, PDS, nutrition, health and education are essential for poor women to take part in poverty alleviation and empowerment-oriented programmes. It is also required to convert increased income into improved well-being for themselves and their children.

Another lesson is the need to focus on both income enhancement and (unnecessary) consumption reduction for

---

[45] The DWCRA programme has suffered because of a lower budget for capacity building of groups, as well as for appointing adequate staff for social mobilization (Murthy et al., 2002).

poverty reduction and women's empowerment. While income enhancement strategies are central to poverty reduction, the study has strongly pointed out that the extent to which an increase in the household income gets translated into well-being depends on the extent to which leakages do not take place on alcohol consumption as well as practices like dowry. By far, most poverty reduction programmes of government and NGOs have excluded the second agenda. Male alcoholism, gambling and dowry also have a significant impact on violence against women. Increase in dowry is closely linked to son preference and female foeticide.

Finally, the study points to the institutional context of fostering women's/dalit empowerment and poverty reduction (and its feminization). It points to the centrality of a process-based rather than a target-driven approach. It also points to the need for inducting committed, competent and socially sensitive personnel into the project management. The induction of sensitive Indian Administrative Service (IAS) officers and experienced NGO activists into UNDP's Project Management Units at both state and district levels, and recruitment of (adequate)[46] people from NGOs or universities at the cutting edge in the villages has really paid off. Needless to say, such a bottom-up process cannot be unleashed in a short time span; a minimum period of 10–15 years is required.

References

IFAD (International Fund for Agricultural Development), 1999, *Completion Evaluation Report of Tamil Nadu Women's Development Project*, Rome: IFAD.

Mayoux, L., 2001, 'Microfinance Impacts in Enterprise', *Impact News*, 3 (November): 2–4.

Murthy, R.K., Ramachandran, A., and DWCRA Research Team, 2002, 'Towards Women's Empowerment and Poverty Reduction: Lessons from the Participatory Impact Assessment of Development of Women

---

[46] Field staff to group ratio of one full-time staff per a maximum of 80 SHGs seems essential; this has been better adhered to under the SAPAP than the DWCRA.

and Children in Rural areas in Andhra Pradesh, India', UNDP (Mimeo).

Murthy, R.K. and Rao, N., 1997, *Addressing Poverty: Indian NGOs their Capacity Enhancement in the 1990s*, New Delhi: Friedrich Ebert Stiftung.

Murthy, R.K. and Sankaran, L., 2001, *Denial and Distress: Gender, Poverty and Human Rights in Asia*, Bangalore: Books for Change.

Oxaal, Z. with Baden, S., 1997, *Gender and Empowerment: Definitions, Approaches and Implications for Policy*, Sweden: Swedish International Development Cooperation Agency.

SERP (Society for Elimination of Rural Poverty), 2003, *Velugu: Voices of Women*, Hyderabad: SERP.

Shiva Kumar, A.K., 1995, *UNDP's Gender Related Development Index: A Computation for Indian States*, United Nations Children's Fund (Mimeo).

Wieringa, S., 1994, 'Women's Interests and Empowerment: Gender Planning Reconsidered', *Development and Change*, 25: 829–48.

Woolcock, Michael, 2000, 'Friends in High Places? An Overview of Social Capital', *Insights*, 34, http://www.id21.org/insights/insights34/insights-iss34-art02.html.

3

Micro-credit and Women's Empowerment: A Case Study of SHARE Micro-finance Limited

Anuradha Rajivan

Background

It is widely believed among development practitioners that micro-credit and, more broadly, micro-finance[1] contributes not only to poverty reduction but also to empowerment of the poor. Many fringe benefits are seen by protagonists as flowing almost automatically from micro-finance interventions, such as changes in gender equations in favour of women, improved health and nutrition, improved education, increased self-reliance, even better management of natural resources.

Based on these beliefs, a number of micro-level, micro-credit models are currently in operation in different parts of India. A common feature has been the promotion of self-help groups (SHGs) through social mobilization, composed mainly of women, which start with pooled savings for internal rotation, and eventually receive and repay loans. NGOs, government agencies and banks have been promoting SHGs, within three broad approaches. In the first approach,

---

[1] Also includes other financial instruments such as savings, insurance, financial intermediation, etc.

micro-credit is seen as an entry point or complementary activity to mobilize people and sustain interest, though the principal objective is something else such as promoting literacy and education, enhancing maternal and child health, facilitating watershed development, catalysing women's empowerment, or reducing child labour. In the second approach, micro-finance is used as the main tool for poverty alleviation. The nation-wide, centrally sponsored Swarnajayanti Gram Swarozgar Yojana (SGSY) scheme is a notable example, apart from programmes of several NGOs. In the third approach, the relative strengths of the government, NGOs and banks are sought to be combined under an umbrella organization promoting multi-purpose SHGs, where micro-finance is an input along with systematic training and capacity building in virtually any subject of concern and interest to the members. One example is the Tamil Nadu Women's Development Project called *Mahalir Thittam* ('women's scheme').

This paper examines whether, and to what extent, micro-finance interventions, when used as tools for poverty alleviation, impact on women's empowerment. It is based on a case study of the experience of SHARE Micro-finance Limited (SML) in Andhra Pradesh, southern India. It raises two related sets of questions:

❖ To what extent can micro-finance be seen as a tool not only for income poverty alleviation but also for women's empowerment? Even if the primary concern of a micro-finance agency is something else, particularly poverty alleviation, does women's empowerment occur? If so, to what extent? Are there limitations on what can be achieved 'incidentally'?

❖ Does increase in income through micro-finance flow into the hands of women? Are there benefits to women beyond incomes? What are these benefits? Do these benefits flow from access to micro-finance per se, or from the integration of micro-finance with the process of social mobilization resulting in women's groups? To what extent is the nature of social mobilization, and the kind of capacity building that takes place in the process, important in determining the type and extent of women's empowerment?

These questions are examined here by analysing the perspective and approach of SML, the design and management of SML's micro-credit programmes, and the changes in the lives and situations of women members of groups promoted by SML.

Methodology

The methodology adopted for the study relied heavily on intensive field investigations and direct observations spread over eight days, rather than a structured sample survey. The attempt was to identify qualitative changes and bring out the perspectives of poor women.[2] To the extent possible, voices of the poor women and men are directly reported. Other key stakeholders such as staff members, community members and bank officials were also met during the discussions. Secondary data and reports on SML were also reviewed.

Detailed focus group discussions were held with 48 SML staff members (eight from the head office and 40 from field offices); in addition, 38 SML staff members were met briefly. Of the SML's 13 field districts, two were covered as part of the study, and of the eight branches in these two districts, four were visited. In one branch (Perecherla), a workshop was held in which 210 members from 68 centres[3] and 401 groups took part. In the villages, focus group discussions were held with 86 mature members (with over one year membership and with credit access) from 33 groups. Visits were made to households of 13 women members for in-depth discussions on intra-household impacts. Interviews were also held with 27 indirect stakeholders such as husbands and members of village communities to understand their

---

[2] The author carried out the investigations, in the absence of a budget for hiring and training field investigators. Help was provided by the SML head office personnel who facilitated field visits. They were open, free with information, and enabled easy access to groups and field staff.

[3] Each centre comprises eight groups, and each group comprises five people.

perceptions of the impact. Also, 32 new members and non-members were met to compare differences between them and mature members.

An attempt was made to capture as much variation in the geographic and economic context as possible within the time and cost constraints. Hence, of the two districts, one (Ranga Reddy) was a dry and less developed district and the other (Guntur) was a relatively fertile and more developed one. The study area for branch and village visits was finalized in consultation with SML. SML personnel also helped in translation and identification of locally relevant issues, but within the terms of reference given by the United Nations Development Programme (UNDP). Perceptions of the field workers were actively encouraged. Their comments and those from members and other family members contributed to detailing and refining the questions. In the villages, it was ensured that the time and place for the investigations was as consistent as possible with the normal life of the people being investigated, to minimize disruption and the creation of a feeling of hierarchy between the researcher and researched. For example, groups were visited during their normal meeting hours, usually in the late evenings when they returned from work. Those who needed to leave halfway through the meeting were free to do so. The researchers would sit at the same level as women and use a dialogue process, allowing the flow of conversation to determine the sequence of questions, rather than throwing questions in a predetermined order. At times, the researchers withheld some questions where appropriate to avoid embarrassment or backlash against women.

Perspective and Approach of SHARE Micro-finance Limited

History of SML

SML was founded in 1999 by the Society for Helping Awakening Rural Poor through Education (SHARE), an NGO registered as a society in Andhra Prdesh. SHARE's experience in managing vocational training programmes for the rural poor in the early 1990s convinced its founder that upgrading skills among the poor in the absence of access to finance has very limited impact. Around that time he had also heard about Grameen Bank's rural micro-credit operations. Wanting to test the Grameen model in Andhra Pradesh, SHARE, as a registered society, started a small action research project[4] in 1992 with two branches, one each in Kurnool and Guntur. This provided an opportunity to design and plan lending methodologies, information systems and staffing patterns. Like the Bangladesh model, very small affinity groups of five persons were facilitated through a process of social mobilization, with only women as members. Around eight such groups from the same village were encouraged to meet jointly at a common centre on a regular basis. In the mid-1990s, SHARE borrowed funds from the National Bank for Agriculture and Rural Development (NABARD) and the Small Industries Development Bank of India (SIDBI), two national banks, as well as Friends of Women's World Banking (FWWB), enabling increased outreach. During 1997–99, SHARE's first major expansion took place, taking the number of branches to 17, and the number of groups to 3,582, with 17,910 members.

To access larger funds, facilitate growth in micro-finance operations and promote commercial viability, SHARE decided to register a public limited 'for profit' company called SML. This registration took place in April 1999. SML is also registered with the Reserve Bank of India (RBI) as a non-bank finance company (NBFC) which will enable it to mobilize savings (deposits) from its members directly once it completes three years of establishment, demonstrates Rs 50 million as paid-up capital, and is credit-rated. Around the same time, in October 1999, SHARE India MACS (SIM) was established as a mutually aided cooperative society (MACS). SIM mobilizes the savings of all SML members as permissible under the MACS Act.

SML has purchased the loan portfolio of SHARE Society, branch by branch, in phases over one-and-a-half years and

---

[4] This project was funded through a grant from the Asia Pacific Development Institute, Malaysia, and a soft loan from the Grameen Trust, Bangladesh.

currently owns most of it (over 90 per cent). SHARE's balance portfolio is limited to two branches in Guntur, which
were not transferred to SML as the funding agency (Rashtriya
Mahila Kosh) did not lend to a 'for profit' NBFC and because
some of the funds received were for a long term on soft terms
(at 2 per cent interest from the Grameen Trust), which would
be prudent to continue. The future plan is to phase out lending operations of the society once the loans are repaid, with
the areas/clients to be serviced by SML. SHARE would then
restrict itself to capacity building based on grant funding.
SML itself is in the process of promoting new companies
(both for profit and non-profit) for expansion and diversification within and outside the state. This study focuses on
SML alone, the main micro-finance growth trajectory of
SHARE. SML's growth trajectory is summarized in Table 3.1.

SML Perspective on Micro-credit as a Tool for Poverty Reduction and Empowerment

SML's mission is to mobilize resources to provide financial (credit and savings) and support services (capacity
building) to the poor, particularly women, for viable, productive, income-generating enterprises, thus enabling them
to reduce their poverty. The management of SML views
micro-credit as the single most critical input for poverty
reduction. At the same time, formal financial institutions
and the government's subsidy-based micro-credit programmes have not been able to meet these needs. Hence,
regular access to micro-credit on reasonable terms with simple procedures, quick disbursements with full and frequent
(weekly) repayments, is seen as the critical input for poverty
reduction. As per SML's understanding, access to micro-credit
enables households to use their skills in income-generating
activities, helps them generate surpluses and slowly expand into multiple activities, thus countering seasonal and
activity-based risks.

SML has targeted its micro-finance programme only at
women as global experience shows that it makes good

TABLE 3.1

Growth in SML's Micro-credit Operations

(starting under SHARE and growing into SML)

Item	1993–94@	1998–99@	1999–2000^	2000–2001#	2001–02 by November 2001#
Districts	2	5	6	11	13
Branches	2	17	20	29	53
Villages	18	592	851	1,013	1,497
Staff	15	200	273	267	556
Centres	17	931	1,553	1,992	3,217
Groups	41	3,582	7,477	11,732	18,888
Members	205	17,910	37,235	58,690	94,374
Active clients	117	14,155	30,629	48,868	73,675
Credit disbursed (cumulative, in million rupees)	0.28	130.20	316.24	544.19	893.52
Repayment of due credit (percentage)	100	100	100	100	100
Operational self-sufficiency (percentage)	11	87	90	110	104
Financial self-sufficiency (percentage)	10	71	74	86	96
Cost/money lent	1.41	0.13	0.09	0.09	0.07

Sources: SHARE records for 1993-94, 1998-99 and 1999–2000; and SML records for 1999–2000, 2000–2001 and 2001-02.

Notes: @ data relates to SHARE; ^ SHARE operations start getting taken over by SML, data combined for SHARE and SML operations; # SML data.

economic sense (women are more responsible, better at accepting discipline, and better at repayments than men) and as a higher percentage of income generated goes to the family. Women's empowerment is seen as a secondary outcome of poverty reduction, when the credit inputs to the household are routed exclusively through women, which in turn brings them recognition and a voice within and outside home. Thus, though SML does not have women's empowerment as its primary objective, it believes that this will happen on its own through the strategy that SML adopts. Discussions revealed an understanding existed within SML that 'empty tummies cannot be interested in empowerment'. It believes that mere training on gender issues without financial inputs and income generation will be of little use. Since operational and financial self-sufficiency are underlying operating principles, expenditure on matters not directly related to improved repayments, such as gender training of staff and members, is not encouraged. No special linkages are sought with organizations working on women's empowerment.

Organizational Structures, Staffing and Capacity Building of Staff

The managing director of SML is supported in the day-to-day operations by eight departments: administration, training, monitoring and evaluation, field operations, planning, finance, human resources, and entrepreneurship development. A manager heads each department, with assistants reporting to him/her. The field operations are more complex. A branch covers on an average 61 centres of eight groups each. Each branch is a profit centre headed by a branch manager (BM) who functions with the support of assistant branch manager (ABM) and field credit officers (FCOs). Four to five branches together form an 'area', headed by an area manager (AM). The AMs are supervised by the divisional manager of field operations, who in turn reports to the manager of the department of field operations.

The staff at the head office is highly qualified, with members holding postgraduate degrees in commerce, management and finance. Some are also chartered accountants. In the field, FCOs are recruited from among people with 12 years of schooling or more. While recruiting FCOs, attitudes and aptitude for training are considered more important than formal qualifications. New recruits are taken young, between 18 and 24 years of age, and start as FCO trainees. Trainees are confirmed in their posts only after they undergo formal training and direct on-the-job exposure, and pass a test. This ensures that they pick up the needed skills for SML's operations.

Though all the clients are women, the proportion of female staff is low at the branch/area offices. Of the 510 staff members in the field, only 5.3 per cent are women. The sex composition at the head office is more in favour of women with 27 per cent of the 48 persons being women. In the field, only now a beginning has been made to appoint women staff, especially for office work. The reason given is that fieldwork involves travelling to villages, using two-wheelers, and working to suit the timings of the clients. There is a perception that women may be unable to handle these work schedules and may have to be accompanied by a male staff member (in the evening) adding to avoidable costs.

The work atmosphere is congenial, combined with strict discipline. The immediate supervisor closely monitors the work of staff under him or her. Suggestions from lower levels as well as members are encouraged, appreciated and discussed. This helps foster team spirit at all levels. Personnel policies like two-wheeler loans purchase of television at branch offices, dining facilities and promotion opportunities help keep staff morale high, leading to low staff turnover. Some staff members have in fact moved into SML from the private sector.

SML places considerable emphasis on building staff capacities. The aim of all staff training and exposure is to make the members effective micro-finance service providers to clients. All are expected to share a common set of attitudes, values and work culture, and to learn the skills needed for their posts. New recruits start with a two-day orientation on group formation, targeting and motivation. They learn to conduct weekly centre meetings and solve local problems. They are imparted basic skills in accounting and in procedures of SML. The training department coordinates all training programmes for staff as well as client members. Apart from induction training, there are workshops and in-service training programmes for existing staff. Course material development for FCOs, branch managers, AMs and internal auditors is taken up. The staff is exposed to concepts in micro-finance and the current developments in the sector. Accounting, computer applications, planning, and budgeting are taught. Every opportunity to improve capacities of staff at minimum cost is seized.[5]

Group Building and Micro-finance Interventions

Group members receive support in the form of capacity building, ongoing micro-credit access, and a facility to deposit their micro-savings.

Process of Group Formation, Management and Decision-making

SML's entry into a new village and the setting up of a new branch or centre start very systematically with an assessment of the potential for micro-credit. After a village survey to assess the population, landholding, percentage of poor, existing credit facilities, types of income generation activities and transport facilities, and discussions with village elders, a report on potential for a micro-credit programme is sent to the head office. A senior person from the head office is then sent to the area with support staff for a more detailed survey. The concerned AM/BM scrutinizes the survey reports. If at

---

[5] For example, a young head office staff member was deputed to accompany this researcher for part of the fieldwork to enable her to observe and learn.

least 40–50 poor families with demonstrable business potential are identified, a new centre starts.

Once a village is identified for a new centre, the process of social mobilization starts with a public orientation meeting by SML staff to explain the criteria, rules and benefits for/of group membership. Some days are allowed to the people to think about the micro-credit programme. Women are encouraged to form themselves into groups of five. Then the FCO visits the house of each planned member of the group to verify that the membership criteria (discussed later) have been properly followed. Once preliminary groups are formed, members are exposed to compulsory training. Thereafter a potential group undergoes a re-interview by the BM and a final Group Recognition Test to finalize its membership under SML. Unique numbers are allotted to groups and its individual members that pass this test, which aid in monitoring. Weekly group meetings are conducted by SML (for loans) or SIM staff (for savings).

Membership Conditions

As discussed earlier, for reasons of efficiency, poverty reduction and women's empowerment, SML targets only women. Both women and men agree with this decision (Box 3.1). Another key condition for eligibility includes a 'means' test through a questionnaire and physical verification of income and assets to ensure that the household is really poor.[6] Apart from this, group homogeneity is promoted through encouraging neighbours and women of similar ages to join. However, two members from the same family are not accepted, in order to avoid concentration of power and resources. Caste or religion is not taken as relevant criteria. In practice, mixed caste and religious groups as well as single denomination groups are found, based on the habitation pattern and proximity of residence in the village.

Most membership criteria were applied in practice. An independent survey (IFPRI and NIRD, 2000) showed that, on

---

[6] Asset holding should not exceed Rs 20,000 (approx. US$ 430); per capita income should not exceed Rs 350 (approx. US$ 7.5) per month.

BOX 3.1

Men's Opinion on Forming Groups with Men

'It just can't happen. Men will not sit together ....'
'Women work hard and repay. Men spend a lot of money on hotels, friends ....'
'Men may come together until the money is received. Then you can watch them dodge the repayments!'
'I'm telling you all this. Now it is up to you. If you still want to give men money, go ahead .... Don't say I did not warn you!'

an average, the clients of SHARE were worse off at the time of selection of beneficiaries on most indicators of economic status as compared with non-clients. Around 85 per cent of clients came from the bottom 20 per cent households, showing a substantial and genuine poverty focus. However, further disaggregation of the data showed that while the *average* level of a poverty indicator was lower (that is, worse off) for SHARE households as compared with non-client households, the *poorest* of the non-client group were worse off than the poorest of the clients. So, while a majority of the members are indeed poor, the absolute worst-off cases are probably getting excluded. Credit may or may not be the best first tool in many such cases.

In some groups the age gap between members was found to be high, but this did not seem to deter smooth group functioning. Theoretically, women-headed households (WHHs) were expected to be encouraged to join as members. Among the 86 long-duration members who were contacted, 9 per cent were found to be widows or abandoned women. But there was one centre (in Nandivelugu village) which had excluded all such cases for fear that they may not be able to adhere to the financial discipline of weekly repayments.

Exit Options and Member Replacement

A member is free to leave a group if she so wishes. A group may also remove a member under certain circumstances.[7]

---

[7] Most groups have rules to the effect that a member who does not comply with group rules, attend regularly, or repay loans can be removed

The most common reasons for the exit of a member were reported to be migration (of several months at a time or permanent), local disputes, political differences and non-co-operation at home. In one case, a member got a regular job on humanitarian grounds after the death of her husband. The group decided that she was no longer poor and removed her. However, she still keeps in touch with members as it was an amicable exit. When a member leaves, the savings amount is paid back with whatever interest is due and loan repayments are separately collected. The remaining members then identify suitable women to replace the dropouts.

Capacity Building

Capacity building of clients is done with the objective of converting non-creditworthy women into creditworthy members of small groups. While no separate training manuals have been prepared, group members are given seven days of training covering subjects such as savings, credit norms and procedures, zero tolerance for non-repayment, and joint liability in case of delinquency. Group and centre leaders are taught leadership skills that help them manage their respective groups/centres. Weekly meetings are used as the most important forum for ongoing building capacities of clients. However, groups do not conduct meetings on their own (unlike in the case of SHGs of other organizations). Rather, a staff member from SML conducts a common centre meeting for all groups in that centre. In addition, at least once a year, a workshop is held at branch level which brings together a few members from each centre and provides a forum for sharing of experiences, confidence building, planning and managing their businesses, and solving problems. Workshops are also used as a forum for cultural activities,

---

from membership. However, no such case was actually observed where a member was asked to leave for these reasons. In some cases, members were removed because they were no longer poor, but they kept in touch with the group (example cited).

strengthening public speaking skills and spreading awareness regarding health and education. Sometimes officials
like the district collector are invited for interactions.
Women have used such opportunities for articulating the
needs of their villages to the district administration and
getting their grievances addressed.

Profile of Leadership and Leadership Rotation

Each group selects its own leaders. Generally the members
choose the most educated woman or the one with high self-
confidence, ability to articulate, and a trustworthy nature. Of
the members, the leaders tended to be relatively economically better-off. However, there was no domination in access
to credit. The procedures of SML required that the leader
take her loan the last. This was also well understood by the
members. Leaders were responsible for mobilizing weekly
repayments and savings contributions. Leaders were proud
of their positions and took their responsibilities seriously.

Rotation of leadership is supposed to take place annually
or at least once in two years. This principle promotes transparency and accountability and develops a second line of
leadership. However, in the groups visited this was not normally followed. Members reported that they had faith in the
existing leaders. By and large, SML tended to go along with
the members' view so long as the existing leader was ensuring discipline and repayments. However, if the same
member continued as a leader for too long, the staff did stress
the need for change.

Savings

The amount to be saved is left to the discretion of the group
members, though it is common for all group members. Most
groups save Rs 10–20 per week. Those who wish to save
more are permitted to do so. Savings based on encouraging
individual thrift are collected weekly and centralized under

the SIM. Each member has her own passbook under SIM for the savings account. Once SML is registered as an NBFC, it plans to handle savings as well. The role of SIM and SML may then need to be clarified.

Discussions with members revealed that members are also saving outside SIM (hiding money at home, placing it in banks, etc.), indicating that members, by and large, tend to save the minimum amount possible so as to access the loans. However, there were also a few examples of members who saved more with SIM than the norm of their group. Women were allowed to withdraw amounts required for needs other than income generation from their savings. On an average, savings per member with SIM stood at a little over Rs 1,513. As of November 2001, the cumulative total savings amount with SIM stood at Rs 142.80 million for 94,374 members. From this, cumulative disbursements were Rs 138.82 million. Thus, the rotation ratio of savings stood below 1 (0.97).

The disadvantages of centralized savings in SIM (from the women's point of view) rather than group managed savings are the lack of perceived ownership of a common fund, no development of skills in collective decision-making and funds management, complete reliance on SIM for accessing funds for consumption and emergencies, interest rates restricted to what SIM can pay (6–7 per cent) as against the far higher rates available through internal rotation (24–36 per cent, as observed in the case of classic SHGs). However, there are advantages too (both, from SML's and women's perspectives): at any time the exact availability of funds is known and pooling can allow better financial intermediation and investments.

Credit Rules

Loans are given after four weeks of group functioning. To begin with, two members from a group are provided first-cycle loans of Rs 5,000 or less as general loans at 15 per cent interest. Once weekly repayment is established, after another four weeks, the next two members get their loans.

Finally, the group leader receives her loan after another four weeks. This completes the first cycle, and then further cycles follow with larger amounts of loans. Applications for loans are processed during weekly meetings. Actual credit disbursement takes place at the branch office so that staff does not have to carry large sums of cash. A member has to go to the branch office (till April 2001 to centre meetings) only once a year to collect her disbursement. Each member has her own passbook under SML for keeping track of loan taken and repayments made. No physical or financial collateral is required. The group's social collateral is treated as adequate guarantee (all group members sign on the form before disbursement), together with a signature of the 'guardian' (husband, father, brother, son, mother, or another family member considered suitable) of the woman at the time of disbursement. In case no male relative is available, a female relative is readily accepted. When enquired about this practice, the reason given was that when women are away for extended periods (for example, during delivery or illness), it is the husband or another family member who is expected to continue with the repayments. SML wants to avoid situations where the husbands deny knowledge or responsibility for the loans in their wives' absence. The interest rates are reasonable, ranging from 10–15 per cent per annum depending on the purpose of loan (when compared to 100 per cent in the case of moneylenders) while at the same time allowing enough margin for SML to be viable. Repayments start from the week immediately following disbursement and are collected at the weekly meetings.

Actual Lending Operations

Currently, seven types of loan products are on SML's books: general loans, supplementary loans, seasonal loans, housing loans, sanitation loans, special loans, and small enterprise loans. Table 3.2 provides details on the nature of each kind of loan, interest charges, repayment schedule and share of the loan in total lending. As can be seen, the general loans of around Rs 5,000 are the main products for financing

TABLE 3.2
Loan Products and their Cumulative Relative Share

Loan type	Period	Interest rate (percentage)	Repayment system*	Nature of security	Number of loans and percentage	Million rupees disbursed (percentage)
1. General loan (Rs 5,000, for small-scale income generation activities)	50 weeks	15	50 equal weekly instalments	Nil (group's social collateral)	164,392 (79.74)	784.24 (87.83)
2. Seasonal loan (like agriculture)	50 weeks	15	50 equal weekly instalments	Nil (group's social collateral)	28,692 (13.92)	75.31 (8.43)
3. Supplementary loan (Rs 2,000, working capital support for general loans)	25 weeks	10	25 equal weekly instalments	Nil (group's social collateral)	11,376 (5.52)	24.47 (2.74)
4. Housing loans (Rs 7,000–15,000)	200 weeks	15	200 equal weekly instalments	Nil (group's social collateral)	1,019 (0.49)	7.71 (0.86)
5. Special loans	15 weeks	5	15 equal weekly instalments	Nil (group's social collateral)	542 (0.26)	1.08 (0.12)

Loan type						
6. Sanitary loans (Rs 4,000, for sanitation)	50 weeks	15	50 equal weekly instalments	Nil (group's social collateral)	75 (0.04)	0.01 (0.002)
7. Small enterprise loans (Rs 10,000 for loans for enterprises larger than general loans)	50 weeks	15	50 equal weekly instalments	Fully secured	56 (0.03)	0.06 (0.007)
Total					206,152 (100)	892.88 (100)

Source: SML internal records, November 2001.
Note: * In all cases, repayment commences from the week following disbursement.

income-generating activities. Responding to demands for larger loan sizes for income generation, a new loan product being tried is the small enterprise loan repayable in a year. Even though this loan size appears small as compared with the demands made by mature borrowers (Rs 10,000–40,000), it is certainly a step in the right direction. If SML can mobilize funds for same, it will expand availability for such loans. Currently, no consumption loan is available. Members are allowed to use their savings from SIM for this purpose, though very few actually avail of this facility.

In all, as of 30 November 2001, of the 94,374 members there are 73,675 with live loan accounts. The total number of loans is 206,152. Thus, on an average, a member has received 2.8 loans. Taken together, the loan sizes are small, averaging Rs 4,528, and ensure that better-off people are not attracted.

Nature of Productive Enterprises and their Sustainability

An overwhelming majority of the enterprises is run by the women themselves or jointly by the husband and wife. Group activities are not the norm. It was also observed that member households took up more than one income-generating activity to cope with seasonality, spread business risks, and to repay weekly instalments. This contrasts with the SGSY approach that either encourages group members to take up a common and single activity or form groups of persons already engaged in a similar activity.

Because of the cautiousness with which women deploy funds and make choices, the increases in income are small (low risk, low return), especially in the beginning, but by and large sustainable. As members gain confidence, the small loan sizes impose a restriction on the size of enterprise. Expansion of the secured small enterprise loan may help in this regard. On their own, one household was found to have accessed higher level of funds under the Prime Minister's Rozgar Yojana scheme (Rs 25,000) which helped it purchase an additional grinding machine and tie up electrification. Tie-ups with commercial banks were not seen. SML does not get into the issue of strengthening backward (for example, raw material) and forward (for example, market) linkages. However, the annual branch-level workshops organized by SML do provide a forum for information exchange across centres and interactions with specialists invited to participate.

Mechanisms for Record-keeping and Accounting

The staff of SML and SIM maintains records and accounts. Other than an attendance book where members present sign their names, all other records are available only at the branch offices and these are updated every week, no doubt very promptly, by the field staff and sent to the head office. In all the branches visited, updated records and accounts were found. No capacity building inputs are provided to members on bookkeeping or record maintenance. However, the members have all been taught to sign their names. This undoubtedly has given them self-confidence. But it could also give them a way of signing off documents without fully understanding what they are accepting. A beginning, at least, to keep minutes of the weekly meetings could be made to help members eventually maintain their own records and accounts. Even in groups where all members are illiterate, they could seek the help of their daughters to help them with the writing.

Women's Experiences in Accessing Loans

Women report the enormous value of regular access to credit (as against none or one-time access) to themselves and their families. They found the procedures simple; there was no need to make repeated trips. The SML field staff had already helped them in filling out the single form required and obtained the signatures of the other group members at a previous weekly group meeting. They did not find it a problem to bring an additional family member to sign (preferably 'guardian') at the time of collecting the money. There were no complaints about delays or leakages. Some women reported initial hesitation in joining because they were not sure about their ability to repay every week. Others reported that they did not really believe the SML staff when they were told that loans were being given without collateral at reasonable interest rates. But once the first few loans were actually disbursed in the village, the information spread and membership increased. Weekly payments were not considered a problem as it reduced their interest burden and actually eased repayments.

Savings–Credit Linkages

Except for the precondition of weekly savings, there is no operational linkage between the size of savings and the size of credit. Members with very low savings also get equal access to the loans. While it may appear that SIM collects resources from the poor, SML actually lends far more than SIM collects. Overall, credit (through SML) to savings ratio has not only been well above unity, it has even increased from an already high 5.4–6.3 between August 2000 and November 2001,[8] showing that SML credit has grown faster than SIM savings. As in November 2001, the amount of credit disbursed stood at Rs 893.5 million, while the amount of savings collected was only Rs 142.8 million.

Credit Plus Interventions

Facilitation to groups to take up other issues like alcoholism, participation in gram sabhas (village assemblies), and standing for local body elections is outside the scope of SML's operations. Similarly, the facilitation of linkages between groups and other organizations like district/mandal

---

[8] These figures were noted during MC-RIL rating, a micro-finance risk rating and risk assessment exercise by Micro-credit Rating and Guarantees India Limited, which gave SML an alpha+ rating grade, valid up to September 2001.

administration, the district rural development agencies (DRDAs), gram panchayats (village local self-governance unit), village development officers and village administrative officers is not part of SML's activities. While SML does not discourage group members from accessing benefits from other agencies, it does not play any role there. With respect to forging linkages between group members and formal sector banks, SML perceives that banks do not provide any credit to the poor, hence it is stepping in to fill the gap. Thus, it views itself as a substitute to banks.

Sustainability of SML

The primary thrust of SML is on financial sustainability. This is efficiently ensured with the overall repayment rate consistently at 100 per cent (all braches) and a steadily increasing overall operational self-sufficiency that stands at an impressive 104 per cent (percentage varying across branches) as on November 2001 (Table 3.1), indicating more than full cost coverage. In fact, SML also takes into account inflation and the implied interest subsidy,[9] as against actual cost of funds to SML to monitor its financial self-sufficiency in real terms that stands at 96 per cent.[10] These ratios help the institution in remaining sustainable and accessing commercial funds from India and international sources for its operations. Though sustainability of empowering processes is not the main focus, reliable and ongoing access of members to credit has resulted in some near permanent lifestyle and attitudinal changes among women and men, as discussed later.

---

[9] An interest subsidy arises when rising prices lower the purchasing power (value) of money, whereby the money interest rate agreed today is worth less when it is paid back at a later date. Thus, the borrower in fact pays lower (real) interest than indicated in the original contract.
[10] Though not required in India, this more stringent standard is useful for SML to attract international funds.

Changes in the Lives of
Individual Women Members

Poverty Reduction

A vast majority of the activities are micro-enterprises yielding net incomes ranging between Rs 30 and 150 per day (as reported by the women). This is higher than the typical wage earnings through *coolie* work of Rs 20 per day. The increase in income is higher in the case of mature members than new members. A recent study by Cashpor (cited in Gibbons, 2001) covering 125 mature clients from three branches found that 76.8 per cent of SML's mature clients had seen a reduction in their poverty status, with as many as 38 per cent moving into the 'non-poor' category from 'very poor' or 'moderately poor'. This is an impressive reduction in poverty. Of those with whom interactions were held for this study, 100 per cent of the mature members confirmed significant income increases and better living standards through access to micro-credit. By contrast, among new and non-members, only 22 per cent reported increased incomes. Moreover, these income increases among mature members were stable enough to help poor households face crises, mainly because of multiple income sources and variety of activities undertaken through multiple small loans. Again, as per the Cashpor study, 82 per cent of the mature clients with three or more sources of income had experienced significant reduction in poverty, as against only 47 per cent with a single source of income (ibid.).

Self-confidence and Ambition

The first change that attracts the attention of an observer is an enormous increase in self-confidence among the participating women. This is in sharp contrast with women who are non-members or have newly joined the groups. Members who are in their third or later cycle of loans are very articulate, not at all hesitant while talking to strangers, can confidently face audiences and questions, and like to be well groomed. There is also a discernible increase in ambition for themselves. Those who have taken two loans want a third and larger loan since they want to expand and diversify their source of income. Women have also started wanting better lives for their children. They discourage their sons from dropping out of school and even send them to university or for technical/vocational education. Many also want to let their daughters study. In the voice of a member: 'Earlier we never thought about such things. My older daughter was married at 16. Now I want my younger daughter to study as much as she wants to.' Members listen to talks on television, which inspire many to value education for the future benefit of their children.

Men also observed changes in women. The husband of a member commented about his wife's (a 4-year-old member) transformed personality: 'She signs her name. She has learnt how to talk to senior officials. She wishes people. She has become disciplined and brings money into the family. What is bad about it?' The SML staff noted similar changes. Said a young FCO:

Initially, the members used to talk crudely or roughly. After a couple of years their style and behaviour was much more cultured and they have learnt how to communicate with higher officials and seniors. In areas populated by Muslims, women hardly came out of their homes, but now they attend centre meetings regularly with others and go out for marketing. In one case, a Muslim woman is even going to Hyderabad and Mumbai for her cloth business.

In fact, one senior member, Ms Razia of Indira Nagar Colony, is now on the board of SML.

Control over Income, Assets and Expenditure

Though the loans are all in the name of the woman, there are various combinations of participation in business ownership: wife supplying resources and labour for husband's business; joint ownership and running of a family business by husband and wife; wife running her own business with active support from the husband; husband joining the wife after giving up previous work; wife running her business with passive support or mere acknowledgement by husband; and a widow or abandoned woman running her business by herself. Concomitantly, the extent of control over business assets and income arising thereof is inherently variable, with the latter combinations allowing for greater control.

Women with a relatively longer-term membership (two years or more) said they were free to buy personal things without consulting their husbands. For example, one woman stated: 'If I want to buy a sari, I just do it. I don't ask. I tell him later.' Other members confirmed that this was so in their cases also. New members and non-members who did not yet have their own income stream necessarily relied on explicit consent from their husbands for any purchases. Decisions regarding expenses on food and cooking were generally with the women, even before membership. But additional earning by women has changed the diet patterns and eating arrangements within the household. Senior members explained how they gathered *punlukura* (or *gonkura*) leaves, cooked them, and ate them with rice or *rotis* earlier. In contrast, now, they say: 'We go to the market and actually buy vegetables', or 'We also eat meat items once a week now', or 'One of the members sells us vegetables and even guavas', or 'Earlier children ate first, then husbands, and I ate last what was leftover, but now we all eat together— after all I am also earning! But sometimes if children are hungry, they still eat first!' As the entire family was eating better, girl children were also getting to eat more than earlier.

Women now have a say on utilization of income contributed by them. In Udumeshwaram village, a member observed: 'How can I be questioned when I am giving the money?' She had repaired her house and purchased a fan. On spending income for personal needs, the women said, 'What do you think we spend on? It is mostly for the family or for the business! But we can easily buy small things, like bangles, for ourselves.' About husbands, they said, 'They spend on hotels, cigarettes and drinks. When they meet friends, they spend. It is not like women.' The men also agreed with this assessment.

However, on major capital items, members universally said that they would consult their husbands and take a joint decision. If, for example, they had to dispose of land or incur capital expenditure on equipment or undertake house improvement, it was a joint decision. One woman was surprised by the question and retorted,

> How is it possible for us to buy an asset without the husband's consent? After all, he would also have to ask me if he wanted to buy or sell something big! In any case you don't give us the loan without his signature!

Gender issues and women's empowerment are not seen as areas where men are pitted against women. Rather, women interpret the situation as one of expanding spaces and choices for themselves and getting recognition and respect within and outside the household.

Support from Husbands and Spread Effects

In the very early stages, there was some reluctance on the part of men and they doubted whether SML was genuine. However, this attitude is hardly visible today. Not only is there support, in case after case, husbands come forward to say how they encouraged their wives' membership. Some of the remarks made by husbands of members are: 'At first I had this doubt—you don't know us. How are you going to give loans without surety? Now we believe, after the money has started flowing.' Another said, 'I'm the one who encouraged my wife to join.' To a specific question about what was negative about the groups, the reply was, 'What is there to dislike? How can I invent shortcomings when it is all good?'

In only two cases, men were found unwilling to support the programme. In one case, the woman (from a Muslim household) had gone ahead and become a member anyway, using her young son to co-sign. In the other case, the man said he was not keen that his wife joins groups. But he still wanted to find out the benefits, so he had come for the discussion. Perhaps after a period of observation, his wife might become a member.

Spread effects are clearly visible, and evident in the growth in micro-credit operations of SML (Table 3.1). In all villages visited, the number of member borrowers has grown. People from non-SML villages come to observe SML centre operations to start similar activities there. Often men were found to take the lead.

Work, Labour and Leisure Choices

The first change is the reduction of wage labour in favour of becoming owner-managers. As one member put it,

> Coolie work is coming down. We used to work from eight in the morning to six in the evening for Rs 20 only! And we had to carry our food tied in a cloth! Now we can choose how to spend our time and earn more money.

A member in Udumeshwaram village who had already taken two loans (Rs 5,000 for a sewing machine and Rs 9,000 for a flour mill, supplemented by a loan from the Pradhan Mantri Rozgar Yojana) and had fully repaid both, wanted a third loan for a hairdresser's shop for her husband. He was a wageworker in someone else's barbershop. She explained: 'If we own a shop, I can also go there and do hairdressing for girls.'

Women have started enjoying leisure activities. 'I bought a tape recorder to listen to music', explained a member from Yenkepalli. Others said they watch television now that they have electricity. However, some women thought they worked more than before, as 'even at night, we think about our business'. But these choices of how many hours of work to put in for their businesses as against other activities were their own. Moreover, hard physical labour seems to have declined.

Non-market Work and its Sharing within the Household

In activities such as household work and child care, by and large no reduction of load for women was seen. Most women replied that they were used to doing such work, and that they had not thought about sharing. However, there were some exceptions. In Gumastanagar, a visit to a member's house-cum-grinding mill showed that the husband had gone shopping for the household while the member was at the mill waiting for customers. She showed this researcher around her house where there was a fan and some furniture and a kitchen equipped with a gas stove. The use of cooking gas had reduced the time and drudgery of firewood collection as well as cleaning. In another case, in N.T. Rama Rao (NTR)[11] Nagar in a Muslim weaver's family, the husband came forward to explain: 'I make *dosas* and *idlis* for the hotel when my wife is at centre meetings.' It was the fourth year of his wife's membership and she had already taken three loans. He had given up his work as a construction labourer and joined his wife's business. On the whole, men are assisting more in enterprise activities than domestic chores.

Access to Public Resources

Changes in attitudes towards girls' education have already been commented on. If one considers the sphere of health, in instances of serious ill health as well as for sterilization operations, members and their families do access government hospitals and health centres. There is, however, a preference for home remedies for minor ailments. This is also common among new and non-members. While the quality and timeliness of health services have been reported to be variable, expectations from 'free' services are also not high.

Women themselves have little or no systematic access to technology or training. Skill training for members and facilitating access to technology is not part of SML's agenda. However, there is a great interest in these areas. Women are very interested in upgrading their skills to improve their businesses and make quantum jumps in their enterprises. Some have accessed training programmes of the rural development department of the government on their own. But such examples are few, and this is a gap that could be

---

[11] NTR was a well-known film actor, who later went on to become a Chief Minister of Andhra Pradesh.

redressed. Yet another unfulfilled need is improved access to, and quality of, housing. This need is met to a small extent by accessing SML's housing loans. Increased incomes are not enough for such improvements, and expansion of housing loans and mobilization of government programmes for housing is essential. In one colony, members were living in government constructed cement houses.

Women's Physical Mobility

Borrower members, including those from Muslim households, travelled much more freely in connection with their businesses, both within and outside their villages. There were no objections from family members regarding attending weekly meetings in the village or workshops at the branch level. If marketing or procurement involved travel outside the village/district, and in a few cases, even outside the state, women were doing so. They were also staying out late. One member from Mangalagiri village remarked, 'Now women can move freely up to 8 p.m. or even 9 p.m. because it is for business. Money is coming in! Who will object?' Such opportunities were far less for non-borrowers. However, travelling for pleasure was not reported as is observed in Tamil Nadu where members have pooled money and undertaken group holidays or pilgrimages.

Visiting their natal households was common among all women, not just members. For example, it was common for them to stay up to even six months with their mothers for their deliveries. Similarly, visits during festivals or religious occasions were common. Even during illnesses, women routinely sought rest and support from their natal households. In fact, among some members home visits have reduced due to business preoccupations, including in cases where the parents lived in the same village.

Breaking Social Barriers

More than half the groups were of mixed castes (for example, Scheduled Castes and backward classes together in one group) or religious groups, resulting in far greater interaction across community lines. This has helped break down social barriers within groups. At the beginning of each centre meeting, the members and SML staff took an oath that included a line on non-discrimination on the basis of a person's community background. The members were proud of the mixing with different caste groups. In Yenkepalli, the women listed out the various communities (Gollas, Mudras, Mala, Madiga) and observed: 'We are all together. There is no problem at all. It is not relevant. We are all poor.' A centre leader from N.T. Rama Rao Nagar said: 'We have Hindus, Muslims and Christians! It is not important.' A member from Gumastanagar village remarked, 'Whatever be our caste, we all have to die in the end! And meanwhile we all have to make good money to live! How does thinking about things like caste help? You tell me!' Members also interacted outside centre meetings, independent of SML. For example, in Udumeshwaram, a member explained how, when her mother died, all others from the centre had come 'to console and help me when my mind was upset'.

SML staff reported marriages between children of members, often without dowry but rather on the basis of expenditure sharing. Members and SML staff reported a specific case from Venigandla village, Guntur, where the centre leader's daughter had married a group leader's son. It is significant that the families agreed even though there was an old enmity between them arising out of a murder case where they were on opposite sides. The women met each other regularly in centre meetings that led to their children falling in love. The marriage took place without dowry. The dispute is also behind them now. However, so far, marriages continued to be on caste/religious lines, including in the case last mentioned.

Control over their Own Bodies

Questions on alcohol consumption and domestic violence initially resulted in complete denial. Slowly, members made revealing remarks such as: 'Because of our self-respect now this does not happen', or 'There is group support, so husbands are more careful' or 'Men have expectations about future loans, so there is no need for us to face beatings'. In Mangalagiri, a member proudly described a specific case: 'I know of one member's drunkard husband. He took her money. It was she who beat him up and took it back!' Another member added, 'Now we can at least talk back freely. We threaten them: we can survive well without you!' Thus, it appears that while domestic violence does exist, women's financial independence and group identity has helped in coping with it better. The remarks also indicate that, perhaps, the frequency and intensity of violent episodes may have gone down.

There could also be changes in the way parents-in-law treat their daughters-in-law. SML staff narrated the case of a young widow in Guntur. She was ill-treated by her marital family, causing her mental distress. After she joined a group, she first took a small loan for just Rs 1,000 to start petty trading in canteen items. Her second loan was for a buffalo. After her third loan she expanded and diversified to start a small restaurant. Once she was financially secure, her parents-in-law started helping her with the business.

On choices regarding number of children, the majority (84.8 per cent) prefers a small family size (one or two children), regardless of whether women were long-duration members or new/non-members. The reasons given were revealing: 'Indira Gandhi said so'; 'We can't afford many children. Who will spend on bringing them up?'; 'It's not good for women's health'; 'If we have too many children, we would have to make them coolies'; 'Where is the time to take care of so many if we have to do our business?'; 'The television showed that there is nothing wrong with having girls.' It appears that a combination of economic, social and health reasons have contributed to a preference for smaller family, this being an overall trend effect.

Individual enquiries regarding actual family size revealed that there was a gap between the desired and actual number of children in the case of 59 per cent of members. In 51 per cent of the cases, actual fertility was higher than desired, and in 8 per cent, it was lower than desired. Detailed interactions revealed that younger women (35 years or less), regardless of the duration of membership in groups, were better able to actualize their preferences to have less children as compared with older women. It is age (showing a trend effect) rather than duration of membership that seems to contribute to control over fertility. It is interesting that even among older women, many replied that they like the trend towards less children and felt that two children were enough. The common reasons given by the older women for the gap between the preferred number of children and the actual number were: 'We were waiting for a male child' or 'My father-in-law and mother-in-law insisted on a son.' But some young women said that group membership helped them decide on their own without succumbing to pressures from elders.

On contraception, the adoption of terminal methods by women was nearly universal, as against the usage of temporary methods. While younger women tended to undergo sterilization operations after two children, there were about half who had done so after three or four, either after the birth of a son or after giving up hoping for a son. All the women with whom the subject was explored confirmed that (a) they discussed the matter with their husbands before the operations; and (b) it was the woman's idea or a joint decision between husband and wife. No case of vasectomy was reported.

On the preferred sex of children, the desire for a male child persists. When the issue of reasons for preferring a male child were explored, the replies were: 'Girls are an expense because of dowry'; 'They go away after marriage, and are of no use to parents'; 'The family name continues with the sons'; They provide security in old age.' During discussions in NTR Nagar, a new member complained that she had two daughters when another member of four years emphatically said, 'I have three children, all sons! Now I want a daughter!'

While a son preference is common, longer-duration members were also able to counter many reasons: 'Girls continue to look after parents even after marriage. Don't we, now that we have money?' or 'Girls provide good security for their parents, better than sons, when they have their own business'. The discussions led many members to understand that they themselves were already helping their parents in many ways, more so after achieving economic independence.

Changes in Position and Status of Women's Groups in the Community

Participation in Political Spaces/Processes

Political participation, as voters, was nearly universal but on an individual basis, rather than as groups. While most women make up their own minds, they are influenced by discussions in the community, husbands' opinions, and money paid by candidates. Only in Nandivelugu village did group members reply almost unanimously that they took money from both parties (Rs 100 each) and voted as per the directions of their husbands. There was only one exception who said: 'My husband and I discussed. Then, to be fair, I voted for one and he voted for the other.' (They had taken money from both factions!)

Women had also started participating as candidates, especially in the local body elections. This had been spurred by the policy of reserving one-third of the seats for women. Discussions with SML staff (FCOs) at Tandur branch office revealed that there were many examples of group members standing as candidates and two specific cases where members had been elected to the office of the *sarpanch* (panchayat head) in their villages (Gottika and Devanur). 'We hope to see a Member of the Legislative Assembly one day from our groups', said one staff member. In Yenkepalli branch too, examples were narrated of members who contested from reserved women's seats, but lost by narrow margins of one or two votes. In Mangalagiri area, the vice-president in one of the gram panchayats (Pathuru) was a member. An example was reported of a member who had stood and won from a general seat (R.R. Nagar), which was a significant development. But in Nandivelugu, there was not much political interest. Women's replies to questions of standing for elections were: 'We have not yet thought of this' or 'Standing for election needs investment, but there is no guarantee of winning!'

On the quality of candidature, it was commonly felt, in both Ranga Reddy and Guntur districts, that while it was women's reservations that had helped them come forward in greater numbers as candidates, it was the self-confidence built due to group membership that had contributed to SML women being seen as 'genuine' candidates as against the 'dummy women' candidates controlled by dominant interest groups. Also, where members stood, there were genuine contests. It was reported that earlier, in many villages, there was no real election at all as everything was 'fixed' and a unanimous result declared. The increase in genuine contests was seen as a significant change that was taking place due to group membership.

Attendance in gram sabhas was the exception. Most members said they did not know when a meeting was convened. They felt it was not announced or properly publicized. Some felt that this might be deliberate. There was a general feeling that attending might not be of much use if they were not going to be consulted. Groups do have the potential to start making the gram panchayat accountable to them as is observed in Tamil Nadu where, very often, it is the women's groups that are the major participants.

Overall, the conclusion is that political participation continues to be on an individual basis or through support of systems (family, community groups, payments, etc.) outside the group. This may be because SML itself has not paid attention to this aspect.

Use of Collective Strength

Given the increased confidence levels and willingness and ability to take charge of their own lives, women's groups do have the ability to start negotiating for their own interests by participating in discussions with local bodies, presenting their needs to the *mandal* or district administration, and networking with other groups outside their centres. But promoting this systematically was outside the scope of SML's sharply focused micro-credit management agenda. Nevertheless, there are scattered examples of groups using their collective strength to redress a grievance or advance the interests of their villages.

In Ranga Reddy district, some groups reported approaching government officials including the local collector and asking for water supply and road improvement. 'Because of the group we have learnt how to talk. None of us are scared anymore!' Due to their disciplined behaviour and genuine needs, the collector gave them a patient hearing, accepted their demands as legitimate, and ordered the concerned officials to take up relevant work. One husband said, 'Only the women come forward now. Earlier, none of us would approach higher officials!' In Guntur district, a member had a problem with the local ration shop. The man did not serve her properly and threw her ration card on the ground. Instead of picking it up, she marched straight to her village and gathered the group members. Together they went to the *mandal* revenue officer, filed a complaint, and got the grievance redressed. In a case of police harassment, again in Guntur, where the police picked up a member wrongly, the group intervened collectively and got her released.

Overall, due to the fact that top-level officials from state government recognize women's groups as a key tool for poverty alleviation, there is increased visibility and recognition of women's groups. Based on this principle, groups under the Development of Women and Children in Rural Areas (DWCRA) scheme have been promoted by the Government of Andhra Pradesh like elsewhere in India. Government officials invite not just DWCRA women members to participate (which at times overlaps with SML groups), but also members of groups formed by other organizations. The women members of SML are aware of this and use it for addressing collective village needs.

Changes in the Wider Socio-economic Environment

Changes in the Economic Environment

Two significant changes are observed in the wider economy: a sharp reduction in dependence on moneylenders and a diversification of the rural economy. The immediate advantage of alternative credit access on a regular and reliable basis for consumption, emergency, and business needs has directly contributed to members redeeming their previous high cost debts by the second or third SML loan. Freedom from moneylenders has also given them back their self-respect. In case after case, the researcher was told how even for Rs 1,000 they had to make several visits to the *patel* (upper-caste moneylender) and plead with him before he released the money. Not only were the interest rates charged exorbitant (ranging between 60 and 120 per cent per annum), but as the women said, 'Our husbands were also at the beck and call of the patels. They made our men sweep their houses and yards and work on their fields for low wages ...'; or 'Sometimes, we borrowed Rs 900 in the morning and repaid Rs 1,000 by the evening of the same day! On top of that we had to provide collateral!' The interest rates were so high that even if the principal was written off, the moneylenders would still make profits on interest collections alone.

SML field staff explained how there was some resistance initially from moneylenders who tried to discourage the women from joining. Moneylenders were reported to say: 'How long can SML provide loans? They'll give you once and go away, but we are here permanently.' Moneylenders also approached SML staff and advised them to go away from their villages saying that the women would not repay. SML staff rose to these challenges and convinced members that they were also in the business on a long-term basis. This message has gone down well among the members. No reduction was observed in interest rates charged by moneylenders as an effect of competition from SML's credit operations. Local enquiries revealed that moneylenders were now lending to the poor among non-members and non-poor households, which provided them with adequate business. There was no increase observed in bank lending to women. SML was a bank substitute.

Coming to the second change, a substantial diversification of the rural economy has happened as a result of loans. There is a clear emergence of a service and business sector. Small loans and weekly repayments support income generation activities that yield daily/weekly returns, like trade and other services. Apart from the traditional buffalo-, goat- and agriculture-based activities, a number of new activities have sprung up. The more successful ones include petty shops, bicycle rentals, stone polishing (for floors), readymade clothes, cut-piece shops, fruit and vegetable sales, flowers, mutton shops, *beedi* making, small hotels, tea shops, and so on. Even traditional activities are being given a modern twist. For example, tailoring is linked with stitching school uniforms and embroidery with beadwork. The barber's wife is thinking of women's hairdressing, and weaving *saris* is being combined with weaving *dupattas* and suits. Women within a group select their activities in such a way as to avoid competing against each other or oversaturate the small local markets. All this has contributed to widening and deepening of the local economy.

Changes in Village Poverty Profiles

As women are taking to increased paid work, there is an increase in income and assets in their hands. Particularly WHHs (widows, divorced women, abandoned women, etc.) have tended to benefit, reducing destitution and beggary. Except in one centre (Nandivelugu) WHHs were in most cases actively encouraged to join the groups. SML head office presented the case of a beggar woman in Kurnool district who was practically on the sidelines of society. She was afraid to talk to strangers and scared that people would make fun of her. It took a while to encourage her to join a group but after 15 days of motivation by SML, she did. The first loan offered to her was for Rs 2,000, but she thought it was too much money. She took only Rs 500 and used it to start selling small fancy things like plastic items and mirrors. She earned her first profit of Rs 7, which surprised her but sparked off a desire to improve her situation further. Her successive loans were larger. She graduated from a small basket that was her mobile shop to a pushcart. She is no longer in poverty and has even availed a housing loan. Several such individual stories demonstrate the rapidly changing poverty profiles.

Higher and steadier incomes also contribute to better food and nutrition. Better nutritional situation among women and girls is important on several counts: their own well-being, the health of the future generation, and reduction of loss of work days and incomes. A definitive assessment of the health and nutritional status of poor households would involve anthropometric measurements among growing children (weight-for-age, height-for-age, weight-for-height, etc.) and an examination of clinical signs of malnutrition, preferably over a period, which was outside the scope of this study. However, feedback from member families was illuminating. Diet patterns had definitely changed. There was an increase in food availability; red gram and black gram pulses were additions. There was regular consumption of purchased vegetables such as tomatoes, brinjals and okra, and inclusion of fruits such as guavas and bananas in the diet. Meat was consumed weekly. This meant a greater availability of vitamins and proteins, apart from carbohydrates. Earlier, _gonkura_ leaves and rice formed the staple diet with meats being consumed only on festivals or special functions. Women no longer eat last or the least. They are also more aware of treating their daughters on an equal footing as their sons. These changes can be expected to have reduced hunger and short-term malnutrition, especially among women and girls. Currently, it is taste and general impression about well-being that drive food patterns. If income increases are combined with systematic nutrition education, forging systematic links between group and _anganwadis_ under the Integrated Child Development Scheme (ICDS), the health and nutrition impacts can be strengthened. Groups could even consider monitoring/running _anganwadis_ on a trial basis, depending on local interest.

Women are more conscious and confident about monitoring the public distribution system (PDS) shops. They are less likely to put up with undermeasurements, avoidable stock-outs, or other irregularities. However, they have yet to take over the running of PDS shops as a social or even economic activity.

Impact on Child Labour and Education

In certain occupations, children help their mothers by dealing with customers in petty shops, minding a grinding mill, or painting/repairing the premises. Children help out only after school and during holidays, without affecting their access to education. In fact, in some cases, the children even force their mothers to learn how to write. Hence the easy availability of micro-credit is not observed to increase paid child labour or withdrawal of children from school to augment family income. Rather, increased incomes are used to help children study further.

However, when a child had already dropped out, he did become an earner. But in all such cases it was observed the son was found to work independently, generally as a labourer or in other wage employment, not in the mother's business. If it were a daughter who dropped out, she would be married. No cases of a dropout rejoining school were observed because parents now have additional incomes.

Conclusion

SML's experiences with micro-finance demonstrate that this primarily credit-for-income generation-based model of small women's groups, well-oriented in receiving and repaying loans, closely supervised with trained staff does lead to significant, first-level improvements in the individual lives of members and their households, in contrast to non-members or new members. There are also some beginnings of change in the position and status of women's groups as collectives. In respect of the wider socio-economic environment, changes are observed in respect to dependence on money-lenders, poverty profiles in villages, and a greater willingness to retain children, especially girls, in full-time education. The changes are all considered positive by women as well as men. These developments are taking place in the absence of systematic capacity building on gender or women's empowerment issues. The nature of facilitation for social mobilization and capacity building of group members itself influences the range and extent of empowerment, no less than credit. The potential for change seems to be greater than what has been actualized so far.

There are increases in incomes and assets in the hands of poor women, which is a significant improvement over their pre-membership situation. The benefits from this increase flow to the household as a whole. Other family members, in particular husbands, well appreciate women contributing more money to the household on a regular basis. Consequently, other non-income benefits to women like changes in personality, greater self-confidence and greater say within and outside the house are not resisted.

The consistent 100 per cent repayment rates have not only enabled women to access repeat loans, but also enabled women to be able to rely on repeat loans. Moreover, high rates of repayment combined with prudent cost consciousness has made SML's operations sustainable in the long run. It also makes SML an attractive investment destination for commercial financial institutions, enabling greater resource flow in future.

However, loan sizes are currently small, restricting further growth of businesses. SML is aware of this and in the process of experimenting with larger small enterprise loans for members who have a long and sound repayment history. Technical skill training to improve existing skills and to learn new skills is absent and most women restrict their businesses to what they already know and to local markets. There is no support for strengthening marketing through expanding skills in sales, design, modern packaging, branding, standardization and quality control. These factors also limit business and income growth. Because of the sharply focused objectives of SML and its concern with costs, such support is currently outside their agenda.

Women have greater control over their resources—assets, earnings and savings. A husband cannot sell the asset acquired on the basis of a loan from SML, except with the woman's consent. Women have a greater say in household expenditure, arising directly from their contributions. They are spending on gas stoves and fans that reduce the drudgery of domestic work and thus improve quality of life of family members. However, other independent expenditure on themselves, though more than before, tends to be small, restricted to saris and bangles, with most of their money being used for the benefit of the household or for improving their micro-businesses. For major expenses, women consult their husbands. However, the reverse is true too: now husbands also consult their wives more often than earlier.

A significant change is the transformation of women from low-wage workers to owner-managers. This is widely valued not only because of higher income prospects, but also due to a perceived increase in dignity and control. This change is associated with less time spent in hard labour as well as, in some cases, more time spent on the new work situation. However, more time spent on work is seen as resulting in more returns, and therefore liked by them.

There is an increased cooperation between husbands and wives. While husbands have not started helping in any significant way in unpaid domestic work, they have started helping in their wives' business-related work, especially where the businesses are thriving. Some have even given up their own occupations to join their wives on a full-time basis. While this is seen as beneficial, whether this could eventually lead to a lessening of control by women is not as yet clear. However, women's access to credit, combined with self-confidence, is a countervailing factor, helping to keep control with women. Moreover, SML itself would like to see women retain control so that repayments are not adversely affected. This congruence of interest between SML and members contributes to the first level of women's empowerment.

Increased incomes have resulted in very visible increases in self-confidence and self-worth. Women volunteer to give their opinions, are more articulate, can negotiate better within their households, can present their demands to government officials without hesitation, and can ask questions and demand information. Many report picking up new ideas from the television. Women's mobility has increased and they travel more freely. Other family members consider it legitimate that women stay out late in connection with group meetings or business. But women are not yet commonly riding mopeds and bicycles (as is observed in Maharashtra and parts of Tamil Nadu). Travelling or staying out late for other reasons like tourism or pilgrimage is not reported.

While domestic violence is not eliminated, women members report a decrease, combined with their increased ability to cope with it. They relate this to their increased economic worth. Birth control is almost universally practised, especially among the younger generation. This is more a trend effect, rather than one arising out of group membership. Women are discussing contraception issues with their husbands. While there is a desire for small family size with one or two children, there is still a preference for a male child. Women undergo terminal methods of birth control after the couple has attempted to have a son, often resulting in family sizes larger than desired. Male sterilization is rare, even though simpler and less expensive. However, simultaneously, there is an increase in the value of girls. Younger daughters are more likely to remain in school for longer periods and married later. Increased value for daughters is related to group membership.

As groups, the local village communities have started to recognize women's collectives. They are regarded not only as important sources of credit access and incomes, but also as tools to approach officials and articulate village needs. However, the picture on political/democratic empowerment is mixed. SML, of course, does not concern itself with orienting women on these issues. Voting is near universal, regardless of group membership. While a majority of members seem to be voting as per their own decisions, there are examples of members voting as per instructions of husbands. A far larger number of women are standing as candidates for elections to local bodies than before. While this is primarily a result of reservations for women, rather than group membership, the effect of SML is seen in the quality of candidature. More 'genuine' women candidates are reported to come from out of group members and real contests are reported from constituencies where members have stood. But there is very limited participation in the grama sabhas. Most members reported that they did not even know when the grama sabhas were conducted or what was to be discussed in them. The groups are not yet a democratic force and wooing for votes takes place more on a community basis.

Government agencies and banks do not recognize SML groups for linkages and benefits, perhaps due to SML itself being independent of government, a bank substitute. SML does not facilitate these linkages. The groups see SML as a bank, popularly calling it 'SHARE Bank'. However, in individual cases members are accessing benefits from government schemes. SML is open about this and does not inhibit them from availing these benefits. Some groups have been successful in placing their needs before the relevant authorities and getting them addressed. Such linkages could be more systematically facilitated at group/centre levels in sectors where there is no competition or conflict of approach, for example, for improved access to and a say in the operation of health centres, ICDS services, PDS, water supply, sanitation, education for girls, etc., rather than with SGSY or NABARD's SHG–bank linkage programme.

Changes in the wider socio-economic environment are more significant than changes in groups. There is a sharp reduction in dependence on moneylenders among member households, especially after the second year. The rural economy is getting more diversified as members take to a variety of economic activities. Growth of the service sector is observed. These developments help in combating seasonality factors and business risks, contributing to a widening and deepening of the rural economy. Poverty profiles are changing. More WHHs derive economic and social benefits of group membership. More widows and abandoned women enjoy greater security. However, while SML aims to target poor women, there are also cases where member orientation has not focused on this, resulting in the exclusion of the worst off as they are seen as unable to cope with weekly repayments. Diet patterns have improved with consumption of a variety of purchased vegetables and fruits (as against gathered leaves with rice and *rotis*) and weekly consumption of meat. With an increase in market-oriented work for women, a possible temptation to utilize the help of children to earn more can arise, adversely affecting their attendance and enrolment in schools. But this is not in fact observed. Members are more aware of the value of education, including for girls.

It is husbands who are helping out more than children. Children do help, but not during school hours.

The changes that are taking place flow from the joint facilitation of group strengthening with credit access for women, rather than from credit access per se. Moreover, the nature of social mobilization and the kind of capacity building that takes place in the process of group formation seems to be just as important in influencing the type and extent of women's empowerment. SML's focus being prim-arily credit-based for income generation and poverty reduction, there are limitations to the range and extent of empowerment that can be reasonably expected to take place 'incidentally'. Certain changes are not part of SML's agenda like orientation of women on gender and women's empowerment, orientation of men and building in them skills to cope with changing male–female relationships, deepening democratic participation, and enabling women to address not just their practical needs but also their strategic interests. Hence, it would not be fair to expect them to have taken place.

The conclusion here is that a very good triggering off for women's empowerment has taken place with a strong economic foundation, and a precondition for further change has been established. Now the time is ripe for a more explicit strategy to widen the scope of women's empowerment. Awareness building on gender and empowerment among, both the facilitators and members of micro-finance can help counter historical, patriarchal, socio-cultural and political factors, which prevent women and men from growing up to their full potential and supplementing SML's economic inputs. It is not necessary that this awareness generation be funded by SML. Alternatives could be considered. For example, SML could consider linking up with other relevant agencies and individual specialists on gender for building capacity in this area. SHARE Society itself could work in tandem with SML or set up another wing within the SHARE group. There does not have to be a contradiction between a primarily credit-based and primarily other-than-credit-based approach, as each has the potential to strengthen the other, forging a symbiotic relationship.

References

Gibbons, David S., 2001, *Poverty Reduced Through Micro-finance at SHARE Microfin Limited* (draft, 9 March), Cashpor.

IFPRI (International Food Policy Research Institute) and NIRD (National Institute of Rural Development), 2000, *Assessing the Relative Poverty Level of MFI Clients—Development of an Operational Tool: Synthesis Report for the Case Study of SHARE India*, Washington, DC, and Hyderabad: IFPRI and NIRD.

4

Social Mobilization and Micro-credit for Women's Empowerment: A Study of the DHAN Foundation

Veena Padia

Background

The concept of empowerment is being used increasingly as a tool for understanding what is needed to change the situation of women and other marginalized sections of society. The proponents of micro-finance consider economic empowerment as an entry point and a road map towards overall empowerment. It is believed that non-economic benefits flow automatically as a consequence of this approach. This chapter examines whether extending micro-finance along with a process of social mobilization is sufficient to foster a process of poor women's empowerment using the case study of the Development of Humane Action (DHAN) Foundation.[1]

Intensive field visits and investigations and direct observations formed the basis of examining and assessing empowerment processes unfolding at individual and collective levels. It was not possible to use a structured sample survey due to lack of time. The attempt was to identify qualitative changes taking place among the women through their own voices, and the voices of indirect stakeholders such as community

---

[1] A profile of the Foundation follows later in the chapter.

leaders, government functionaries at the village level, bankers, and the staff of the DHAN Foundation.

Members and leaders at the group, cluster and federation levels were met as groups, and issues such as the process of group formation, decision-making, savings and lending, and financial and social sustainability were discussed. Some issues were discussed with individual members and non-members in their respective houses, as they were better discussed in a confidential atmosphere. Themes falling under this category included intra-household decision-making, division of labour, workload and mobility. Participatory exercises were used for these discussions, and a comparison was made between the situation before and after the micro-credit intervention to discern changes. This was supplemented by a comparison of the situation of the members and non-members to examine whether these changes were part of a general trend, or arose because of the micro-credit intervention. Informal discussions were also held with primary school teachers, *anganwadi* workers, local administrators, bankers, local law protection officers, village leaders and male relatives to ascertain their opinions on changes in women's lives and villages. Further, senior functionaries of the DHAN Foundation, programme leaders, leaders of federations and staff members of the clusters were met to validate the collected information and also to understand the long-term perspective of the organization. A review of secondary literature also helped in drawing conclusions.

The DHAN Foundation operates its micro-finance programme in Tamil Nadu, Pondicherry, Andhra Pradesh and Karnataka. It is called the Kalanjiam Community Banking Programme. The *kalanjiam*s or self-help groups (SHGs) at the village level have been federated at the cluster and block levels. Of the 20 registered block-level federations, three are urban-based, one is semi-urban-based, and 16 are rural-based. Three of these federations, all in Tamil Nadu, have been selected for the study. High incidences of poverty, child labour and male alcoholism are common to all districts. At the same time, there is a lot of diversity in the federations and the areas they function in. The Pothigai Vattara Kalan-jiam (PVK) federation located at Madurai West block in Madurai district is a relatively new (1999) and semi-urban federation, with 60 per cent of its population dependent on agricultural labour. Female infanticide and foeticide are not uncommon in this area, and the sex ratio is in favour of males. The Mugavai Kalanjiam Mahalir Vattara Sangam (MKMVS) federation, registered in 1995, operates in Mandapam block in Ramnad district. The block is situated in a coastal belt, and constitutes one of the most backward areas of Tamil Nadu. Muslims constitute roughly 50 per cent of the population, the rest being mainly Hindus. Unlike in Madurai West, women here outnumber men, due to male migration to more prosperous areas in and outside Tamil Nadu. The Kadamalai Kalanjiam Vattara Sangam (KKVS) federation, registered in 1995, functions in Mayiladumparai block in the backward Theni district. Dalits and tribals constitute 24 per cent of the population. Theni is also known for its incidence of female foeticide and infanticide.[2]

Within each federation, groups of different degrees of geographic remoteness and composition were selected. The discussions held in households, SHGs, clusters and block federations covered a total of 378 women, including 14 with whom intra-household dynamics were examined through participatory tools such as mapping of the gender-based division of labour and resources (Table 4.1).

The study, spanning two weeks, cannot claim to capture the impact of the entire programme of the DHAN Foundation (which is vast in nature), or all the dimensions of its impact. Nevertheless, it offers important lessons for policy-makers and practitioners. Before delving into the findings, an overview of the perspective of the DHAN Foundation on development and women's empowerment, as well as its micro-credit programme, is provided.

---

[2] Theni has a child sex ratio of less than 900 as per the 2001 census. That is, less than 900 females in the age group 0–6 are found when compared to males (Rajalakshmi, 2002).

TABLE 4.1

Comparison of the Daily Routines of a Member and Her Husband

Member's daily routine		Husband's daily routine	
Activity	Time	Activity	Time
Waking up	3 a.m.	Waking up	7 a.m.
Sweeping, cleaning, cooking, bathing, caring for cow, eating breakfast	3–7 a.m.	Bathing and eating breakfast	7–8 a.m.
Walking to the field for work	7–8 a.m.	Agricultural labour/felling wood	8–10 a.m.
Agricultural labour, collecting fuelwood	8–10 a.m.	Resting in the field	10–11 a.m.
Resting in the field	10–11 a.m.	Agriculture labour in the field	1 a.m.–2 p.m.
Agricultural labour	11 a.m.–2 p.m.	Returning home and eating	2–3 p.m.
Returning home	2–3 p.m.	Sleeping	3–5 p.m.
Cleaning vessels, washing clothes, cleaning cowshed, milking the cow	3–5 p.m.	Gathering food	5–6 p.m.
Cooking dinner and other household work	5–7 p.m.	Bathing and eating	6–7 p.m.
Watching television or sleeping	7 p.m.	Chatting with other men in village	7–9 p.m.

Perspective and Approach of the DHAN Foundation

The DHAN Foundation was initiated in October 1997 and incorporated under the Indian Trust Act (1882) in January 1998 with the objective of bringing highly motivated and educated young women and men into the development sector to promote rural innovations. The DHAN Foundation functions in 17 districts of Tamil Nadu, Andhra Pradesh, Karnataka and Pondicherry. It was created as a spin-off organization from the erstwhile NGO called PRADAN (Professional Assistance for Development Action) to expand and deepen its base in southern India.

The aim of the DHAN Foundation is to reduce poverty in its area of operation. Its mission is to build institutions for development innovations and to upscale interventions for impacting livelihoods of the poor, thereby enabling the poor to overcome poverty and realize their aspirations. This mission emanates from its core organizational values such as 'grassroots action', 'enabling', 'innovation', 'excellence' and 'collaboration'. It seeks to promote three kinds of institutions to achieve its mission: institutions for fostering development innovations, institutions for upscaling these innovations, and institutions for human resource development. The last institution seeks to attract young professionals to the development sector with a focus on strengthening their skills and competencies to undertake development work.

The DHAN Foundation therefore does not deliver services to the poor but supports the poor to articulate and realize their choices through building institutions and capacity. As part of this strategy, the DHAN Foundation has formed the institution of *kalanjiam*s (name given to SHGs, literally meaning 'mud bin used to store grains') and *vayalagam*s (tank farmers' associations) at the village level, which in turn are federated at the block and district levels. *Kalanjiam*s are formed only with women, while tank farmers' associations comprise both men and women. The Community Banking Programme (CBP) for women and the Tank Fed Agricultural Development Programme for farmers are implemented through these two institutions, respectively. The strategy of the DHAN Foundation is to introduce a theme in the community, support it, and move to the next theme. For example, after successfully introducing and upscaling community banking and tank-fed agriculture, it has moved to two new themes in the recent years: the nurture and training of young professionals for development work (through the DHAN Academy) and promotion of information technology for the poor.

The DHAN Foundation considers micro-finance services as essential tools for poverty reduction. The primary focus of their CBP is to enable poor women to access and control financial services such as savings and credit by promoting localized self-managed institutions. The programme seeks to penetrate the financial market in an area through a policy of coverage of all the poor and replacing the services provided by informal sources of credit. Once the poor start utilizing the savings and credit services, it will help them link up and bargain with and influence the mainstream financial system. In the DHAN Foundation's perception, for effective poverty reduction, micro-finance services have to be managed by women, reach out on a large scale, and engage with and influence the government and banks.

The staff at all levels recognizes women's powerlessness and secondary status in all domains, and believes that this status is closely linked to their low economic status. Though the DHAN Foundation has actually not used the word 'empowerment', it does realize that empowering processes are set in motion as a result of its CBP and other activities. It believes that women's empowerment is about women expanding their access and control over resources, increasing their sphere of decision-making in democratic spaces in the community, and gaining control over their own stories. The DHAN Foundation holds that women learn in their own way and at their own pace, and it is best to not short-circuit the processes. For this purpose, it has adopted a four-generation strategy in its CBP. The first generation process entails social mobilization followed by financial intermediation, the second involves promotion of livelihoods, the third focuses on promotion of businesses, and the fourth entails addressing of civic and gender issues. The DHAN Foundation believes that 10–12 years are required for the fourth generation to be reached. The generation gap may, however, be reduced in the case of new groups as they learn from the experiences of the older ones. On the whole, it may be interpreted that, for the DHAN Foundation, economic empowerment is the entry point for unleashing empowerment in other spheres.

The DHAN Foundation believes that staff has to be highly competent and committed to facilitate such a process of innovation and institution building. Hence, it recruits people with professional qualifications,[3] who are willing to work for the development of the poor, and puts them through a rigorous induction and training process. A unique feature of the DHAN Foundation (like that of PRADAN, or Professional Agency for Development Action) is that the staff at the cutting edge (village level) are from such backgrounds. Field-level staff is allowed to reflect its voices and concerns through structured and unstructured interactions with those at higher levels. These interactions are further developed, refined and validated through their experiences of working with poor people. All staff members whom the researcher met adopted a scientific method of social analysis, were willing to learn continuously, displayed good communication skills, and possessed the ability to cope with tensions and conflicts. They had a strong sense of ownership over the organization. However, the long hours the team puts in on a day-to-day basis may lead to tensions and stresses in the long run. A noteworthy point is that the DHAN Foundation has a policy of gender-balanced recruitment, due to which women are found in non-traditional domains such as agriculture as well in senior levels of the organization.

Community Banking Programme

The CBP began in 1989 under PRADAN when a modest beginning was made in forming 20 SHGs in 11 villages of Tamil Nadu with a total membership of 286 women. After

---

[3] For example, many of its staff hold masters degrees in social work, rural management, or agriculture sciences.

the establishment of the DHAN Foundation in 1998, a revolutionary movement was initiated based on a decade of community banking experience. The year witnessed the celebration of the *kalanjiam* movement and women taking oaths to spread the concept to all poor women and also to reach 100,000 women within three years. During 1999–2000 itself, the movement covered 33,000 additional families. Cultural teams have been set up from among the members for spreading the concept. As of December 2001, the programme had been successful in promoting over 6,100 SHGs in almost 2,000 villages with 400 cluster development associations (*kalanjiams* coming together from two or three villages) and 20 block-level federations. At that time, there were over 100,000 *kalanjiam* members. The setting up of a *kalanjiam* foundation has been proposed as a separate thematic institution to upscale the CBP and reach a million poor over the decade.

The focus of the CBP is to create sound local financial institutions managed by women at the hamlet, cluster (two or three villages), and administrative block levels and to link these with mainstream financial institutions. The key activities under this programme include the following:

✦ Organizing poor women into groups of 15–20 (*kalanjiams*) and giving them an opportunity to share their experiences on the nature and causes of exploitation.
✦ Mobilizing their own resources through savings and managing these for their own benefit through internal lending.
✦ Regular interactions, exchanges and exposures with other *kalanjiams* and groups organized by other organizations to promote collective learning.
✦ Linking women's groups with formal financial institutions, with the credit being managed by women as a group; the relationship is one of clients and not beneficiaries.
✦ Building leadership qualities through transferring the roles and responsibilities to women to manage their own groups and activities over time.
✦ Skill building and training in specialized business activities (dairy, poultry, charcoal, etc.) and financial management.

→ Forming women-managed financial institutions at the village, cluster and block levels to gain mass strength and power, to form linkages with government institutions at these levels, and to address credit needs that cannot be met by *kalanjiam*s at the hamlet level.

Group Formation

As apparent, community banking operates at the hamlet (*kalanjiam*), cluster and federation levels. The executive committee (EC) that manages the group comprises the president, vice-president, secretary, joint secretary and treasurer chosen from the *kalanjiam*s by the consensus of all members. The secretary is responsible for looking after operational and administrative matters while the treasurer takes care of cash and accounts. Members of the EC divide the banking, monitoring, evaluation, expansion, training and community development activities among themselves. Once five to six *kalanjiam*s in a contiguous area have attained stability in their operations, they are encouraged to meet periodically and share their experiences. Over time, as more *kalanjiam*s join, these meetings are formalized and a cluster association comprising 15–20 *kalanjiam*s is formed. Each *kalanjiam* nominates three representatives to the cluster body, of whom seven are elected into the EC. The task of the cluster association is to form new groups, monitor the progress of existing groups, resolve conflicts within and between groups, and train group members. It also helps groups create bank linkages and acts as a forum for civic issues.

The federation comprises 150–200 *kalanjiam*s. Federations —registered as societies or trusts—get support for three years from the DHAN Foundation. The general body of the federation consists of all the leaders of the member *kalanjiam*s, from whom 11 are selected to the executing committee. The primary objective of the federation is to strengthen and sustain the primary groups and mobilize external funds from banks and apex financial bodies. They also act as support bodies for training and managing specialized services such as insurance, health and education. They promote economies of scale in enterprise activities and strengthen bargaining and negotiating powers of women with banks, government, and external agencies. By promoting direct elections to ECs from *kalanjiams*, federations promote leadership development.

Within the overall structure, each level operates as an autonomous body. Each level has to cover its costs itself. The autonomy is to ensure that the group and its leader take responsibility for group activities, own the programme, are aware of cost coverages, and develop community and financial management skills. It also ensures a transparent system. Through this process of decentralization, members and leaders develop the abilities to ask questions, negotiate and analyse and manage finances.

Governance and Management of Groups

The norm of one person, one post is followed to avoid burdening any one person. Normally, SHG leaders graduate into cluster leaders and cluster leaders into federation leaders. This process brings in the experience of the local context and strengthens the ability of leaders at the SHG and cluster levels to take on greater responsibilities. Once a leader graduates to a higher level, a new person fills her post. This process gives the opportunity to all members to develop leadership skills over time.

While women members take on governance roles, local staff members are appointed for maintenance and management functions. One group accountant keeps the record for five to six *kalanjiams*. However, money transactions do not take place through the accountants, who are merely facilitators for writing accounts and keeping records. Similarly, the cluster appoints cluster accountants and cluster associates. The costs of the staff at each level are borne by the groups out of their own resources. There are around 1,500 local staff members working at the group, cluster, and federation levels. Currently, the groups spend a total of Rs 3 million per month towards staff salaries. In essence, these groups are also creating employment opportunities at the local level.

Targeting of Women and the Process of Group Formation

Women members are primarily landless agriculture labourers, masonry workers, construction workers and petty shopkeepers/vendors. Families are organized into three categories, based on their economic threshold: survival, subsistence and self-employed. Almost 80 per cent of the women belong to the survival and subsistence categories, depending heavily on wage income. They are budget-deficit households, indebted before joining the group. Village mapping and wealth-ranking exercises are undertaken in the village before group formation. An effort is made to target all the poor in the gram panchayat and in an administrative block so that 100 per cent coverage of poor is ensured.

Once the target households are identified in each hamlet, women from these households are formed into homogeneous groups of 15–20. Homogeneity here refers to economic homogeneity. The DHAN Foundation has chosen women, rather than men, because they are poorer, occupy a secondary status, and are seen as better finance managers. The process of group formation initially takes five to six months, but over a period, lesser time (three to four months) is required as one group learns from another. Social issues like female infanticide and suicides are taken up in the beginning to build confidence and rapport amongst women, and only when rapport is built are micro-finance activities introduced. In the initial stages of the programme, the DHAN Foundation staff facilitates the groups, but over time the cluster leaders take over this responsibility. After the process of initial grounding, a 'quality check' is carried out followed by the process of (informal) registration with the federation for obtaining a group code. This code is further sent to the DHAN Foundation for consolidation of data for the Management Information System (MIS)[4]. Bank accounts are opened after six months of

---

[4] The Management Information System (MIS) refers to an organized assembly of resources and procedures required to collect, process and distribute data for use in decision-making.

informal registration and books of accounts are introduced. The norms for group functioning such as savings amount, loan amount, interest rate, meeting schedule, meeting agenda and group leadership are decided by the group themselves.

Meetings and Attendance

In semi-urban areas, women prefer to meet generally at 10 a.m. as they are free from household work by then. Most rural groups prefer to meet in the afternoon, once they have finished wage/agricultural work. Groups meet on a monthly or fortnightly basis in semi-urban areas, and on a monthly basis in rural areas. In Ramnad district, however, a fisherwomen's group meets four times a month, as they need frequent loans for fish vending. Rural groups normally meet outside the village, under a large tree. In semi-urban areas, women meet in a common garden or open space. One of the groups visited meet in the temple courtyard. Menstruating women do not attend the meeting, as it is a social taboo to enter the temple during such times. In another group, some women do not attend meetings because they are held at the house of a better-off member; the very poor women feel un-comfortable there.

Members attend meetings regularly; those not attending take permission from the group or inform the leader in advance. Some groups have evolved the practice of imposing penalties for not attending meetings. It was observed that the quality of participation of women in the semi-urban areas is higher than that in rural areas. Unlike many parts of rural areas, women in urban areas sit in a circle, which helps maintain eye contact. The participation level depends to some extent on the degree of literacy. Normally, younger women (25–32 years) are the most enthusiastic, initiating issues and playing facilitating roles. Middle-aged women also involve themselves in discussing issues, while women who are extremely poor, infirm, elderly and/or illiterate tend not to participate in discussions.

Savings Mobilization

The DHAN Foundation considers savings as essential for the viability of groups. Savings help the group to generate resources for internal rotation as loans, as well as to leverage credit from mainstream banking institutions. Savings also enable members and groups to build capital for their own development, in a manner that suits their own needs. In the beginning, members saved Rs 5 per month; now they save up to Rs 100. Each group has its own rules on how frequently savings are collected; some gather them every week, some every fortnight, and some every month. The total savings of all the *kalanjiams* is Rs 106.7 million as of March 2001, a substantial growth over Rs 62.7 million in March 2000. The average annual savings per member increased from Rs 55 in 1991 to Rs 337 in 1995/96, Rs 1,329 in March 2000, and over Rs 1,500 by December 2001. In older groups, the average savings per member range from Rs 3,000 to 5,000. The savings of all *kalanjiams* are 51 per cent of lending, indicating the extent of people's rotation of funds.

Two types of saving products are available for members through the groups: primary savings and diversified savings. Primary saving is the regular contribution that members make, which is used for internal lending. The amount is flexible, based on the ability of each member to save. It cannot be withdrawn until the death of the member or discontinuation of the member from the group. Diversified savings, on the other hand, are optional and can be withdrawn easily. They are often used for specific consumption needs such as education, marriages, festivals and social obligations. These take care of seasonal fluctuations in income and expenditure, and ensure food security during emergencies. Rural women save from their own earnings or wages. Women in semi-urban areas save by curtailing certain expenses, such as tea or tobacco. Sometimes, men help in contribution of savings, but they do not seem to reduce unnecessary expenses.

Credit Services

The CBP provides a range of services to meet different consumption and production credit needs of the poor. Credit for food security and social security like health education is considered credit for consumption. Small loans (up to Rs 2,000) for this purpose are available at an interest rate of 3 per cent per month. Loans above Rs 2,000 are provided at an interest rate of 2 per cent per month. The loan outstanding of all the *kalanjiams* has increased to Rs 207.5 million as of March 2001 from Rs 119.6 million in March 2000. The average loan per member ranges from Rs 2,500 to 2,800.

Loans vary in proportion to savings. Usually, during the first year, loans are eight times the savings amount (savings tend to be small then). After the first year, loans up to five times of the savings are considered (savings are large by then, and the actual loan amount may be larger than the first loan). The number and amount of loan of each member increases as the group ages. In older groups, members have received between five and seven loans starting from Rs 100–200 to Rs 20,000–25,000. There is no physical collateral required for availing a loan. Indirectly, savings work as collateral, as savings are used for adjusting defaults on the part of members. There is flexibility within the programme for usage of multiple loans concomitantly. Repayment instalments are fixed flexibly on the basis of purpose and quantum of loan.

Table 4.2 shows that the pattern of loans taken by three members: one from a new semi-urban group, one from an old semi-urban group, and one from an old rural group. It more or less indicates the general pattern for the members studied. The trend is normally to graduate from smaller to larger loans, and from day-to-day consumption to production loans. However, consumption loans related to life cycle changes or housing may be required (marriage, dowry) even after production loans have been taken. Whenever an asset such as housing is created through the loan, it is in the name of women. It is, however, a point of concern that some of the loans are for gender-insensitive purposes, such as

TABLE 4.2
Pattern of Loans Taken by Three Members

Sequence	Loan taken by a member of new semi-urban group		Loan taken by a member of old rural group		Loan taken by a member of old semi-urban group	
	Purpose	Amount	Purpose	Amount	Purpose	Amount
First	Grocery	200	Consumption	500	Medical expenses	200
Second	Repayment of debt	1,000	Buying goats	10,000	Grocery	500
Third	Fees for daughter	2,000	Marriage of grand daughter	10,000	Repayment of old debt	5,000
Fourth	Agriculture	500			Wedding of daughter	10,000
Fifth	Lease of land	10,000			Son's education and repayment of old debt	20,000

dowry, or expensive social ceremonies that embarrass adolescent girls (puberty ceremonies).

The major impact of lending is seen in redeeming loans from moneylenders, which are often taken at exorbitant interest rates of 10–15 per cent per month. Moneylenders refuse loans to the very poor unless they pawn small assets; even then, they lend only after greatly humiliating the loanee. Members also pointed out that it is for the first time they had access to repeat loans, which has increased their confidence in themselves. A few members however reported that they continue to depend on moneylenders for small loans of say Rs 50 when required urgently; these are available only through moneylenders. There were also instances of self-exclusion. For example, Pushpa, a widow in Neelmegham group, sat quietly in a group meeting. When asked about her loans, she said that she had availed only two small loans for consumption and fulfilling social obligations. Though she does need money for repairing her house, she did not take a large loan as she felt that she did not have the capacity to repay the loan.

Repayment rates on internal loans are impressive, ranging between 80 and 94 per cent in the first six months of group formation, and 100 per cent in case of groups over six months old. Repayment rates by groups to banks for external loans range from 98 to 100 per cent, which is much higher than prevailing repayment rates with respect to bank loans. Not surprisingly, a branch manager of a bank opined: 'A hundred small but standard accounts are preferable to one large non-performing account.'

Members can reschedule repayments during emergencies for up to three months, but after that there is pressure to repay the instalment. Penalty for non-payment of instalments can be Rs 20–50 for each instalment. If they fail to pay up this fine, they risk losing the group membership. Some women stated that there are conflicts with their husbands over repayment during lean income months. Usually, all women take the consent of their husbands before availing the loan to ensure joint responsibility of repayment. In older groups, loan sizes are perhaps greater than absorptive capacity, with instalments coming to Rs 800–1,000 per

month for those availing large loans. There is a need
to look at rationing the credit according to absorption
capacity.

Insurance

Insurance services are very vital for the poor because of
their vulnerability to ill-health, accidents and death. Almost
each adult member in a poor household is an earner, and a
calamity befalling any member adversely influences the
family cash flow. The federation operates life and accident
insurance, medical insurance, and housing insurance
programmes. Before initiating insurance in a federation, a
detailed analysis of death rates over the past five years is
conducted. The DHAN Foundation staff discusses the details of each insurance product with the federation leaders,
and each federation is encouraged to create a separate insurance fund. This also helps the member's family to repay
the loan in the event of the member's death. Some federations have formed links with insurance companies to offer
other insurance products. A premium of Rs 100 per year is
to be paid by each member for life and accident insurance,
which covers their own natural death and that of their husbands to the tune of Rs 10,000 and accidental death up to
Rs 25,000. There is flexibility of providing premium in three
instalments for very poor women-headed families. The DHAN
Foundation is conscious of the need to reduce the premium
amount over a period so that more poor people can be covered. It plans to encourage older groups to pay premiums
out of common funds.

There are some areas pertaining to insurance on which
more clear consensus should be formed. For example, on
the death of her husband, a young widow was entitled to get
insurance coverage. Her father-in-law wanted the insured
amount as the man who died was his son, while the father
of the widow also wanted this money for remarrying her.
This obviously created much conflict. It needs to be reiter-
ated that in the case of a husband's death, the widow gets
the money, and in case of death of the woman too, the girl
child gets the money.

Management Information System, Record Keeping and Monitoring

Given that the CBP deals mainly with money, the need for strong financial systems is obvious. Record keeping and MIS from the *kalanjiam* to the cluster level and from the cluster to the federation level allow for detailed financial analysis and monitoring. Financial analysis at the federation level is conducted through the Dhanam software, especially designed for this purpose. At the DHAN Foundation level as well, the data is consolidated for all federations with the help of a software developed specifically for this purpose. Each *kalanjiam* is viewed as an autonomous financial institution that maintains its cash books, vouchers, member ledger, general ledger, demand collection and balance statements, members' passbooks, receipt book and minute book. The group accountant, appointed by the group, maintains all updated records. The respective EC members monitor the working of the group accountant and cluster accountant. The accounts are discussed in the *kalanjiam* meeting and the EC members cross-check the entries made by the group accountant. There is a clear-cut policy on accounting procedures that aid such monitoring. Though illiterate, leaders remember transactions or try to cross-check them by showing them to their school-going children. Nevertheless, 15–20 per cent of the groups are not regular in submitting MIS records on time.

Another kind of monitoring is through quality checks by cluster leaders. Quality checks entail monitoring to see whether regular meetings are held with members staying till the end of the meeting, whether all members participate in discussions, whether savings and lending operations are carried out as per rules, and whether repayments are made on time. In the process of quality checks, the cluster leaders often revive defunct groups by solving conflicts. Groups, for example, become defunct due to issues like default by some members in repayments and other members refusing to repay if some members have defaulted. Sometimes conflicts arise due to poor and better-off people being members of the same group, and ensuing differences over who should get loans. Cluster leaders then explain the importance of repayments and homogeneity among group members and provide information on SHG concepts, often managing to revive defunct groups.

Internal auditing of the groups by the EC and clusters is done once every three months. An external audit is conducted once a year at the group-, cluster- and federation-level accounts. Provision for loan loss and bad debt is maintained at the group level in order to cover any delinquency. Groups and clusters are not registered bodies, but the auditing reflects any problems and mistakes in accounts. During the external audit, the EC members, group accountant and cluster accountant are present. Such external audits help the groups and clusters enhance credibility, helps create direct linkages with banks, and also builds up women's capacity for management and account keeping.

Capacity Building and Training

Training of *kalanjiam* members takes place in regular meetings. Training is sequenced, starting with modules on financial management, record keeping and administrative aspects. This phase of training is spread over five months. Training sessions on linkage building with banks and government are conducted for one to two months. Refresher courses are conducted once a year. Exposure visits to other projects, exchange visits to other groups within the project and annual Mahasabhas are other opportunities for learning. All staff members are associated with organizing capacity building programmes. The staff members are exposed to experiences across the nation through the DHAN Academy. Besides the DHAN Academy, there is a separate Kalanjiam Training Centre (KTC) to groom women volunteers as cluster associates through a 42-day training. In addition, NGOs, bankers, government agencies, and training and academic institutions alike come to learn from the DHAN Foundation's community banking experiences. Thus, the DHAN Foundation is emerging as a support institution to intermediary organizations as well, in addition to supporting *kalanjiam*s, cluster bodies and federations.

Training programmes for members and leaders have built up the capacity of the members in financial administration and management. However, there is a need to create greater awareness of the impact of the interplay of various types of oppressive social structures such as gender, caste and class. Some training modules now take into account these issues but the awareness is yet to percolate to the member level, where it is in the process of being implemented.

Sustainability

Integral to the DHAN Foundation's mission of building institutions and upscaling is the issue of sustainability. The concept of sustainability can be discussed in three respects: financial, institutional and social. Financial sustainability implies that not only do revenues cover the costs of running the operation, but also help create sufficient reserves for contingencies. Each *kalanjiam* has to cover its cost from the very first day. The DHAN Foundation supports cluster associations for two years and federations for three years. After this period, these structures need to be self-sustaining. Besides this, out of the common fund, the *kalanjiam* sets aside funds for education, health and village development. The revenue sources for *kalanjiams* include membership fees, difference in interest rates between what is paid on savings (around 12 per cent) and what is charged on internal lending, and difference in interests between what is paid on loans from banks and clusters and what is charged to members (around 6 per cent). *Kalanjiams'* expenditures include the group accountant's salary, audit charges, cluster and federation fees and creation of risk funds. In spite of all these costs, *kalanjiams* run at a net profit and manage to create reserves. Their reserves increased from Rs 5,000 at the initiation of the programme in 1991 to Rs 27.4 million in March 2001. Under a proposed policy, earnings through interest differentials will not be accumulated at the cluster or federation level, to avoid conflicts and centralization of power. This will help the *kalanjiams* strengthen their position, expand their sense of ownership, and ensure accountability of the cluster and the federation to their members.

Financial sustainability is not an end in itself but the means of reaching a large and growing number of women. The outreach of the CBP has increased from 20 groups and 286 members in the year ending March 1991 to 6,051 groups and 95,000 members in August 2001, with major growth from March 1998. The *kalanjiam*-level growth, in essence, could well be defined as institutional sustainability, given its lack of dependence on the leadership of any particular person. It has become a self-propelling movement, responding to poor women's need for micro-finance. Besides expansion, women members have started managing the operational aspects of the programme. Women manage collection, disbursement, default, accounting, staff appointment, auditing, as well as interaction with banks and government agencies. Women have also addressed social and civic programmes in the villages. Long-term sustainability can be achieved when women members respond to the changing environment and also when the aim of women's poverty reduction is achieved. Besides lack of economic opportunities, on the one hand, the vicious circle of poverty is also the result of forces like lack of awareness, education, child labour, early girl marriage, early childbirth and practices such as dowry system, female infanticide, desertion of women and unnecessary expenditure on social ceremonies including attainment of puberty and ear-piercing. As long as these systems persist, the programme will continue to add to the category of the poorest within its ambit. These social issues have to be addressed in order to make a long-term sustainable impact on poverty. The DHAN Foundation has to move towards a broader livelihood approach that comprises capability, assets and activity required for a means of earning.

Empowerment Impact of Micro-finance at the Individual Level

The impact of the CBP is clear and tangible in its outreach to the poorest of the poor in backward and remote locations and in its success at curbing the abusive practices of moneylenders. The process of selecting the poor is rigorous. Participatory rural appraisal (PRA) techniques (including wealth-ranking exercises) are conducted in a village to identify the poor. Suitable deletions are done to ensure that the poorest members are included. The poor are further classified into the survival, subsistence and self-employment categories. The lending policy is also adapted to each category. As discussed, the groups have mobilized substantial resources, and repayments stand at an impressive 98 per cent. A cadre of leaders has been built up from among poor women. With the backing of collectives, women are emerging more confident, are more mobile, have greater access to public space, and exercise increased control over financial resources. The creation of the *kalanjiam* movement led by the poor women has given them a sense of achievement.

These changes are described in detail in the following sections, beginning with changes in the lives of individual women, and then women as a collective.

Access and Control over Private Resources: Credit, Savings, Assets

The programme has provided poor women the space and opportunities to gain access to resources. For many women, this is the first time that they have savings and loans in their own names. This has enabled women to feel more secure during emergencies. Some of the loans have led to creation of assets (house, land, trees), and it is mainly women who own these. Women do take the consent of men for obtaining the loan and for the purpose for which it is to be utilized, but this has not taken away from their enhanced economic status within the family. Wherever women are managing the activity initiated through the loan, they have better control over household decision-making compared to women doing unpaid work in the family or waged work. The fact that *kalanjiams* provide the family with access to money has countered the initial resistance of men to women attending *kalanjiam* meetings, where women discuss social issues as well.

Women members are able to access bank credit and talk boldly with bank officials. Having displayed good repayment records, they are attended to promptly. Over the years, they observe an attitudinal change among bankers towards lending to poor women. Some members even telephone the bank manager, wanting to know the status of their applications. Commercial and cooperative banks and financial institutions such as the Housing Development Finance Corporation (HDFC) and the Housing and Urban Development Corporation (HUDCO) lend to groups, not individuals. Access to housing loans through apex bank linkage has enabled many women to own houses in their own name.

A few issues need to be looked into. Most productive loans taken up by women have been used for very small-scale activities (petty shops, land cultivation, dairy, small trading, flower selling, rope making). With notable exceptions, these activities become a joint activity for men and women in male-headed households (MHHs). Yet another concern is that the economic benefits have not been experienced evenly. Women who head their households have greater control over income and assets created through the loan than women in MHHs. But as their sons become older, they often take over. At times, women heading households are the ones more disadvantaged than women in MHHs. Kartamma's voice captures it best:

> I cannot afford to own any asset from income generated through loans taken as I need to spend for my daughter and granddaughter. My daughter is a widow at 20; my son-in-law committed suicide as he was in love with another woman.

Many of the positive changes pertaining to access to resources and to leadership are higher among group leaders than members, and among members who have taken repeated loans.

Control over Labour and Income

To understand the nature of work that women and men do and their workloads, an exercise of mapping daily routines of some men and women was undertaken in all the three federations visited in September 2001 (Table 4.1). Women work seven to nine hours more than men on a typical day. Surprisingly, despite the longer hours, women do not admit that they work more than the men in their households. Men are considered by women as well as by other men as working harder, and as the bread-earners for their households. Women, on the other hand, are considered supplementary earners. They are expected to do all the household work, unless their girl children start helping them. Men's participation in household work is found only in few cases, and is restricted to fetching water (if the source is far away) and breaking wood for fuel. No choice is available either with respect to what productive work women can do, as it is shaped by the norms on division of work between men and women. For example, with respect to agriculture, women are allowed to do only weeding, transplanting, and harvesting as per the division of labour; these tasks fetch lower wages than ploughing, which only men do.

While husbands of members accept their wives' unpaid work within the family, they do object to the unpaid work that members do for *kalanjiams*. The husband of a cluster leader commented to the researcher: 'My wife is already overworked at home. She should not take on additional responsibility.' The member, however, continues to work despite this opposition, showing women members' increasing autonomy. Such responses of husbands to their wives' leadership in the groups may actually reflect the blow to the male ego, rather than a concern for the women's well-being. Gender sensitization for men is hence essential.

Daily routine mapping also revealed that men have more leisure time than women. As soon as a man is free, he cycles or walks to a tea stall or a common place where other men assemble. Women use their leisure time to sleep, listen to the radio or watch television—nothing beyond that.

Men's wages range from Rs 40 to 100 per day, depending on the kind of work they do, while women's wages hover around Rs 25 per day. Men and women get work for six months as agricultural labourers. Men migrate to nearby states like Kerala or adjacent urban centres in Tamil Nadu during the lean agriculture period, but women have no work then. Women members think that men's work contribution is more important than theirs as it brings in greater revenues. They do not value their (unpaid) housework. Women's control on wages and expenditure for personal consumption is very low. As women say, 'We spend only for our homes.' Men, on the other hand, spend on themselves and have higher control on expenditure. Women seem to have a fair amount of say on small household expenditure, but they have to take the consent of their husbands for major expenditure.

Access to Public Resources: Education, Child Care, Health

Along with the CBP, an effort is being made to introduce functional literacy. Seventy per cent of *kalanjiam* members are now able to write their names and sign, while 30 per cent still make do with thumb impressions. Women members do recognize the importance of educating girls, but do not make sustained efforts in this direction. The general opinion is that since girls will anyway get married, the benefits of education are not going to accrue to the natal families. Other reasons include distance to the high schools and lack of good and safe transport facilities. Some cases of daughters of members studying up to Class XII are seen in semi-urban areas, but they are more the exception than the rule. Loans are taken for higher education of sons but not daughters, even if the latter are performing well at academics.

In all the areas visited, women are aware of child care services and send their children aged 0–3 years to the Integrated Child Development Services (ICDS) centres. They also avail of the facility of supplemental nutrition for lactating mothers. In some places, women complain about the quality of food but never challenge it. A close convergence between the *kalanjiam*s and ICDS centres is advisable to strengthen child care services and nutritional security of women and children.

Women support the primary health centres during polio vaccination campaigns but do not seem to utilize the services on a regular basis. First aid training provided by federations, associates, or staff to 59 women in the PVK Federation has enhanced the health and hygiene of member households. The trained women are now able to serve 59 villages in their area. Traditional birth attendant training in one area has helped women conduct safe deliveries, but these developments are area-specific.

Access to New Skills and Technology

Access to training on administration and financial management has enhanced women's ability to manage the *kalanjiams*. Individually women are more aware and better able to analyse, question, and negotiate their interests within and outside their families. They have greater confidence to deal with difficult situations in their day-to-day lives.

In urban federations, women have accessed new technology in the area of low-cost housing. Women members of an urban federation are building a training centre with the support of HUDCO. Access of rural women members to new technology seems lower.

In the MKMVS Federation, (older) women did mention that they now need skill-building training to earn more. This is an area that the DHAN Foundation may like to consider.

Women's Control over Reproduction and their Body

Almost all the women with whom discussions were held were married as soon as they had attained puberty. They were not fully aware of the implications of marriage. Even now, many girls are married by the time they are 17. Most women in the 45-plus age group have borne 10–12 children, half of whom died after birth due to malnutrition and lack of access to proper care. Issues of infant, child and maternal mortality require attention in the coming years.

All women were aware of family planning. In contrast to the middle-aged and elderly members, members in the age group of 20–30 years have undergone family planning operations after bearing two or three children. In fact, one women member stated: 'I went to the hospital and got myself operated upon without my husband's consent. He did not talk to me for a week. Later he was happy with my decision.' Therefore, a gradual change is visible. There is, however, no evidence of spacing between children. The burden of contraception also seems to fall mainly on women.

Most women were aware of ultrasound tests that provide sex determination facilities, but none openly admitted to being party to female foeticide. Preference for male children is very strong. In Kadamalai block, female infanticide is widely prevalent. This has been curbed substantially due to the DHAN Foundation's intervention. In order to support women with girl children, the federation gives Rs 2,000 to a mother of two daughters.

In all the areas visited, it was not uncommon to find some women members deserted by their husbands (Box 4.1). The reasons ranged from giving birth to female children to husband's entering into extramarital relations. The latter was common in the case of men who migrated in search of work. The dowry system is another social practice that keeps women always under the control of men and indebted throughout life. There are also various social rituals pertaining to puberty, which not only pull poor households into debt but also violate the right of adolescent girls to a life of dignity.[5] Wife battering is another form of violence experienced by women members. Many women reported that earlier they used to be beaten for even attending *kalanjiam* meetings. This has not only stopped, but there has been moderate reduction in wife battering after women's association with *kalanjiams* and also because the role of women has widened in the family. There is a need for the DHAN Foundation to initiate specific programmes to combat violence against women and girls within families.

Women's Control over Mobility

Women's physical mobility has expanded by attending *kalanjiam* meetings and training programmes as well as

---

[5] The entire village comes to know that the girl has attained puberty, which can be embarrassing for her.

BOX 4.1

```
┌─────────────────────────────────────────────────────────────┐
```

Achieving New Heights

Rajalakshmi, 41, is the treasurer in Kadamalai Federation. She has studied up to Class VIII. She got married at the age of 15 and soon gave birth to a daughter. At 19, when she was pregnant for the second time, her husband left her, thinking that she would bear a daughter again. However, she gave birth to a son. After being deserted, she stayed with her parents. She says that women who do not live with their husbands are neither respected nor invited to any festival or ceremony. As a result, she had to face a lot of flack from her family and society. Initially, she was not even allowed to work or go out of the house.

Rajalakshmi became associated with the *kalanjiam* seven years ago. She has now moved out of her parents' place and lives alone with her son. Within the *kalanjiam*, she moved from group leader to cluster leader and became the treasurer of the federation three years ago. Today she has the confidence and courage to face anything. She provides training to cluster associations. When the managing director (MD) of her federation was absent in the last year, she conducted the meetings of the federation. She feels proud that her signature is required along with the MD's for encashing the federation's cheque. She has learnt to appraise the proposals. She also keeps a check on cluster workers through field visits. She has successfully negotiated a Rs 8 million loan from HDFC for housing purposes. She has been taking the lead in addressing civic issues such as water, electricity and streetlighting.

Today, Rajalakshmi is highly respected and has access to the police, the block development officer, the collector and the bank manager in her town.

through visits to banks. Enterprise activities have also contributed to enhanced mobility as they involve visits to local and distant markets. Women members have travelled to villages and cities they had never seen before. Unlike in the past, they now travel without their husbands, either alone or with other women. For the first time in their lives, they visit places such as banks, block development offices, collectors' offices and police stations. The local policemen trust the *kalanjiam* women and have made them members of the village committee called 'Friends of Police'[6] set up by the

---

[6] 'Friends of Police' is a group of village members (male and female) constituted by the police department to provide information and to support the system in curbing social evils such as illicit liquor processing. This group also conducts awareness programmes on such issues.

government. Enhanced mobility and interaction has increased women's confidence, courage and access to knowledge and information. While men do not entirely approve of these changes, most do not object either as economic benefits accrue to the family. Some of the men even wait at the bus stand with a bicycle for their women who come late after attending the meeting. But in some instances women have gone out on *kalanjiam* work against the wishes of their husbands and sons (Box 4.2).

BOX 4.2

Vellaiyammal: Rising in spite of Opposition

Going by Vellaiyammal's calm expression, one would not believe the difficult times she has been through. Fifty-five-year-old Vellaiyammal belongs to Vemboor village, Theni district. She studied up to Class V, but had to discontinue because of her marriage. She was married at the tender age of 10, even before she had attained puberty. Her husband was a labourer engaged in woodcutting, carpentry and masonry. At 13, she delivered her first child, followed by 10 more, of which eight died. She managed to carry on, until her husband got into bad company and started consuming opium. Soon his health was severely affected. He started to beat up Vellaiyammal and ask her to buy opium for him. Thus, she started working as an agriculture labourer after 16 years of marriage. She and her son (who by then had also started working) could not provide for the family. Meanwhile, her husband died due to worsening health. After that, she married her two sons and one daughter and stopped working.

At this point, the DHAN Foundation staff came to her village for group formation and the village women agreed to become members if Vellaiyammal was appointed the leader. She soon took up the operations of the *kalanjiam* and gradually got involved in forming new groups. Her son, however, tried to stop her from going to other villages. Once it was raining heavily when she went to conduct a group formation meeting. Her angry son closed the door and didn't let her in. She had to sleep outside her house. Undeterred, Vellaiyammal continued her association with *kalanjiams* and became the cluster leader. She attended many leader meetings and started engaging in quality checks of *kalanjiams* in her cluster. Her sons started loading her with additional work so she wouldn't leave the house. However, she did the work and also attended to the *kalanjiam* work.

Gradually, Vellaiyammal has started visiting banks herself to demand bank loans for *kalanjiams*. She is also called upon as a trainer for many programmes. Her work on expansion of *kalanjiams* has continued and with the help of members she could form 150 *kalanjiams* within three years. She was also involved in the process of registering the KKVS Federation and was made its president in 1997. She never hesitated to raise her voice wherever she found mistakes. She even opposed the managing director of the federation and challenged him to dissolve one of the groups in her village.

Vellaiyammal took up the issue of opium cultivation and was successful in burning the opium plants. She also arranged for mass destruction of the local arrack-making centre. After her having addressed these issues, even the police department accords due respect to her. She has acquired the confidence of talking to the district collector, the superintendent of police and bank managers. She would like to serve the *kalanjiam* till her last day.

Access to Decision-making and Leadership Space

Most aspects of decision-making have already been commented upon, such as decision-making on credit, assets, expenditure, work, mobility and reproduction. If one examines other areas such as democratic participation, women members in both semi-urban and rural areas exercise their votes, but the decision on whom to vote for is influenced by political promises and pressures from male members.

Overall, it is observed that women in semi-urban areas are able to speak and assert their rights within the family and outside more than women in rural areas. The sphere of decision-making is wider among women who head their households than women in MHHs. Women's confidence and ability to assert their needs is higher in older groups than in newer groups. The practice of rotation of leadership has enabled most women members of older groups to shoulder larger responsibilities.

Empowerment Impact at the Collective Level

The name given to the groups (*kalanjiams*) has become well-known in the villages and within the overall community. The success of the *kalanjiams* in achieving such a social space is indeed laudable. As a collective, the *kalanjiams*, cluster associations, and federations have successfully taken up a range of issues, such as access to water, road repairs, and access to electricity. These issues are non-controversial in the sense that they benefit men and women. There are, however, some issues that challenge male power that have been taken up by the groups; these are elaborated here.

Access and Control of Political Space/Processes

Many cluster leaders are getting ready to participate in panchayat elections, with the backing of the groups. Women, in particular leaders, are looking for their own space to make an impact so that they can be heard and can negotiate with the government. Panchayats at the local level now recognize *kalanjiams* and invite the group leaders to attend gram sabha meetings. In some villages, the panchayats have provided the *kalanjiam* with space for conducting regular meetings. In gram sabha meetings, *kalanjiams* have taken up infrastructure issues such as access to electricity, drinking water facilities and roads. In some instances, wherein such initiatives failed, *kalanjiams* have used their own funds for meeting such needs. In the area of the PVK Federation, the chronic drinking water problem in Genguvarpatti village was solved through the efforts of cluster committee leaders and *kalanjiam* members. Whether this is the right approach needs to be questioned. *Kalanjiams* need to be encouraged to make gram sabhas more accountable, rather than delivering services themselves. Questioning the elected members in gram sabhas will make women more confident and lead them towards political participation.

Government organizations also call for representation of *kalanjiams* in their meetings and committees (see Box 4.3 for the opinion of a government official on the groups). In one block, the federation took up the challenge of constructing 150 toilet buildings, which men could not finish. These women have now decided to take up the contract of road construction with the panchayats.

BOX 4.3

**Discussions with a Block Development Officer
in Mayiladumparai, Theni: A Gist**

I have lived in this area from birth. I come from a very poor
family and have personally experienced poverty. I am aware of
how the poor are victimized. I have witnessed a sea change
among women belonging to *kalanjiams*. These poor women are
participating in social activities and have been able to approach
government officers on a number of community issues. I occasionally see men beating their wives for attending *kalanjiam*
meetings. Perhaps men are threatened because women are coming together and getting recognition. Men need to become more
sensitive and should allow women to think independently. Since
many members are illiterate, they still lack clarity on economic
activities that could be taken up. I find that women above 45
years with experience are more mature and can take up advocacy roles. Over the years, government officers' attitudes towards
these women have also changed.

Assertion of Gender Identity and Interests

The *kalanjiams'* participation in locally elected bodies and
government bodies is just one indication of their growing
collective strength. On the complaint of *kalanjiam* women
in Kadamalai block, the police raided the village and arrested several men for illegal arrack distillation. No sooner
were the men released that arrack distillation resumed.
Fuming with anger, the women broke all the mud pots used
for distillation and even burned the opium plots.

Most *kalanjiams* comprise women from different caste
groups, and some include women from different religious
and ethnic groups. Past resistance to sitting together has
been replaced by a feeling of solidarity among members.
The *kalanjiam* meetings, festivals and Mahasabha celebrations are conducive in breaking class, caste and religious
barriers. Numerous examples of initial rifts and conflicts
between members on the basis of caste, which were subsequently resolved, were cited during interviews. Women were
quite upset when the issue of caste hierarchies was discussed. They were very categorical in saying that they had

forgotten such differences and did not want to be reminded of them.

Collective Strategies to Address Basic Needs

As mentioned, in urban areas, there is greater awareness of the importance of education and girls' education. Some urban groups have initiated collective programmes in this regard. For example, the Shri Padmavathy Mahila Abhyodaya Sangham Federation in Tirupati has started a *Vidyadeepam* programme for girls' education. This federation has also started a school for the children of *kalanjiam* members.

Similarly, the MKMVS Federation, the oldest one, has taken up health programmes in the Ramnad district. In a regional family welfare conference organized by the District Family Welfare Board, 65 *kalanjiam*s and cluster leaders and barefoot health workers from the MKMVS Federation participated. The Federation also organized some awareness camps on the reproductive system, HIV/AIDS and water-borne diseases. In Theni district, the Kadamali Kundu Vattara Sangham federation played an active role in the government-sponsored comprehensive health check-up programme for the poor in rural areas. In the PVK in Madurai West, 59 members were provided with training and first aid medical kits and they, in turn, provide services to 52 villages. Though there is a growing awareness on the need for strengthening health services, a concerted strategy is yet to emerge.

Collective Interventions in Markets

In Thoppaiyapuram village of Kadamalai block, some *kalanjiam* women have started a collective dairying enterprise with 30 cows, and formed linkages with Kerala milk chilling plants for marketing. Women are managing this activity successfully by hiring men for selective activities, and they have full control over the milk sale proceeds. Support services such as arranging for veterinary doctors are provided by the federation. Cases of collective enterprises are few but lead to greater income, and can have considerable demonstration impacts.

While there are many examples of the collective powers of the group, perhaps the most notable is how federation leaders and members question the Managing Director of the DHAN Foundation if they do not agree with his views or suggestions.

Changes in the Larger Socio-economic Environment

At a wider level, a change in approach of bankers and government towards poor women is distinctly visible as a result of the CBP. Caste and religious barriers are breaking down. There has also been substantial reduction in the turnover of local moneylenders. In fact, this is one of the major achievements of the CBP. There have been instances wherein moneylenders have been challenged by the *kalanjiam* members for misappropriation of poor people's money or charging exorbitant rates of interest.

The incidence of poverty is reducing among group members. Successive smaller loans have enabled poor women to emerge from debt and enjoy strengthened food security. Existing income has been protected through access to loans, but increase in income is felt only when women have taken loans for business activities. There has been no perceptible change in the consumption pattern of the members. Women members are aware of obtaining food grains from the public distribution system (PDS). There is evidence of groups strengthening quality and arresting malpractices in the PDS in Mandapam block, but this is not a large-scale movement. The nutritional status of members' children appears satisfactory, though this has not been ascertained through anthropometrical measurements. There is definitely scope for groups to create systematic links with the ICDS programme to strengthen health and nutrition impacts. Girls' education and girl child labour at home is another area where impact is not visible. On the whole, the impact on poverty is visible in individual cases. It is difficult to comment on the changes in the poverty profile of the area where the DHAN Foundation works.

Inferences and Conclusion

The biggest contribution of the DHAN Foundation is in establishing women-managed financial institutions at multiple levels. Instead of becoming a micro-finance institution, the DHAN Foundation has provided exemplary support services to the poor, enabling them to own their own financial institutions. The design of the CBP has intrinsic strengths such as retaining a narrow and strategic economic focus, using women's saving as an economic base, linking savings to credit from day one, linking groups to banks, delinking governance from administration, making each tier an autonomous body, graduating leadership from lower to higher levels, and applying financial and institutional sustainability criteria to all activities.

If one were to assess the performance of the DHAN Foundation vis-à-vis its own objectives, its achievements become quite apparent. Promoting institutions to reach scale is one of the objectives of the DHAN Foundation. Reaching 100,000 women in 6,100 SHGs in 2,000 villages of 16 backward and drought-prone districts of southern India in a decade reflects the commitment and conscientious efforts by the DHAN Foundation. The *kalanjiam* programme has become a movement in itself, with a momentum of its own.

The broader aim of the DHAN Foundation is to reduce poverty. Towards this end, it has evolved effective targeting strategies such as identification of poor blocks, remote villages within these blocks, and vulnerable households within the villages through social mapping and wealth ranking methods. Groups like the landless, dalits, tribals, marginal and small farmers and women who head their households are key constituencies. The economic impact of the CBP is felt in terms of sharp reduction (though not elimination) in dependence on moneylenders by the members, which directly reflects reduction in income leakage in terms of high interest rates. Another visible impact is redemption of pawned assets, leading to reduced vulnerability to poverty. Life and medical insurance programmes have also reduced vulnerability arising out of ill health, death, or accident of earning members. Seasonal dimensions of poverty are less visible than earlier due to expansion of livelihood strategies and availability of consumption loans. However, some concerns do remain. Income enhancement is visible only in cases where productive loans have been taken, not just once but several times. Often income increase is less than what is required to come out of poverty, as activities with low income generation potential have been taken by women to avoid risks. Yet another concern is the use of loans by members for expenses like dowry and puberty and ear-piercing ceremonies, the repayment of which may plunge women back into poverty. While repayment rates have been over 98 per cent, there are instances where members have borrowed from moneylenders to repay.

Though women's empowerment is not a formal objective of the DHAN Foundation, it is assumed that with access to economic resources and institution building such a process would unfold. There is evidence that building financial assets like cash savings and productive assets in the women's own name has enabled the women to have larger control on their own lives. Some women have moved from unpaid and wage work to self-employment. Many now retain substantial control over their earnings. All these economic processes have given them a niche in gaining recognition within and outside the family. The economic activities have also expanded women's mobility by taking them to new places to meet new people and institutions, and that too without male accompaniment. At the same time, attention needs to be paid to who is bearing the burden of repayment and savings. The responsibility seems largely to fall on women, at times through cutting down their consumption of tea and betel nuts. Improvement in women's income has led to some decline, but not total elimination, in domestic violence. Neither has it fundamentally altered the gender division of reproductive or agricultural work.

At the collective level, the three-tier structure of the CBP—*kalanjiam*, cluster development association and federation—acts as a support structure for women for sharing information, experiences, as well as emotional issues. The group meetings, apart from acting as forums for financial transactions, give women the opportunity for co-learning and developing functional literacy skills. The norm that one person can occupy only one leadership post has created the opportunity for all women in older groups to develop leadership skills, thus contributing to their confidence and skills in negotiation for practical needs (drinking water, roads, streetlights) vis-à-vis the government, panchayats, and other organizations. Functional skills in financial management are also strengthened through leadership rotation. Within the overall structure, each level is an autonomous body, leading to both decentralization of power and management of finances. Impressive achievements at all three levels are the breaking of caste hierarchies and the emergence of strong gender identities among women. Irrespective of caste, women have come together to take on issues of illegal arrack distillation and opium cultivation in the area. Women now plan to put up candidates for contesting panchayat elections. Community institutions, the government, and elected panchayats now recognize that the women's groups are a force to reckon with. One of the leaders of its federation, Chinnapillai in fact received the prestigious *Stree Shakti Purashkar* (women's empowerment award) for 1999 from the Prime Minister of India.

While at the collective level many empowering processes have begun, there are some areas where concerted action is needed. Convergence between the groups at different levels with the government health system, child care and nutrition system, and PDS is essential if improved income is to lead to better access to basic needs. Currently, this is happening in some localities only.

Many of the above gains in women's empowerment at the individual and collective levels are more visible in semi-urban areas than rural areas, and among women who head their households than women in MHHs. Several men respond to these changes in their wives' lives with resistance in the initial stages, but with time the resistance declines in most cases as women bring economic benefits to the family. In some instances, women persisted with the group and in leadership positions, despite opposition from their husbands, revealing their growing power within the family.

While the empowerment processes have begun through the DHAN Foundation's economic interventions, it may be worth highlighting the key assumptions that it needs to challenge in the coming years if the full potential of this process is to be achieved. The DHAN Foundation believes that economic interventions can lead to empowering changes in other domains as well. There are limitations to the extent and spheres of women's empowerment that can be expected to take place out of an exclusive micro-finance intervention. As Srilata Batliwala (1994) puts it, 'There is often an assumption that power comes automatically through economic strength—it may, but often does not, depending upon local gender relations and class/caste relations.' The DHAN Foundation as a supporting, facilitative body is fully aware of this. The time is perhaps now ripe to initiate non-economic interventions to strengthen women's positions within and outside the family.

Yet another assumption is that economic inequality between men and women can be bridged without touching the reproductive sphere. The anti-poverty approach (Moser, 1989) underpinning the CBP does not link economic inequality between men and women to women's subordination in the reproductive domain. It focuses only on the productive domain, that too with a distinct focus on furthering income equality. The anti-poverty approach is consequently indifferent to women's strategic gender needs in reproduction, which apart from being essential for achievement of economic equality, is central for women's control over their bodies. Issues that need to be considered include sharing of responsibility for domestic work and child care, as well as women's control over biological reproduction. Otherwise there is a danger that women will not have the time to engage in marketing. Women's participation in new economic activities in addition to reproductive work (and old economic activities) will increase their work burden.

Underpinning the income enhancement focus is the assumption that improved income will lead to improved human capabilities. This assumption need not always be valid. Two basic elements of human capabilities are education and health. The DHAN Foundation, through the Kalanjiam Foundation, could consider providing specialized training through focused group discussions on the need to send girl children to school, on barriers to women's/girls' health, on reproductive health of adolescent girls, and on legal and economic literacy. It should see education as broader than acquiring reading and writing skills. Women should be given training on legal and economic literacy, combating domestic violence, and questioning persistence of puberty ceremonies. At the same time, men need to be sensitized on gender concerns, in particular on women's subordination in reproductive and productive spheres. The Kalanjiam Foundation with proper professional support is ideally suited to take up this gender advocacy role. It is these challenges that the *kalanjiams* have to accept with the support of the DHAN Foundation.

References

Batliwala, Srilata, 1994, *Women's Empowerment in South Asia*, New Delhi: Food and Agricultural Organization, Freedom from Hunger Campaign and Asian-South Pacific Bureau of Adult Education.

Moser, C.O.N., 1989, 'Gender Planning in Third World: Meeting Practical and Strategic Gender Needs', *World Development*, 17 (11): 1799–1825.

Rajalakshmi, T.N., 2002, 'Legislation: Against Gender Bias', *Frontline*, 19 (2), 19 January–19 February.

5

Awareness, Access, Agency: Experiences of Swayam Shikshan Prayog in Microfinance and Women's Empowerment

Soma Kishore Parthasarathy[*]

Introduction

Women's forays into new realms of activity related to economic development, specifically savings credit groups (SCGs), often mistakenly called self-help groups (SHGs),[1] have led to their enhanced participation in group-based activity and interaction in public spheres. This study seeks to examine these processes and their impacts on the lives of women, to trace the extent to which newly gained public

[*]This study was undertaken as a participatory exercise with the Swayam Shikshan Prayog (SSP) team comprising Laxmikant Mavladkar, Devyani, Anuradha and Kishori from the Latur district team and Leela Somvanshi, Naseem Shaikh, Mukta Salunke, Laxmi Fulsunder, Jaishree Kadam, Babita Koli, Vimal Shinde and Anita Mule from Osmanabad district team.

[1] The term 'self-help groups' (SHGs) is currently used to imply an economic entity that organizes its own economic functions, whereas the origins of the nomenclature within the women's movement dates back to earlier decades of women's quest for autonomy and assertion of reproductive rights. SHGs existing today are rarely of the kind that addresses issues of autonomy, being primarily a means to save for family well-being and poverty alleviation.

spaces and voices have translated into empowerment in women's private lives. SCGs mark a shift from the dependency framework[2] of micro-credit. In this process, women are often short-changed, defined in an instrumental manner (as frugal and creditworthy) and become a means for addressing macro-economic goals of liberalizing economies. Innovative approaches and a clear perspective towards using the SCG to bring about a change in the status of women is often a link that does not get addressed in a patriarchal framework.

Empowerment processes are not stimulated in a vacuum. The organizational perspective and management systems can either deter or nurture the processes of empowerment through practices of exclusion or inclusion. The case of Swayam Shikshan Prayog (SSP) clearly illustrates the organization's perspective on the politics of development and its commitment to bringing women's voices to the centre of development. SSP is an NGO working in partnership with women's SCGs in five districts[3] of Maharashtra in central India. Headquartered at Mumbai, the organization's operations are managed and implemented at the district level, which is the unit of planning. District teams comprise senior staff members/resource persons with sectoral-/issue-based responsibilities, assisted by other staff members. SSP has moulded the approach of the initiatives towards SCG promotion through a two-pronged approach: (a) improvements in livelihoods for women and their families through savings and credit activity; and (b) creation of women-centred institutional spaces to address women's strategic needs for agency and negotiation.

SSP's involvement in SCGs dates back to 1989. Earlier it was part of another NGO called SPARC (Society for Promotion

---

[2] Groups that have focused only on credit without first insisting on a thrift component have been promoted by external agencies for purposes of credit disbursement, and are therefore dependent on the norms and systems established by the promoter. Savings and credit groups have a degree of leverage and autonomy in comparison since they initiate operations based on their own capital, with a basis for ownership—however minimally articulated.

[3] Latur, Osmanabad, Solapur, Nanded and Amrawati districts.

of Area Resource Centres) which works with the urban poor in 20 cities in India. In 1989, SSP separated from SPARC and set up a learning network of rural NGOs in Maharashtra by facilitating exchange visits. SPARC–SSP had pioneered the practice of SCGs in SSP, a learning network of rural NGOs in Maharashtra. Initially 30–40 NGOs/grassroots-level organizations participated in these exchanges wherein a group-centred learning approach was facilitated. A marked shift occurred in the organization's role and mandate following the earthquake on 30 September 1993, when SSP began its direct interventions in Latur and Osmanabad districts. The community-driven rehabilitation strategy that was adopted focused on the key elements of building local capacities and skills instead of a 'brick and mortar' approach to reconstruction. Village development committees (VDCs) were formed with the participation of existing community institutions and women's groups as facilitators to manage the rehabilitation effort. Women leaders were selected and trained as *samvad sahayaks*[4] or village communication assistants to ensure entitlements and involvement of women in planning and designing of houses and liaison with the government. Women's groups at the centre of the community participation strategy for reconstruction gained space on formal fora and came to be acknowledged as key players in village development and reconstruction.

Following the earthquake rehabilitation project in 1998, SSP steered the women's groups and communities in a broad-based community development strategy. Women's collectives started addressing their savings and credit needs and those of their families, as also practical survival needs, and to participate in community initiatives through their interface with the Mahila Mandals (MMs). From March 1998, SSP has focused its work to provide support to MMs to form groups and initiate savings and credit to address their

---

[4] A number of these women were leaders of Mahila Mandals formed under the government's 'Total Literacy Campaign' and had fallen into varied stages of inactivity. SSP sought to activate them once again by investing in capacities of their leadership to work with gram panchayats on village development issues.

survival needs.[5] MMs represent the 'face of development' in women's groups to address community problems as well as being involved in developmental initiatives in the village, like the provision of drinking water, housing, health, education, and dealing with social and legal issues. The SCG creates opportunities for economic advancement and is also an integral part of the MM; through this linkage, women who are members of both these fora are able to raise issues related to their needs. Today, SSP partners with over 700 SCGs with over 12,000 women members in Latur, Osmanabad and Solapur districts of Maharashtra.

The key elements of the processes initiated by SSP are as follows:

✦ Focus on horizontal learning through sharing and exchanges of each other's knowledge and on the centrality of women in the generation of knowledge.
✦ Decentralization, by which the systems of management are focused on the lowest rung of the SCG, while SSP is involved in the more complex tasks requiring higher levels of management.
✦ Ownership of institutions in the hands of women, and capacity enhancement to facilitate management of the same.
✦ Emphasis on the processes of learning and practice towards achievement of sustainable outcomes; spread and outreach for greater efficacy as well as visibility.

Methodology

It was decided that the study would be undertaken as a collective process, facilitated and led by the researcher with the district teams, which were hence actively involved in the design and data collection. The study was viewed as a

---

[5] While SHGs allow women to meet their credit and livelihood needs, MMs are legally registered women groups working to access basic services, village development and local self-government.

learning input for the organization and as an opportunity to initiate inquiry into aspects beyond financial and quantitative gains. It could help develop a conceptual understanding to examine and track the changes in the lives of the women and their communities. The focus has been on understanding what empowerment has meant in women's lives from their perspective. The organization, its approach, its strategy and its initiatives have also been examined in that context, to discern the significant aspects that have enabled or limited the space and processes of empowerment.

Since SSP's work in terms of direct implementation was initiated in two districts (Latur and Osmanabad), these form the universe of the study. It was decided to concentrate on the 300 groups that were at least two years old, and to draw a sample of 10 per cent of the groups across the two districts, based on their levels of development as assessed by the organization. Thirty groups were selected from the two districts for study through focus group discussions (FGDs) based on a checklist of questions. Group discussions were held in eight villages by the research team leader to orient the field workers to the methodology for the FGDs. Discussions were also held with women who are not group members to assess their perceptions about the impact of the SCGs on their lives and communities. Discussions with family members and leaders were conducted in sample villages. The primary data and information gathered in the course of the field interactions and interviews was recorded and translated (from Marathi). Efforts were made to ensure that the actual views expressed were captured in totality rather than summarized or interpreted by the researchers.

The researcher-workers were encouraged to maintain objectivity by conducting the discussions with groups other than their own villages and clusters. They were cautioned not to influence responses by prompting; their role was to be that of asking questions, probing: how, why, what, and then what did you do. Meetings were held with the group only when at least 50 per cent of the members were present at the beginning. Village profiles were prepared to give a holistic picture of the villages' background: population/demographic characteristics, occupational patterns, characteristics of the area, proportion of women linked to groups, any special initiatives taken by the group or by women in the village, etc. This also enabled an understanding and distinction between those activities that could be attributed to the SCG and subsequent initiative and others that had been either pre-SCG or independent of the SCG initiative. The researchers conducted discussions as a team, so that process documentation and discussion and probing for details could be done simultaneously, and crosschecks were possible. Thereafter, discussions were held with the other community members and family members so that women experienced no pressure or proxy interpretation of their experiences.

Apart from these primary data sets, the following also revealed information: discussions with clusters and federation leaders; interviews with resource persons/agencies; data collection; and review of existing records and literature with the organization.

Design and Management of the Micro-finance Programme

As a network, SSP facilitates NGOs and women's groups to work together to create effective strategies that address access to resources. Sakhi Gaon Samitis are the village committees initiated by SSP to integrate concerns and membership of MMs and SCGs by providing a continuous forum for ordinary women to bring up their concerns for debate and action. They are expected to provide leadership support to elected women panchayat members to function independently and act as a pressure group. The Sakhi Parisar Samiti is a form of cluster networking and platform for women leaders belonging to MMs and SCGs as well as elected members from 10–15 villages. Such networks also exist at the block level. Cluster and block networking is supported by 15 Mahila Mahiti Kendras (MMKs) (women's information centres), operationalized through the sub-programme to lead local development by modelling need-based services in health, education, socio-legal aid, skill training and networking for enterprises among groups.

The pyramid of self-learning institutional structures for empowerment is supported by the SCGs and MMs at the base and the Sakhi Mahasangh at the apex block level. The Sakhi Mahasanghs are grassroots women's federations promoted as community-owned institutions to sustain the economic base of SCGs to further the objectives of social and political empowerment. The Mahasangh's main objective is to facilitate the economic and social empowerment of women belonging to rural poor communities. The formation of the Sakhi Mahasangh, Latur was based on a need expressed by SCGs to link with banks and other financial institutions (FIs). Learning through exposure visits and exchanges with the Covenant for Community Development (CCD)[6] and the Mahakalasam Federation at Madurai helped to establish the first Mahasangh at Nilanga promoted by SSP. The process of building the first Mahasangh was a learning opportunity for women leaders on how to manage independent institutions. The board of directors was elected by member groups at the SCG's annual *melava* in 1999, from the leadership of the SCGs. After the formation of the Sakhi Mahasangh, they finalized its rules and regulations, the byelaws of the Mahasangh, and the eligibility of member groups. The main responsibility of the Sakhi Mahasangh is to collect share capital, membership fees and external credit to finance loans for livelihoods for member groups. Around 40 groups are members and shareholders, and have contributed Rs 1,000 each to the capital fund. Federation rules were evolved by Mahasangh women on the basis of their learning from the CCD and Mahakalasam, and modified to suit their needs.

With five federations existing and two more under way, SSP facilitates inter-federation learning and exchange. The

---

[6] CCD is an NGO based in the Madurai district of Tamil Nadu which works with tribal communities for enterprise development and herbal remedies.

Mahasangh's administrative costs continue to be borne from programme budgets. The interest collected on loans extended by the federation is shared by the SCGs and the federation, and 5 per cent interest is assigned to the credit fund, to cover the Mahasangh's administrative costs. For this to be viable, however, the scale of operations of the Mahasangh would need to be upscaled substantially. Gradually, it is expected that the Mahasangh would be recognized as credit-worthy and would be able to mobilize credit from banks and other FIs.

Savings are the foundation on which SCGs are built. Financially, they represent the resource base on which the group is built. Socially, the collection of a member's savings represents the need for a secure place to keep savings and pooling resources to address emergencies. As the group evolves, members generally become focused on loans. Savings are a vital element of vulnerability reduction in times of crises. SSP's role at this stage is to ensure that not only do the regular savings grow, but also that the group creates savings products that respond to members' short- and long-term needs. In the long term, members may save for the marriage or education of a child. In the short term, groups are encouraged to put aside extra savings after the harvesting season to meet expenses towards the next agricultural cycle. Groups need to ensure that savings are not kept idle.

Up to March 2000, over 5,407 loans were taken from the groups for consumption and productive activities. Women perceive both types of loans as necessary for everyday survival. SSP's effort is to ensure that groups continue to be the mainstay for crisis/emergency loans for members. These are usually short-term loans for health/illness, electricity, rent, travel, marriage, family functions, etc. Productive loans are mainly for agriculture, buying livestock, self-employment/trading and other economic activities. Besides receiving loans from groups, members in mature groups had the advantage of getting larger loans from banks and federation. Here again, monitoring the ranges of loans, the number of loans and the purpose of loans and the seasonality helps group leaders and SSP to see the extent to which loan products are refined to respond to the needs of members.

SSP's attempt is to analyse the changing loan profile and find out reasons for low utilization, slow movement toward productive credit and imbalance in credit for emergencies and economic activities. The reasons are then discussed with all members. A time line is worked out for redressing gaps. Loan monitoring depends entirely on the detailed analysis of financial indicators. The group meets all operating costs. Donations and fines are collected. Whenever required—for travel to banks, government offices, meetings and other programmes—women collect money. Other group members give one rupee per member every month to meet operational costs. While some groups distribute dividends to members, other groups prefer to keep the interest earned intact and reinvest it for loaning.

When group members are asked if repayment is good, they usually say it is. What they mean is that all loans are repaid. When groups reach stages III and IV, it is expected that they monitor repayment through analysing demand collection and balance (DCB). For this, SSP currently ensures that at least the groups that access external credit maintain records that show them the demand for credit, collections made in the current month and outstanding balance. Members in these groups need to be aware of repayment schedules so that they can repay both the principal and the interest on time. The group has to record the loan agreement including the dates on which instalments are due. This means that repayments have to match with what is stated in the agreement.

Interest rates are usually between 2 and 5 per cent per month. In the first two years, high rates are applied because this contributes to the group corpus. However when group members begin to take larger production loans, they find 5 per cent too high an interest rate. So group interest rates usually come down after one-and-a-half to two years to stabilize at 2 per cent per annum.

Transparency and accountability are a function of the records maintained by the group, the decision-making process, and whether or not all members are aware of the rules and all the decisions taken. Byelaws are not written down but SSP has evolved a set of 40 questions. As the group matures, both members and leaders are able to use these questions as a checklist to monitor their progress. While financial accountability is a primary concern, SSP's emphasis is on active participation of all members and developing collective leadership, which is accountable to group members. Similarly, cluster meetings act as platforms to ensure peer accountability between groups.

Collective Leadership

If SCGs are seen as means for social and political empowerment, then it is essential that members' leadership qualities are nurtured and they understand that they are active participants in group decision-making. Currently, the Sakhi Bachat Gats have two group leaders: a president and a secretary. Earlier, these roles were not differentiated. In the last two years, SSP has ensured that the secretary is trained as an accountant, while the president is the manager. Active members participate in cluster meetings and take on the following tasks within the group: collecting savings, collecting repayments, counting the cash, and going to the bank. Collective leadership ensures that more and more members have the opportunity to take on responsibility for the decisions taken by the group, financial transactions, safekeeping of the cash in hand, and attending the cluster-level meetings are common issues which are taken up.

Over 1,857 group leaders were trained in 65 cluster-level SCG training workshops. Group leaders are trained on financial systems: how to keep records, write accounts, etc. Similarly, the importance of transparency in functioning through group meetings, giving loans to all members is emphasized. Leadership training with an emphasis on collective leadership is promoted. Special workshops are held for the following groups: groups prepared to link to the federation, member groups of *taluka* federations, groups linked to the SHG–bank linkage scheme, and enterprise development workshops for women entrepreneurs in SCGs.

Cluster workers are part of the SSP outreach team, and play key roles in mobilizing women, initiating new groups, information networking, operationalizing the management information systems (MIS), tracking financial transactions, group processes, trouble shooting and providing 'hands on' training for groups. The SSP district team attends meetings of 'problem groups'. Member conflicts, lack of transparency in loaning, and lack of accurate records are problems that are tackled on the spot. This provides hands-on training and support to group leaders and cluster workers. Other problems such as family conflicts, social tensions between various factions, and developmental requirements are also expressed at such meetings. It also establishes the value of group functioning.

All groups conduct savings and loan meetings every month. SSP's perspective is that groups need to exchange the 'hows' of group functioning. Reporting to peer groups at the cluster level increases accountability in financial transactions. At the same time, new ideas are exchanged on how group leaders solve conflicts, how collective leadership is mobilized, how records are written, and how women are promoted to take up enterprises. The learning menu was expanded to include market study tours and livelihood exchanges.

Monitoring SCGs

SSP's attempt is to create a monitoring process that incorporates indicators that assess financial services provided by groups to members as well as the empowerment processes that support women to re-negotiate their positions within the community. Assessing financial transactions is relatively simple because the questions being asked are concrete and have answers that are quantifiable. Monitoring empowerment processes, on the other hand, is more complex as it is difficult to quantify such processes. A good monitoring system attempts to locate only those aspects that are identified as priority areas. When groups are formed, they usually take about three to six months to regulate their day-to-day functioning (mobilizing phase). By the end of the year, it is expected that the group be stabilized (stabilization phase). The SSP field team usually looks for the following six signs:

1. Is the group meeting regularly?
2. Are members saving regularly?
3. Are savings being collected at the meeting?
4. Is the group size between 15 and 20 and do all members attend meetings?
5. Does the group have record books in which transactions are noted?
6. Are loans given in meetings?

At this stage, the emphasis is on building mutual trust through group rituals, meetings, savings collection, and the loans that go out in meetings. Once formed, groups usually take at least two years to consolidate their work. During this period, group members have usually gone through several cycles of borrowing and repaying loans, have adequately developed systems, and understand and practise byelaws to manage funds and group processes. Both aspects are necessary if the group is to move on to Phase III in which it takes credit from mainstream FIs.

The caution in Phase III is that the group needs strong financial systems and a mature leadership that ensures that external credit can be managed and repaid through the group fund. If the group is not mature, external funds could destroy the systems created. SSP's role is crucial at this stage. Groups are prepared to link to the federation as well as the banks. Both involve similar processes of financial accountability. Group records are changed to record external credit transactions as well. It is at this stage that loan agreements include repayment schedules that members have to adhere to. This is a new kind of financial discipline where not only members are accountable to the group, but the group is also accountable to an external agency.

While SSP takes on the responsibility to monitor the overall credit programme, cluster workers, group leaders, and the

SHGs themselves acquire the skills and tools to assess their own work at every stage. SSP tries to create a monitoring process that depends on multiple sources of information. Group records are one source. In Phase I (mobilization), SSP earlier ensured several things that are monitored by cluster workers. SSP's role is moving towards Phases II, III and IV to ensure that the groups have a dynamic decision-making process and good rotation of loans. The SSP worker has an important role to train cluster workers and group leaders to monitor processes. Cluster workers are key to ensuring that the financial transactions are recorded within groups, tracked and recorded at the SSP database, which is computerized in Latur and Osmanabad districts and maintained at the district level.

The financial monitoring focuses on whether funds are being utilized, rather than lying idle and the extent to which all information on financial transactions are recorded and transparent. The data generated for SCGs focuses on the financial transactions of the groups. Recently, an attempt was also made to record and measure group performance by qualitative indicators. The checklist of issues for performance assessment includes the following:

- Monthly meetings: Meetings held regularly, regular attendance by members.
- Decision-making: members' awareness, participation in decision-making, whether leadership is collective or controlled by one or two members.
- Loan portfolio: Range of loans (size), number of members who access loans.
- Savings: Regular savings by members, excess savings.
- Interest rate: Whether groups have reduced interest rates.
- Repayment: Default, reasons for delayed repayment, etc.
- Loan decisions: Production or consumption, need-based or preference to savings.
- Group records and accounts: Accounts kept regularly, accurate and updated.
- Issues discussed in meetings: Conflicts and problems in relation to credit, access to social issues, women's issues, development concerns.

✦ Access to external credit from banks: Whether groups have accounts, submitted applications, follow-up on loan purpose, etc.
✦ Involvement in village development activities: Collective action, linkage with gram panchayat, planning and implementation of schemes, infrastructure development, etc.
✦ Linkage to government: Contact with officials at district and *taluka*, access to below poverty line (BPL) schemes, such as the Swarnajayanti Gram Swarozgar Yojana (SGSY).
✦ Participation in learning programmes: Participation and conducting community programmes, *melavas*, etc.
✦ Enterprise development: Promoting micro-enterprise and group enterprise with women members.
✦ Linkage with federation: Preparatory process and involvement in federation activities.

Banks are institutional actors that SCGs must link with. SSP has designed a process that helps groups to build long-term relationship with local banks and establish its credibility. This is monitored both in terms of contacts made and credit accessed by the groups. The following milestones indicate where the group is positioned:

✦ Opening bank accounts.
✦ Interacting with the local bank.
✦ Interacting with banks at multiple levels.
✦ How groups are treated in the bank—the '*cup of tea*'[7] indicator.
✦ Loan applications.
✦ Access to bank loans.
✦ Repayment of external credit.

Nurturing SCGs as 'Learning Fora for Women'

The SCGs have set in motion two kinds of learning processes. The first has to do with collectively managing resources.

---

[7] Group leaders believe that the offer of a cup of tea by the bank manager indicates their acceptance of women as equals and is indicative of a level of cordiality and respect accorded to group leaders.

The second has to do with mobilizing and organizing, where the SCG provides the means to bring people together on a regular basis since savings have to be collected regularly, and provides a space for women to share day-to-day problems. As women's groups mature, they swiftly make the transition from addressing household concerns through credit, to participation in the public sphere, where they address community issues such as water, sanitation, healthcare, poverty alleviation, and the public distribution system (PDS). The financial activities of these collectives provide women with both the confidence and the resource base to intervene in local development processes. Apart from the rigour involved in the process of savings and credit, they are able to articulate the merits of decisions and negotiate their point of view on a wide range of issues. The collective resources and identity also give them the confidence to broaden their horizons to enhance physical and social mobility. For instance, women have taken bridge loans[8] from the SCGs for the construction of toilets as part of a government-funded sanitation programme, and have negotiated the installation of the hand pump in their own *basti* (settlement) in a lower-caste area instead of the upper-caste area.[9]

Entrepreneurship is promoted among women primarily based on traditional skills and livelihood activities. Apart from these, women have also taken up trade and retail activities on an individual basis, such that they can be combined with agricultural and other labour work. The focus of the organization is currently on exploring opportunities for collective enterprise to enable communities to address sustainable livelihood needs and enhance economic opportunities. In this initiative also, as in other activities that the

---

[8] These refer to advances drawn from the group against sanctions received for government support on development works to individuals. These resources are then returned once the individual receives reimbursement. This serves to mitigate the long gestation period of receiving government assistance between sanctions and actual release of funds.
[9] Discussions in Vadval village, Latur district.

organization has undertaken, the focus is on enhancing women's capacities to undertake entrepreneurial initiatives and enable them to take their own decisions, rather than being dependent on the organization.

In all its activities, SSP has sought to address the learning and capacity building needs of women's collectives in rural areas through horizontal exchange and learning, networking, and peer learning exchanges. The SCGs served as effective platforms for social mobilization as well as a supportive space for poor women to learn about collective mobilization, managing, and exercising control over resources. Often the women's groups felt challenged to take giant steps after they had heard of achievements and lessons from those who had moved ahead in the process. *Melavas* or information fairs, study tours, and exposure and field visits have clear methods, goals and outcomes. Pilots and cluster networks provide spaces for sharing and innovation. Linkages with formal institutions are the current steps in the process and key objectives as well as strategies of SSP. The example of Gujnoor is a case in point (Box 5.1).

While groups are enabled to manage their own financial and other affairs, this also leads to another set of dynamics, which consists of the dominance of the literate in leadership positions as office-bearers and therefore as decision-makers. As a result, neither has group leadership rotated, nor do the group members consider that to be an option, although some groups mentioned that they had raised questions relating to the integrity of the leaders and wanted a change in leadership. Leadership and its consequent learning thus become confined to the literate who are invariably from the better-off section of the community. However, as women gain confidence, SCGs act as platforms for collective decisions. While the organization provides opportunities for capacity development through access to information and development of new skills that equip them for the new roles, women leaders progress to lead information networks at the cluster, block, and district levels. Women's knowledge is made visible through workshops and exposure visits.

BOX 5.1

The Case of Gujnoor

Gujnoor Tuljapur *taluka* has a population of 650 persons. SCGs have existed here for three years. Women's financial status is greatly improved through taking loans and undertaking small businesses. Although the women came together with some apprehensions, they started collecting cash and depositing it in the bank, but didn't know what to do further. Once Madhur *tai* (pronounced *taai*) from the organization visited the village and taught them how to keep accounts, the group started giving loans. Suglabai Shivappa Mulge started a grocery shop, since most of the population had shifted to the highland after the earthquake. Three women took loans for goats. Some women took loans to buy fowls and buffaloes and for other small businesses. So far, 15 women have taken loans from the Mahila Saving Group and started businesses. These village women have started visiting other places too and are learning from other women's experiences. They are learning about ration, gram panchayat work, village development, and so on. They want to join the gram panchayat for village development and public work. Annapurnabai Shivram Vaghmare is the village *sarpanch* (head of the panchayat). Women have decided to support her and take her help to achieve success. Annapurnabai is also a member of the saving group. The gram panchayat is active since the last two years, under her leadership. There is sufficient water but the pipeline needs repair, and Annapurnabai plans to get it repaired soon.

Dealing with Violence

Various instances of crimes and violence against women did emerge in the course of the research team's discussions with groups, such as wife battering, desertion, bigamy, rape and alcoholism. But the women mentioned these only when discussions were more open-ended and unstructured. On further inquiry, it was found that women leaders were dealing with these cases on an informal basis by talking to the elders and men in such households. They, however, did not consider it desirable to discuss these incidents in their meetings. In fact, in one instance after our discussion, the group leader[10] gathered the courage to confide in the SSP staff member that she was a victim of domestic violence but was unable to bring up the issue with the group for fear of losing credibility in her group. Women of Vadgaon[11] spoke in hushed tones about the problem of alcoholism and wife-beating that was rampant in the village, but felt despondent about dealing with it without support from others. They were of the view that by taking up the matter with the *sarpanch* they would be exposing themselves to a backlash from the men in their families and community. But the situation had become so unbearable that they were willing to risk the ire of the men in the community to try and resolve the issue.

As an organization, SSP does not consider it necessary or appropriate to raise issues of violence to a level of community or public debate, since its experience of dealing with violence against women in this way has proven counterproductive in the past. Instead it prefers to deal with issues and cases of violence and crimes against women as the groups consider appropriate and capable of handling. While this is a discreet choice that the organization has made, there is a need to address the issue with a greater sense of urgency than is visible at present.

Given SSP's strategy of building capacities and skills on issues that emerge as priorities in the community, the measures taken hitherto such as legal information camps have been few and sporadic, and need to be accompanied by a more rigorous process of self-learning. In fact, the community leader in Bhosa village, Latur district, who had been on an exposure visit to Gujarat spoke of the Nari Adalat[12]

---

[10] Ramwadi is considered an ideal village for its democratic practices and initiatives in public hygiene and has even been awarded by the government, but discriminatory gender relations and incidence of violence were evident here too.

[11] Discussions held on 29 September 2001 with women of two groups in the village.

[12] An informal alternative justice delivery system, functioning as a women's court that facilitates the negotiation of cases of crimes against and harassment of women. This forum has gained a fair amount of credibility even with the formal law enforcers in parts of Gujarat, since it is a quicker and cheaper option, where women get a fair hearing.

experience and sought the support of SSP in initiating such a process, apart from suggesting that SSP appoint a lawyer to assist in cases of violence![13]

Based on the above, one may surmise that the groups have evolved over a three to four year period to varied levels of strength, with the capacity to deal with a range of issues related to practical needs. By addressing practical development issues of the community, many of which are traditionally male-dominated, women's collectives address strategic gender concerns and enter new spaces, demonstrating their competencies to manage and renegotiating their roles within communities and in the context of the state. However, they are not in a position to deal with the strategic issues of women's status except in a few sporadic instances. SSP views its role as building women's capacities for survival needs and access to resources so that they may build their own fora to deal with issues as they emerge. Thus, while women are provided the support and opportunities to intervene in public spheres, the issues of societal practices and the private sphere of family violence remains largely unaddressed except at the level of legal information.

SSP and Macro Issues

There are boundaries visible in the levels of investment that SSP is willing to make on issue-based interventions, especially with regard to gender and class issues. Issues of minimum wages and employment guarantee for instance have not been areas for sustained campaigning or intervention despite discriminatory practices existing in these villages. However, the issue of ration supply and the PDS have been taken up through a sustained strategy in the past. Issues that are less likely to cause conflict or confrontation are given greater significance over such issues that may cause inter-class or intra-household conflicts and thereby rock the processes that have been nurtured over

---

[13] Discussion with Maya Solte of Bhosa village on 26 August 2001.

the years. This indicates a deeper conflict relating to the role of the organization in creating access to state resources on the one hand and building alternative institutions on the other. The strategy assumes a critical mass approach to resolution of such class and gender issues, while facilitating the creation of institutional options to buffer and challenge the mainstream social, political, and economic fabric. Whether this will ultimately lead to the inclusion of more sensitive issues of violence in the family and discriminatory wage rates being addressed in the long run is a matter of conjecture. The organization, however, needs to examine its own position on these issues to clarify the strategies that it could adopt to facilitate transformatory processes, and moving beyond the existing ameliorative framework.

The majority of staff members who participated in discussions were of the view that lack of resources is the major impediment to women's advancement. Given access to resources and a space for their learning and collective mobilization, they felt that women could and have undertaken significant steps to bring about changes in their lives and that of their families, as well as in their villages. All agreed that women had now gained access to great opportunities, mobility was high, and women articulated public demands for basic services with great skill and confidence. They experienced an enhanced status as economic contributors by virtue of their ability to mobilize resources, augment family incomes substantially, as well as have greater access to outside information. While women have a greater say in their families, staff members were of the opinion that the changes in their social status and attitudes towards women still remain within traditional parameters. According to one staff member:

> We find that women in their households are still doing the same work, have to observe the traditional practices and continue to neglect themselves if they are sick. While there is a change in the situation, their social status is still subordinate and determined by the traditional patterns of patriarchy.[14]

---

[14] Laxmikant Malvadker in discussions at the staff meeting on 23 August 2001.

The staff felt that the organization's efforts should focus on continuing to strengthen the participation of women in public spheres and providing them information and support to strengthen their groups and institutions. In the long run, these efforts would lead to women taking charge of their own lives. While they all accepted and acknowledged that women's health and violence were areas of concern, they did not see the need to focus on these issues for capacity development. Two senior women staff members however differed; in their opinion, it was necessary to deal with these issues and to provide support and capacity development inputs so that women were encouraged to deal with these issues and support each other. Currently, crimes, violence and women's health are not areas of intervention and women did not consider them as the agenda of the groups or the MMs, tending to deal informally with these issues outside the groups. A discussion on the issue of the rivalry between mothers-in-law and daughters-in-law revealed that staff by and large did not see this as a structural problem but as an attitude that women acquire due the lack of their education and exposure. Obviously, greater clarity on gender issues and the structures of gender-related subordination are required for the organization to move into an empowerment framework encompassing these relatively sensitive issues.

SSP's focus, therefore, has been to enhance women's capacities, empower them to engage with development in the public sphere and encourage them to bring about changes in their communities. The underlying assumption is that this would finally lead to a transformation in the status of women in those communities as they gain respect credibility and access to resources. Currently, however, the distinctions between women's empowerment and women as instruments for enhancement of the economic well-being of their families are somewhat blurred as women have gained on a number of fronts in the process of capacity enhancement and access to resources.

Institutional Changes in the Banking Sector

SSP's efforts with specific bank branches have yielded results. Several groups are enlisted in the waiting list for bank linkage as part of SSP's strategy to prepare groups for bank linkage and visibility with the banks. Currently, in Murud cluster in Latur *taluka*, all the groups are in the process of getting bank loans. The SSP team has played a key role in educating bank managers in the region. They have also played a major role in sensitizing middle-level management in the banking sector through their lobbying efforts. In the past year, 89 exposure visits to banks were undertaken by 265 SCGs members to build relations with banks, meet bank officials and bring them to groups, report to banks, deposit group surplus, and understand SHG–bank linkages and other schemes.

SSP has brought about significant changes in the banking sector. It has simplified bank documentation for groups to submit a simple application with details of group loan and a group resolution/agreement to repay the loan. Steps for sanctioning loans to SHGs have been standardized. Wherever SSP has facilitated this, changes are being made in loan procedures by other bank branches as well. As banks increase contact with groups, avenues for further lending have opened up; members recommended by the groups have obtained livestock loans. Information on other group schemes, such as the SGSY, is available to group members from banks. Banks have begun to view groups as business clients instead of beneficiaries of subsidy schemes. Women members recommended by groups have received start-up loans for small enterprises.

Changes in the Lives of Individual Women

The first SCGs that emerged in SSP's work were in those villages where SSP already had strong contacts through its efforts at rehabilitation after the earthquake of September 1993. This motivated women in Latur and Osmanabad districts to form their own SCGs, and seek guidance from SSP. The SCGs formed at this stage followed a pattern of association and membership similar to the affiliations across caste/class lines in the post-rehabilitation stage with a mixed membership, across castes and religious groups and included dalit women. In the 30 groups studied/visited, about 30–35 per cent of the women belonged to the Scheduled Caste category although their representation in leadership positions was lower. More than caste, class affiliations seem to determine the sense of belonging in the groups. Women consciously acknowledge that they are changing social relations through their SCGs.

Only where there is a single-caste group or a single leader are meetings held in common locations on a regular basis, as in the case of Vadval and Ramwadi. In Ramwadi, a number of groups meet together. This necessitates a common locale. Unlike the case of SCGs formed by government functionaries at the instance of administrative directives, SCGs promoted by SSP meet regularly and on a fixed date each month. The venue of the meeting is rotated between members' homes each month in the case of mixed caste groups. Apart from ensuring that there is transparency, this also serves to build social cohesion. 'By participating together we show our elders and children that women can work together despite caste and religion', said one woman in Khandala. Data on leadership and lending by caste is not available but would reveal interesting insights into the dynamics and power relations within groups, as well as social dynamics between members.

Records of the groups reveal that participation in group meetings is fairly high. On an average, two to three women in each group are labourers and are unable to attend meetings regularly; their cases are dealt with flexibly. One group however reported that they preferred not to have such women as members, nor did they give them financial support. In discussions about rules and norms of groups, women have highlighted that attendance is regular even at unscheduled meetings. In some cases, community leaders, young girls and women non-members also attend meetings. More than 75 per cent group members are predominantly in the age group of above 30 years. More than 20 per cent are above 40 years of age and the average age of members ranges from 35 to 40 years. Most members (88 per cent) are currently married and less than 2 per cent are never married and are less than 20 years old. Each of the groups studied had two or three women (10 per cent) who were either widowed or deserted. These women felt that the group provided them with a social space and sense of security.

Procedures for selection of leaders are democratic. Women discuss the criteria for selection of a leader and elect an individual through voice vote or consensus. Active, articulate members who can interact with all others and have the time and capability are selected to leadership positions. 'Women leaders need to be active, intelligent and capable of all work such as managing savings, maintaining records and interacting with banks for deposit and withdrawal of money', said the women from Usturi. Women emphasized personal integrity, honesty and literacy as vital prerequisites, along with management skills, in prospective group leaders.

Group functioning is greatly dependent on the quality of leadership. Leaders run the meetings, share information, and are key factors in resolving problems of groups. They determine the level of democratic functioning and transparency in a group. In most groups, leaders have a significant role to play in determining who should receive loans on priority. However, in most groups we met, the group leaders had availed of loans more frequently and in larger volumes than other members and had also taken target loans from the Mahasangh and/or banks. Leaders also determine the level of interface and involvement in the MM and village development activities. Some active women group members were involved in MM activities and were elected panchayat representatives. This is viewed as a healthy sign, indicating multiple leadership opportunities rather than a centralization of roles and authority.

Participation and Benefits

Access to Information

When asked about who benefits from the groups, more than half the groups stated that while women members were the direct beneficiaries of loans and financial transactions, all women in the community benefited since the group served to create a different environment and opportunity for the advancement of women and girls. Net membership has increased from the initial stage of group formation. Motivation for participation in the SCGs is not based on prospects of economic gain alone. Women reported that learning opportunity and access to information were the main reasons for joining SCGs. Speaking of the unique features of this opportunity as against earlier experiences of SCG operations through government intervention, women stated that the SCGs initiated by SSP provide more than a window of financial support. They prioritize two aspects: (a) access to information as a means of improved livelihood choices, as well as enhanced perspectives (group members as well as their families and community leaders perceive access to information and an enhancement in their world view as a critical value of the SCG); and (b) the sense of belonging to a collective that can negotiate, resolve problems, establish an identity for women and ensure their place in community life and the public sphere.

Women experienced initial resistance from their families. In each group, there were a few women who had started earning and attending meetings without informing their families, for fear of being stopped. Gradually the resistance broke down as women started being acknowledged as the 'gatekeepers of knowledge'. Women contrasted the SCG itself and its operational modalities with their earlier experiences of group functioning. They stated that through SSP they had learnt about management, accounting, and money transaction. This created a sense of self-reliance and ownership of their resources in contrast to the earlier situation where they were dependent on a government functionary.

They have established direct contact with the banks and gained mobility to attend village- and cluster-level meetings and organization-level trainings and even to travel to distant places on study and exposure visits.

Women were able to access information on a range of issues such as government schemes, Panchayati Raj procedures, and the rationing system. The information and discussions on the ration shops and operation of the PDS galvanized the groups in a number of villages into leadership roles. Women used the information to monitor availability, quantities and quality of rations and stocks distributed. They were able to confront the shop owners on a number of occasions and take up the issue at the *taluka* level and negotiate with the administration.

Based on the proactive interventions of the SCGs and MMs on the ration issue, the Chief Executive Officer (CEO) of the Zilla Parishad (an elected local District Council) accorded them recognition and issued identity cards to women leaders. They were thus able to play this monitoring role with greater legitimacy. Based on the information about the norms of the PDS, and the information that women gathered through monitoring of PDS shops, women were able to collate and place this information before the CEO at an 'open forum' meeting conducted by the district administration. This enabled them to gain entry as special invitees to the ration committees at *taluka* level where they could report and ensure action against errant PDS functionaries and shopkeepers.[15]

The ration and PDS issues highlighted the potential of the role that SCGs/MMs could play for family and community members, especially among the economically vulnerable.

---

[15] This situation has however been thwarted since the CEO was transferred and the status of special invitees was withdrawn from the women leaders. The PDS system now stands practically defunct since commodities available offer little relief to the poor, prices not being greatly different from the market price, in keeping with the new policies of the state on liberalization and removal of subsidies. Women are aware of these nuances and the adverse impact of such policies, but have not been involved in any major campaigns on these issues. Nor is the organization engaged in these debates of state economic policy.

Although this effort did not sustain after a change in the CEO, women's awareness on the issue grew. More significantly, it helped motivate women to explore their new-found credibility and leadership as community-level watchdogs for various schemes including poverty alleviation programmes, health and education programmes, functioning of schools, etc.

Women who are not members of the SCGs see a marked distinction between themselves and SCG members. In none of the villages visited did women non-members state that they did not perceive a benefit from the group. Their reasons for not being members lay in their own inability either by virtue of the fact that they migrated for work, not having the time to get away for meetings, or social restrictions imposed on them by their families and communities. One other deterrent was the fact that women who joined an existing group were required to make a deposit of the principal amount already collected by order members. These women also showed some hesitation to join a new group where the systems were not in place. They viewed SCG members as 'active' and 'leaders' and 'voices for the problems of women in the village'. They say that this was based on their ability to access information and act upon it collectively. Women and community members also state that SCG members show greater unity and 'speak in one voice' whereas MMs may be influenced by political lobbies and the women leaders of panchayats may be merely titular members. Thus, women's SCGs are seen as having a more autonomous character with democratic systems of internal governance and management, while MMs are more loosely organized and may be influenced by other forces and factors than the primacy of women's interests.

When asked about who stands to lose by women organizing themselves into SCGs, the most spontaneous response was, 'the *sahukar*'. The moneylenders have used various means to coerce women to take loans: threatened women with not lending to them in the future. The *sahukars* even spoke to bank managers in Nilanga and Vadgaon to discourage them from 'spoiling the market' for them. The others to lose out were obviously the other women in the community, especially the poorest who were unable to join the group due to the burden of work and because they could not save. However, some groups had (40 per cent of the groups studied) made flexible conditions so that some of the women in the poorer communities could continue to be members. They were permitted absence from most meetings, were allowed to come late. They were also provided support to enable them to pay the principal amount to join. This amount was recovered from them in small doses in deferred instalments.

Access to Resources

Participation in SCGs has created access for women to resources to cater to needs of their families in times of crisis and for consumption needs such as household requirements, health care, books and school fees. Apart from group loans, women are able to access resources from the Mahasangh and banks, on the basis of which the economic conditions of their families have improved, and indebtedness to moneylenders has decreased. Women report a greater level of independence in decisions to purchase jewellery or household requirements and manage productive assets. Few women reported purchase of land/fields in their own name, while others acquired cattle and goats. These women also said that they had control over the income from these resources.

More than 50 per cent of the women members reported their work status as cultivators on their household land. Most groups reflect a predominance of women in landowning households, although the majority of these are small and marginal farmer households. About 35–40 per cent membership of the groups is from agricultural labour households. There are few women in other occupations, except in Lohara Khurd, where women are in occupations other than agriculture and casual labour such as *kirana* (grocery) shops, *paan* shops (which keep cigarettes, areca nuts, etc., apart from betel leaves), animal husbandry, poultry and goat rearing, lathes and sawing machines, bangle selling, and so on. Thus it is inferred that the SCGs provide a forum for economic upliftment of women of small and marginal farmer and labourer households, enabling them to attend to consumption needs through small loans, when such need arises. Women members are aware that the poorest are unable to participate as group members, but some groups talked about how they had extended support to more impoverished women by facilitating access to BPL loans (in Kamkheda) and by extending credit at times of crisis (in Ramwadi).

Pandri's women described with pride how they acquired land in their own names. Vadval's women showed off their goats as their assets and wealth. Khandala's women showed us how productivity had improved in the family carpentry unit, although they acknowledged that the sawing machines were not in their names. Women in all groups view their efforts in the SCGs as the creation of new opportunities for their daughters and girls in their villages.

Agency through Access to Resources and Enterprises

Most significantly, women express changes in their perceptions about themselves as members of the SCGs. They view themselves with greater confidence than ever before, in that they are able to provide for their families' needs and are capable of presenting their own points of view even to the male elders of the village and to government officials. Women report changes in their own attitudes about themselves and their status in eight of the villages studied. The opportunity to participate in the meetings of the SCGs gives an exposure to different ideas and perspectives and enables them to develop on opinion. They feel that they receive greater support from their families and more respect as individuals. Extending the concept of their own change in perspective, women state that communities view them as changed and empowered, with the backing of the group supporting them. Their presence is acknowledged in different fora; they get respect from all women. In Mogha Khurd, all women have started feeling an improvement in their status. All women are now respected and women's collective strength is visible to the communities. Women group members and leaders are considered role models and ideals.

With respect to changes in family dynamics, most women report an enhanced role in decision-making in relationships with their husbands. In Talkot, women say their opinions are sought before important decisions are made. Women in Khandala, Ramwadi, Usturi and Ambulga report a decrease in incidences of violence and abuse for group members and other women, despite the organization's resistance to taking these issues on board as part of its agenda. This indicates that whether or not SSP takes on these issues as part of its formal agenda, they are being raised and dealt with in an informal way by the groups. A concerted investment of resources and focus at this point may serve to create a greater impact to address the issue, since groups have moved into situations of greater strength in various ways. In Pandri, for instance, these shifts are more visible. Not only do families take decisions together, but there is also less abuse of women.

Groups have extended credit to non-members in times of illness or daughters' weddings. Ten per cent of the groups studied have also lent to other groups. Support from family members is forthcoming to SCG members to attend meetings and programmes. By and large, repayment of loans taken by women remains the responsibility of women, even if the income has accrued to the family. Most (60 per cent) of the groups report that women repay loans with their earnings from labour and enterprise. Forty per cent of such groups reported that husbands and family provide support if they are unable to repay the loans. Groups state that husbands and family members repay with amounts taken out of the family enterprise and increased incomes. Thus the burden of repayment still lies on the women, indicating that while women's access to credit resources has increased, their control over its returns remains high only when they run the enterprise. This implies that while women are a means for getting credit, their ability to leverage family resources is still limited in the case of investment in family businesses.

Loans have been utilized for initiating enterprises, increasing stocks, or investing in productive assets such as cattle and goats and agricultural inputs such as seeds and fertilizers. They have also been used to purchase cycles. Some loans have been taken for medical treatment, education of sons as well as daughters, house maintenance and construction, laying water pipelines, purchase of motor, and even religious purposes. All these activities benefit the family, but the burden of the debt falls on the women. Women's hesitation to respond to our queries on this issue was an eloquent statement of their contriving burden. Groups do not lend to members for the purchase of gold, clothes, consumer durables such as televisions and air coolers, or alcohol and gambling. Consumption enabling loans are only given when there is no demand for other needs and the money is lying idle.

As they turned to the SCG for small loans to cover crisis needs, families were gradually able to move away from dependence on *sahukars* for small consumption needs. However, when requirements arise for sums beyond the group's capacity, members are still compelled to take loans from *sahukars* in crises. Women do not openly mention this. Only some groups (30 per cent) reported that a few members were compelled to take recourse to higher interest loans from moneylenders, since the volume of credit available from groups was limited.

Group savings or leverage of credit has also not been able to prevent the migration of people at times of drought or those of bad agriculture crops (the rains have failed once the past two years). There has been an analysis of the loan cycle and peoples' requirement at times of drought. In Vadgaon region, groups have broken down, as migrating families demanded their share of the savings. A review of the records of recent meetings reflects some discussion on this issue.

Women have been encouraged through credit availability, coupled with training inputs and exchanges at *melavas* to invest in enhancing their economic status. Women have used available resources to strengthen family businesses and livelihoods such as *kirana* shops, agriculture, *paan* shops, animal husbandry, etc. Along with family occupations, women have also invested in productive assets that they manage and earn returns from. These include poultry and goat rearing, animal husbandry, bangle and cosmetic sales, and purchase and sale of vegetables and other agricultural produce. In the cases of 'own enterprises', ownership is much higher as returns are in their own hands. They say:

We are the owners and workers. In some cases our household members may help in purchase or sale of goods but we must run the business and repay the loans. Along with being entrepreneurs, we are workers and domestic workers and fulfil all these roles.

Women state that in the family's traditional occupations they are part of family labour and have little control over the returns although they may be involved in management tasks.

Although the enterprises translate into more responsibilities in addition to their traditional roles, the women report that their struggle for survival is now less stressful. Women of Usturi would earlier work as labour but are now able to work on their enterprises. In Pandri, women reported that earlier they would strive to finish domestic work and go for labour work, but now this has changed. In Mogha, women have purchased goats and buffaloes with their loans and within a year have been able to purchase more animals and increased their earnings substantially.

Women also report changes in practices over the past few months. Time spent on enterprises has increased and management practices have also improved. Women have diversified to include other activities and the earnings from poultry and animal husbandry have generated surpluses for investment in agriculture and in kirana shops. Increased earnings have enabled women to access resources to cater to needs of the household more efficiently in all cases. Women also have greater resources available to incur expenditures themselves, without having to seek permission from family members and elders as reported in Phanepur. Family cooperation has increased in tending to tasks while women manage the enterprises in Jalkot but they did not elaborate on the sources of support. In Ramwadi, husbands are now more willing to support women in loan repayment than earlier. Husbands and family members are also cooperative in sale and purchase of goods and managing the business if women have to be away at meetings.

Women earlier worked as labourers and moved to seek work in neighbouring villages. New women entrepreneurs in the majority of villages are willing and involved in the sale of products in neighbouring villages products such as bangles and vegetables although most stated that sales within the village itself were adequate. Most women entrepreneurs report higher ability to interact and transact with banks to make withdrawals and repayments. Women are keen to return their loans and take fresh, larger loans.

Literacy

While most group members are illiterate (55 per cent), more than 28 per cent have had primary and middle education. This segment also dominates leadership positions and maintains records and accounts. This vests in them the power to represent the group at cluster meetings, training programmes, and workshops. It gives them greater access to information and confidence in decision-making. Groups that have lower levels of literacy are also predominantly those involved in agricultural labour. This implies that some literate women in such groups tend to remain the hubs, guiding group processes while the others are more dependent on those at the centre.

Literate daughters-in-law create a new dynamic in the group. They are more assertive and their communication styles more formal, reflective of their exposure to school discipline. Older women, including mothers-in-law, did not discourage these young women and watched the interface silently. Thus, although groups openly acknowledged a hesitation to involve daughters-in-law in the group, those that had done so provided openness and a democratic space for all the members.

Family Dynamics and Changing Gender Roles

Interactions with girls (informally and at group meetings) of the group members' families revealed that they took on much of the household workload (cleaning, washing and cooking) when their mothers went for meetings or exposure tours.

But they also expressed that their mothers had become confident and brought in information and resources benefiting the family. Girls stated that since the mothers were involved in the group, education opportunities for them were likely to improve. It has been seen that changing family attitudes towards girls' mobility and education is a major impact of women's greater access to resources and participation in the SCG and other activities.

Girls and daughters perceive changes in women in their growing economic strength as they take more economic decisions within the household and exercise choices in the nature of work they perform for income earning and in task reallocation among family members. Adolescent girls and daughters of women members see them as exercising agency, through newly acquired knowledge of government programmes and panchayat activities, as well as in new roles as office-bearers and members of the SCGs. Women's new roles demand their involvement in various fora, which gives them space to test their skills of negotiation and problem solving. While girls acknowledged that their mothers' involvement in SCG and other collective actions implies that they sometimes have to miss school or do greater amount of domestic chores, they view this as valuable in that the women are paving the way for future opportunities for the girls also. Women leaders of the groups and Mahasanghs represent new role models for their daughters to a greater extent than the panchayat representatives.

Above all, girls value the facts that their mothers bring home new information based on which the family can progress and that women were given greater respect within the home. Girls spoke of the increasing recognition of the value of literacy in the lives of women, due to which they now have more opportunities to attend school. With their mothers' increased economic strength through savings groups and earnings through entrepreneurial opportunities, girls are able to go to school and face lesser restrictions on their mobility. Women's increased social and personal dynamism, ability to negotiate, and their leadership are leading girls to believe that these are and will be options available to them as well.

In their relationship with their children, women report that children are more supportive and empathetic towards their new roles. Children support their mothers in more ways and share work in Raibhar and Gujnur. Viewing their mothers as working, as visibly productive, they feel more confident. 'Girls are more confident now and are feeling stronger. They want to be part of the group now,' report women from Pandri. Women from Pandri, Usturi and Ambulaga who were earlier unable to educate children are now sending them to school. Women in Vadval report: 'Girls are now being sent to school and get better respect and are also given milk, which they were deprived of earlier.' Women in Gujnur say: 'Girls have greater aspirations and are growing up with the idea that they will also work and be active.' The women themselves view the improvements in their status as enabling for girls' opportunities to education and aspirations for new roles. They did not however see the possibility of bringing about changes in the social practices of early marriage and dowry in the near future, as they felt bound by these traditions. Women leaders were keen to address issues of violence and alcohol consumption, feeling that these measures could improve future opportunities for girls.

Although one woman in Bhosa had fought her own battle for right to property and had also reallocated tasks within the family so that her son shared the reproductive chores, she continued to maintain the inside–outside divide. Her son and other boys reported their own experiences of initiating savings groups based on what they learnt from their mothers. None of them were willing to consider changes in gender roles and viewed their mother's new roles essentially as a necessity for family well-being.

Lifestyle Changes

Women in the groups reported changes in their lifestyles. Women would earlier cook once in the day and eat stale food due to poverty and work pressure, as well as low awareness of nutrition values. Meals would be eaten only twice a day; now they consume three meals a day. Houses have been made *pucca* (permanent) and/or repaired and more women are now striving to get houses and land in their own names. Televisions and other consumer durables have been bought, especially in households where women have set up enterprises. Girls are given milk and mother's incomes are being used towards school materials for their daughters. Communities are more alert and aware of issues of discriminatory practices against girl children and admonish each other for any neglect.

By and large, the main support from families comes from other female household members—older and younger sisters-in-law, daughters-in-law, mothers-in-law and adolescent daughters—except in the case of two women leaders of nuclear families whose husbands handled cooking chores when the wives were away. Group leaders mentioned that members would provide support when leaders were out of the village by providing food, grouping cattle and goats, fetching water, etc. Husbands in one village stated, 'We have never eaten so many *laddoo*s as when our women go out for study tours!'

The economic benefits of the SCG gradually break down resistance and family members are also willing to provide economic support for promotion of activities and to attend meetings. Only one of the groups expressed the view that the family did not consider the group work beneficial. Women are now more confident of interacting and negotiating with banks except in Raibhar where the exposure to the bank has been limited to the leaders.

Participation in Planning and Governance

SSP's approach to engender governance processes has revolved around three key processes:

1. Opening up spaces for women's participation, particularly in local planning: The Sakhi Sahyog Manch is a forum

that brings women across fora (SCGs, MMs, elected women representatives) together to work on a common agenda and has the potential of creating deeper bonds to address strategic gender interests at the district, *taluka* and cluster levels.

2. Building women's capacities to address local development agendas by articulating their concerns, interacting with other actors, building alliances among women's collectives and managing local resources: Capacity development inputs for women representatives and leaders include building a perspective and vision of people-led governance; identification and control over relevant information; learning exchanges between elected members and women's groups across *talukas*, districts and other states; best practice identification; database generation; and tool development for participatory monitoring of basic services and community infrastructure.

3. Creating new institutional arrangements responsive to the needs of poor women through partnership with mainstream institutions: Sakhi Gaon Samitis are fora for women to work together to make interventions in the village development process. Resource mapping techniques have been used successfully by women to prioritize their interests and ensure their inclusion in development processes.

The key instrument that enables women to engage in governance is their involvement in the planning process. The planning process starts with the awareness of a problem, a felt need, a shared common concern. This is followed by a situational analysis of the reasons and then a review of the available resources and possible ways of resolving the same. If it succeeds, it is used as a model for future requirements. The next step is to make the model and its initiators visible in the larger arenas of planning. Groups are encouraged to interact with and involve players at various levels of governance, starting with the immediate environment in the community and gradually expanding the spaces of interface to the realm of public institutions and government. SCGs participate in local self-governance along with MM women in local planning and village development processes. Women's groups have mobilized large numbers of women to participate in village assemblies, demanding greater accountability from elected members. Women's collectives are monitoring functioning of basic services, infrastructure and programmes for education, health and social support. Women are mobilizing communities around village development issues. As a result of the sense of community ownership, community contributions and tax collections in areas such as drinking water have increased. Women and elected members participate in meetings at the block and district levels, and provide feedback to local officials. Through information dissemination and networking, women's collectives ensure that local communities are well informed on entitlements and resources for development. The language of group leaders who lead this process reflects optimism, understanding, intent to act, and expectation of problem resolution in the future. Their strength emerges from the support of the larger group and a confidence of their new-found abilities to negotiate at every level.

Women's Political Participation

With the SCGs and MMs increasing their credibility as vote banks and influences on political processes, political parties and candidates seek their support. More than 60 per cent of the groups reported that they were recognized as a strong lobby. The views of the SCGs are sought on critical issues of village development in a number of the groups. SCGs also hold discussions on women's issues and priorities with party candidates in some (40 per cent) villages. Some report that women candidates have stood for election backed by groups and MM members. Women are aware of democratic values and rights and responsibilities through the experience of their own groups, and articulate these in the context of operations of the panchayats as well. Women leaders have also been willing to challenge political fora on instances of malpractice and injustice collectively. While this is evident in the 60 per cent that are the strong groups, other groups are aware of such initiatives and are keen to strengthen their roles in similar ways.

The cluster fora are significant, providing a means for learning for new groups and linkage between groups across villages to collaborate and engage in actions collectively. Women leaders of the clusters and federations were confident of creating a strong lobby on behalf of women in the region's political processes. Women from stronger groups visit new or weaker groups and provide support to address problems. With their leadership, the weaker groups have also been able to access various benefits and streamline their functioning.

Decisions and discussions of the Mahasangh are also made known to all at the cluster meetings. Lending and repayment to the Mahasangh are also discussed. New groups are encouraged to keep records and become members of the Mahasangh and pay their membership dues and shares. The Mahasangh also conducts *melavas* at the cluster level for information sharing and discussions. This motivates new groups to learn and be part of the process, as evident in the cluster meetings we attended.

However, cluster meetings held on a monthly basis are currently focused on information sharing and discussions on problems and transactions. Where cluster workers are newly appointed or weak, problem solving and visioning are responsibilities that the leaders of the Mahasangh (from that cluster or the group leaders) perform, with support from SSP staff. Sustained inputs and rigour need to be infused into the cluster process before consensus building can happen and the cluster emerges as a women's forum with effective skills for bringing about change in a village or regional context. Cluster committees have been elected recently to coordinate the efforts of various groups to work together. Training inputs have also been provided to these committees, as they are envisaged as key fora to redress women's concerns regarding governance and local issues. But there was little evidence of the clarity of roles and vision of the cluster as a women's forum, and much support and facilitation will be required before the cluster as a forum for women can work independently to address gender interests at a regional level. Meanwhile, the federation and the SCGs working in collaboration with the MMs provide the space to address women's needs.

The MMKs are not only places for women to meet, get trained, and plan their activities; they are also the means by which women claim public space and visibility. MMKs have been provided on a cluster level. Groups have negotiated with panchayats for the allotment of land and supervised and facilitated the task of construction. Where land has not been made available at suitable locations, women have even used their own savings, as in Dhutta, to create a MMK as 'a women's office'. However, the ownership of such spaces, and the initiative to organize activities and manage the space, seems to rest with the lead group vested with responsibility of its construction, thereby creating a hierarchy and sometimes rivalries between groups for recognition and allocation of MMKs.

Women visualize these as spaces to conduct their meetings and coordinate with other programmes as well as organize information dissemination initiatives. While the use they are put to may vary from seasonal storage of fodder to conducting immunization and training sessions and cluster-level meetings, groups expressed this as a necessary facility to establish their presence and access greater information sharing opportunities.

Hence, while the Sakhi Sahayog Manch and other fora for women's participation in governance are recent, they have been instrumental in influencing the agenda of panchayats to prioritize the women's concerns for water and electricity in many villages. Their potential to influence political agenda and create opportunities to address women's strategic interests will depend on the nature of support and capacities developed within the various fora to address these issues.

Future Strategies towards Empowerment and Areas of Concern

The SCGs, working in tandem with the MMs, have created a space and environment to address women's needs. Significant changes have come about in the lives of women, especially in the context of access and management of resources. This has brought new opportunities for work and earning, coupled with enhanced skills in the economic spheres as well as created opportunities for leadership, control and decision-making, and women can now lay claim to a space of their own in the economic arena.

The Mahasangh poses a challenge as an alternative designed to suit women's needs for an economic and social forum. On one hand, the SCGs and Mahasangh address the tasks of saving and lending for the survival needs of women and their communities. In so doing, they establish a legitimate role for addressing the strategic needs of women and can provide the fora for raising issues of women's subordinate status. Currently, however, these issues are addressed in the context of a development agenda. These institutions do not address the critical issues of violence and crimes against women in the household and critical questions of health and women status.

The confidence and skills gained by women in the management of resources and negotiation through internal management of the SCGs have prepared women for entry into public spheres to address governance issues. Based on a new confidence, women have entered into public roles and spheres of interaction with the panchayats, with the government and with the market to demand a gender responsive process of governance and development. The questions that women are raising and the agenda currently undertaken do not however address the problems identified as most critical by the women themselves.

In seeking alternative livelihoods activities for women, organizations and FIs need to build on women's traditional knowledge, since this is least likely to cause displacement for women from their niche activities. Viability is likely to be higher in these sectors, provided that opportunities for technological advancements and value addition opportunities are explored. Alternative occupations that are not in sectors traditionally occupied by women will need greater amount of external support for a longer period of time, creating dependencies and disassociation from sectors or realms of knowledge traditionally learnt. This is not being proposed as an argument to keep the poor in a situation of poverty but to enable them to build on existing capacities.

Obviously, greater clarity of perspective and strategies is required at the organizational level as well as with the women before they feel confident to address these strategic gender concerns. SSP's resistance to work with issues that are 'sensitive' and 'personal' may stem from the fact that these issues have hitherto not been their primary agenda. The organization of SCG groups has not required a fundamental questioning of the structures of patriarchy, since it has been limited to the function of access to resources for economic improvement and development. Through this very process, however, women who have come together are raising the issues of health and violence among others as key areas for collective action. The organization is now confronted with these issues of strategic gender interests and must hone its perspectives and strategies to address these issues.

Women are able to cross boundaries across caste and class and pose a challenge to the state in its delivery of services. Political interests are also recognizing the potential power of women's collective and seek their patronage. However, these interventions leave the domain of women's private lives in the household relatively untouched. While a number of groups and women reported support and changing roles, these go hand-in-hand with the reality of the obvious and subtle forms of violence that women are confronted with in their daily lives along with the struggle for family survival.

Dowry harassment and social restrictions on women's mobility have been dealt with by groups based on their own level of confidence and ability to deal with such issues. Some have been able to negotiate changes in relationships, while others have not. Group leaders negotiate with the men based on their credibility. They have in some instances even taken up cases of battering, desertion, rape, etc., to bring cases to the notice of the authorities or to put collective pressure on the perpetrator.

Women are more empowered due to their economic strength and collective experiences, and are now prepared to address issues of status in the personal sphere. There is need for focused strategic planning with groups to address this issue more systematically, based on a baseline analysis. SSP needs to develop perspectives and skills to be able to facilitate processes to address this issue from an empowerment perspective. The strategy adopted hitherto of collective analysis and learning opportunities could well be adopted to address these issues, with the organization playing a facilitative and supportive role in the process. The strategy of working intensively in a district, with large numbers of groups and formation of federations and cluster fora has generated a critical mass which could gradually be prepared to address the strategic gender interests of women.

Women reported the problem of excessive alcohol consumption by men, and the consequent incidence of violence and impoverishment of the household. These issues were however discussed by women in tentative tones. Due to fears of retribution, women are unwilling to raise such issues without adequate support from the cluster and other groups. Negotiation on this issue has been initiated where panchayat support has been forthcoming (Vadgaon). SCGs were not clear about SSP's position on these issues, nor were they confident of their support on these issues. However, it is important that SSP's visible support is available to the women to address these and other issues of atrocities, to enable them to explore strategies and strengthen linkages to deal with these issues. Action on these issues may well create conflict or confrontation with communities, but it would also serve to make explicit SSP's commitment to changing social relations towards the achievement of empowerment in every sphere. Without addressing these issues, efforts at mobilizing women would remain restricted to the achievement of empowerment in a limited arena, and would not enable women to deal with the real challenges to empowerment within their thresholds.

Similarly, class issues are also visible in villages and between groups. Although groups are largely mixed, the predominance of women from better-off households in leadership positions raises the issue of equity and priorities for action. Women in the groups we met acknowledged that the poorest were in fact not represented in their groups, and even within the groups there exist hierarchies of class. An analysis of lending and leadership patterns may enable the organization to develop strategies towards equity. Simultaneously, the development of a deeper understanding of economic processes in a macro perspective would also inform the programme approach of the organization in the interest of the poor. SSP has generally focused on mobilization for economic empowerment and women's subsequent involvement in local planning and governance and taking up social issues in a limited way. It intends to explore primary education for girls and water conservation as new issues of its intervention towards which it has already started visits and interactions with other NGOs working in these fields. Issues of minimum wage, equal wages, or violence are not SSP's main focus. The expectation appears to be of the women themselves taking up these issues in their own time. But some of these issues are critical for women's survival and livelihoods. For instance, issues of wage parity and minimum wages have not been addressed, although SSP staff members are aware of these discriminatory practices. They prefer to take the course of minimum conflict. Without the articulation of these issues in its own approach, however, SSP stops short in its agenda to address the issue of genuine economic empowerment.

Women raised the issue of women's health as a priority in many villages but information on this is meagre, and SSP's efforts to address it have been few. Public health awareness is an inadequate approach to deal with women's health issues although it can provide an entry point. Strengthening its perspective on women's empowerment and linkages with women's health status may enable SSP to define its future strategy on the issue. Group leaders are still at an informal level of financial management, and the support functions to monitor and manage the MIS related to these functions will need to be addressed by SSP for some time to come.

Cluster and federations structures have been created to cater to women's efforts for financial management as well as empowerment. Processes to strengthen these fora to emerge, with a strong gender and class perspective, need to be nurtured with adequate space and time, to enable women to get empowered. SSP will have to assess the learning needs of the leaders at the federation level as well as the areas requiring strengthening in its own team to cater to these emerging needs. Issues of enlarging scale of operation will have to be weighed against the requirement for intensification of these processes necessary for empowerment.

6

Micro-credit and Women's Empowerment: The Lokadrusti Case

Shashi Rajagopalan

Introduction

This study looks at the micro-credit programme of Lokadrusti, an organization based in one of the poorest regions in the country: Khariar, in Nuapada district of Orissa. It explores the space available to women and used by them in (a) their individual capacities, (b) their villages, as groups engaged in savings and credit, and (c) their larger socio-economic environments. Lokadrusti began its work in 1985 as an unregistered group, engaged in development research. Since its registration in 1988, it has been working in the drought-prone southern half of Nuapada (Boden, Sinapalli, and Khariar blocks belonging to Khariar *tehsil*).

Nuapada in its current form came into existence in 1993. Until 1936, it was part of what is Madhya Pradesh today. It then became a part of the erstwhile Sambalpur district. In 1948, it became a part of Bolangir district, and a year later it was included in Kalahandi district. In 1993, it became a separate district. The constant transfer of this region from one district to another has resulted in it being an extremely neglected district.

The 1999–2000 annual plan of the National Bank for Agriculture and Rural Development (NABARD) for the district shows Nuapada as having a population of over 470,000, covering over 100,000 households. Of these, approximately 36 per cent are tribal families, 16 per cent are Scheduled Castes (SCs), around 30–35 per cent are backward castes (BCs), and the rest belong to other castes. The NABARD plan also indicates that as of 31 March 1999, commercial bank (CB) branches in the district together had deposits worth Rs 300 million and outstanding loans worth Rs 190 million, whereas regional rural banks (RRBs) had deposits worth Rs 170 million and outstanding loans worth Rs 120 million; capital mobilized in the district was being used outside the district.

The majority of the population lives in rural areas, and 84 per cent of the families belong to the small and marginal farmer category. There are over 50,000 agricultural labourers in the area. Although the area is one of the most drought-affected districts in the country, it receives rainfall of over 1,100 mm in most years. Khariar lies between two rivers, which makes travel to and from villages in Khariar difficult during the monsoon. Boden and Sinapalli have more forest lands and higher tribal populations than Khariar.

Of the net sown area of 190,000 hectares, around 34,000 hectares are irrigated, mostly through canals and tanks. The remaining 156,000 hectares are dependent on the monsoons for irrigation. Around 38 per cent of the total geographical area lies on steep hill slopes and ridges, about 28 per cent on foothill slopes and uplands, and around 12 per cent on slopes that can be used for some varieties of agricultural crops; only the rest of the land is used for rice, vegetables, maize and small millets. Forest cover is fast depleting in the area.

Lokadrusti has worked on watersheds, water harvesting structures, education, health, group savings and credit, grain banks, seed supply, bank linkages, direct credit provision, agriculture and marketing in the area. Apart from its interventions on the economic front, it has played a significant role in enabling the setting up of bridge schools to help the young, especially girl children, become literate and access the opportunity to enter government schools. It chooses to work primarily with women on most of its interventions, as men tend to migrate seasonally for work, more so than women. Divorced women, women with migrant husbands, and separated women usually had the responsibility of rearing their children and needed interventions to help increase cash inflows to meet family needs.

The three main streams of mobilizing women in each village included (a) the Muthi Chawal (grain banks), (b) the self-help groups (SHGs) or savings and credit groups (SCGs) of women, and (c) the Mahila Samiti or advocacy group, which worked for improved infrastructure and public works contracts and took up the cause of individual women in distress.

Lokadrusti consciously recruits women alongside men on its staff for fieldwork and ensures that they are placed in field stations, taught how to drive two-wheelers, and made mobile. Gender sensitivity training is organized periodically for the staff. Of Lokadrusti's 110 staff members, half are women, belonging to the categories of animators, teachers and coordinators.

Methodology

As the study was on micro-credit and women's empower-ment, it looked closely at the women's self-help SCGs and their impact on women's empowerment. Lokadrusti has helped promote 326 such SHGs in 17 clusters (or concen-trated pockets) in 146 villages, reaching out to over 3,700 women in three blocks of Nuapada. In all, 55 SHG mem-bers, selected at random, were individually interviewed in 20 villages. Of the women interviewed, only one belonged to a family with as 'large' a landholding as six acres. All the others belonged to families with two acres or less, including some that were landless. All the women interviewed came from Scheduled Tribes (STs), SCs or BCs. While most said that they could sign their names, 10 had studied at least up to Class III.

Village-level meetings (with representatives of all SHGs in the village) were held in 20 of the 146 villages, at which more than 400 representatives of 55 SHGs participated. Of the 90 villages with SHGs in Boden, 11 were visited; of the 20 in Khariar, six were visited; and of the 36 in Sinapalli, three were visited. Cluster meetings were formally held in seven of the 17 clusters, at which 43 of the 146 villages were represented, and interactions were held with members and leaders of three other clusters too, at a meeting with leaders of the federation, known as Samajik Bank.

A meeting was held at the collector's office with the project director of the District Rural Development Agency (DRDA). Another meeting was held with Boden's Block Development Officer. A brief meeting with the *sarpanch* of Pharsara village was also organized. Branch managers of the State Bank of India (SBI), Boden branch, and of Kalahandi Grameen Bank, Khariar branch, were interviewed. Where the former branch had savings accounts of several SHGs that Lokadrusti had promoted, the latter dealt with SHGs it had directly promoted.

Self-help Savings and Credit Groups

At the time of the study, Lokadrusti was working with over 3,700 women in the three blocks, around savings and credit activity. Table 6.1 provides an overview of the concentration of women's SHGs and members in the three blocks. The oldest SHG was formed in early 1998 whereas the youngest was formed in June 2001, during the period of the field study.

The 90 SHGs in Boden have formed a federation known as Samajik Bank, which operates a revolving fund for lending to the SHGs for on-lending purposes. Lokadrusti hoped to form three federations in all, one for each block. In all three blocks, SHG clusters have already been formed. Each SHG was expected to accept member savings, access

TABLE 6.1
Spread of SHGs, 31 March 2001

SHG particulars	Khariar	Boden	Sinapalli	Total
Circles	1	1+1=2	1	4
Clusters	4	6+4=10	3	17
Villages	20	56+34=90	36	146
SHGs	77	115+75=190	59	326
Members	903	1,314+813=2,127	691	3,721
Some averages				
Villages per cluster	5	9	12	>8
SHGs per village	Nearly 4	>2	<2	>2
Members per village	>45	Nearly 24	>19	>25
Members per SHG	Nearly 12	>11	Nearly 12	>11

external funds, operate bank accounts, and lend to members. In most SHGs, every member was expected to save a fixed amount every month, usually Rs 10 or 20. The group could alter the amount to be saved in a particular month—decrease it because work was hard to come by, or increase it because the women had managed to get a labour contract. Loans were dependent on need, and not related to amounts saved or capacity to repay.

The job of the cluster organization was to promote SHGs in the area of the cluster, and to try and saturate the area in terms of SHGs and their membership. Each cluster, to the extent possible, was expected to cover villages within a 5–7 km radius. Clusters were demarcated keeping road communication and other interactions among villages in view. Each block-level federation was expected to enforce discipline, tap external resources for on-lending, and undertake advocacy and training. The first (and at the time of the study, only) federation, Samajik Bank in Boden, was set up because Lokadrusti felt that the SHGs were very small and could not raise enough of their own funds to prevent distress sale of paddy and minor forest produce. Lokadrusti lends through Samajik Bank, from its own small corpus as well as from funds borrowed from the local SBI branch.

The SHG members met at least once a month, and often twice. The savings collected by the group were deposited in the group's savings account in the nearest bank branch. The nearest branch could be in the same village, or in a village as far as 7–8 km away. As many of the villages did not have bus facility, to attend cluster meetings and visit banks, the women walked or were taken by their husbands on bicycles. The president and secretary, elected by the members from among themselves, were authorized to operate bank accounts. Groups could lend their own funds to members, and could also borrow from Samajik Bank for on-lending. A second visit in the month was made to the bank branch, when amounts had to be withdrawn for lending to members. The SHGs charged members interest at a rate between 2 and 5 per cent per month. Local moneylenders lent at 10 per cent. To keep calculations simple, some groups asked members to pay Rs 100 as interest for every Rs 1,000 borrowed, at the end of three months. An overview of the financial status of the 17 clusters is provided in Table 6.2.

The figures in Table 6.1 were obtained from the internal reports of Lokadrusti, whereas the figures in Table 6.2 were obtained from formats prepared especially for the study and administered by the field staff. There are small variations in the figures in the two tables, but nothing to significantly alter the observations. One reason for the differences is that some field officers included information on SHGs for a period beyond 31 March 2001.

Together, the women had almost Rs 550,000 as their own funds (savings and interest earned combined). They had loans outstanding to Samajik Bank to the tune of a little over Rs 300,000, while idle funds parked in the savings accounts in commercial bank branches were a little under Rs 400,000. Lokadrusti felt that at least one of the aims of setting up

TABLE 6.2

Financial Overview of SHGs, 31 March 2001

Cluster	Number of SHGs	Number of members	Member thrift (rupees)	Interest earned (rupees)	Samajik Bank loan (rupees)	Total funds (rupees)	Loans with members (rupees)	Bank balance (rupees)
Baklighunti	24	282	57,078	1,088	38,200	96,366	30,174	66,192
Bhaisadani	20	223	22,428	352	22,500	45,280	22,500	22,780
Chikal Chuan	12	122	21,168	309	13,900	35,377	18,400	16,977
Dhammapada	27	308	38,635	639	61,500	100,774	66,809	33,965
Ghatmal	17	186	25,455	690	44,500	70,645	55,378	15,267
Godthala	22	260	35,975	313	5,000	41,288	16,300	24,988
Khairpadar	13	148	13,175	–	–	13,175	–	13,175
Khamtari	16	193	29,555	252	6,000	35,807	15,300	20,507
Khandapara	14	182	9,861	–	–	9,861	–	9,861
Jharnamal	18	196	22,683	665	23,000	46,348	28,841	17,507
Kirekala	21	237	39,239	3,816	10,600	53,655	22,266	31,389
Kirkita	25	306	50,423	888	–	51,311	30,322	20,989
Kotamal	12	138	12,817	100	–	12,917	1,010	11,907
Kusumkhunta	27	348	23,815	–	–	23,815	–	23,815
Maharajor	22	233	27,255	33,993	13,600	74,848	53,487	21,361
Mohulpadar	12	114	24,940	3,047	16,700	44,687	37,058	7,629
Tetalpara	23	262	46,516	885	54,500	101,901	66,488	35,413
Total	325	3,738	501,018	47,037	310,000	858,055	464,333	393,722

SHGs was to demystify banks and, therefore, encouraged SHGs to visit banks regularly to operate their savings accounts.

Samajik Bank charged member SHGs interest at the rate of 1 per cent per month, and the difference in interest was seen as a source of income for the group. Although the interest earned was seen as belonging to all the members of the group, interest had not been credited to the individual accounts of members by SHGs. As Samajik Bank expected the loan to be paid in full at the end of three or six months, SHGs too tended to ask members to pay the full loan amount with interest at the end of a quarter. Samajik Bank lent to SHGs that had a good record of regular savings, and operated their savings accounts well. The first loan from Samajik Bank was expected to be double the members' savings, and, thereafter, the equity–debt ratio was expected to change to 1:3 and then to 1:4. When an SHG had Rs 10,000 of its own funds, it was expected to approach the local commercial bank or regional rural bank directly, as Samajik Bank funds would no longer be available to it. For a repeat loan from Samajik Bank, all the members were expected to have cleared the earlier loan, and the SHG itself was expected not to be a defaulter to the Samajik Bank.

On average, there were nearly four SHGs per village in Khariar, and around two in Boden and Sinapalli. Some villages had as many as five SHGs. Each village had a five-member executive committee, drawn from all the SHGs. This committee was expected to take responsibility for all the SHGs. The president and/or secretary of the village executive committee were/was expected to attend the monthly cluster meetings. The delegates to cluster meetings elected one among themselves as the president of the cluster. In Boden, cluster presidents formed the Board of Samajik Bank, and elected its president.

Cluster meetings were held at a different village each month. However, once a community building (doubling up as storage centre) was constructed, cluster meetings were held there. Samajik Bank or Boden Federation is situated at the field office of Lokadrusti in Jambahalli. SHGs and clusters are not registered, while the Samajik Bank is registered as a society under the Societies Registration Act.

Muthi Chawal and Mahila Samiti

There were three sets of organizations in many of the villages visited: the SHG, the Muthi Chawal and the Mahila Samiti. Lokadrusti started its work among women with the setting up of grain banks, popularly known as 'Muthi Chawal'. In times of need, people used to approach local moneylenders, who accepted as repayment a bag of paddy at harvest worth Rs 400, for every Rs 100 lent. Lokadrusti set up storage centres in villages, so that people could store grain, lend it to themselves in times of need, and sell the excess when the price was right. One of the members in Kotamal village (Khariar), described Muthi Chawal thus:

> We are 13 of us. Every day, each of us, sets aside a little rice. We meet once a month and bring the rice. We keep it in one of the houses. The largest measure brought by a member is taken as standard, and the others make up their contributions to an equal amount. Roughly it works out to 250 gm per house per month. Usually, there are three or four members who straightaway ask for the rice and take it away. For each 4 kg of rice taken, a member must return the 4 kg and a quarter kg for every eight days from the date of borrowing till the date of return.
>
> When we had the food for work programme, they would pay us every eight days. Therefore, most people tended to repay in eight days. Now that that programme has stopped, those who take the rice will probably repay three months later, after the harvest. There are five SHGs with 80 members in our village. Our meeting (Muthi Chawal) usually lasts for two hours and all 80 members turn up. Any extra rice remaining is left at the teacher's house. We probably have 150 kilos left over at the moment, though in most months the rice is taken largely by needy members. This year we did not have any grain harvested. As a result, all the rice contributed was purchased rice, and, therefore, of standard quantity. When we do have our own harvest, we will have different qualities contributed. We will need to decide how best to value the contributions then. We want our Muthi Chawal to last forever.

The Mahila Samiti was conceived as an issue-based organization and one to help get contracts for public works. In several villages, women spoke of having gone to the block headquarters for obtaining seeds, housing (for deserted women), pension (for widows), drinking water facility, approach roads, and so on. Women were also helped to get organized and seek and obtain public works on contract. Almost all the women who were members of SHGs were also members of the Mahila Samiti and the Muthi Chawal. However, the members of the Mahila Samiti in any village consisted of many more women than the members in an SHG.

An Overview of SHGs across the Three Blocks

In Boden, the first set of SHGs was promoted in early 1998. Since then, new SHGs continue to be promoted; some were being promoted at the time of the field study. Several SHGs had a good mix of castes. There were SHGs with members of a single caste, but these were more a result of where the members lived, and less, it appeared, because of any caste bias. With 90 villages and over 2,000 women covered by the SHGs, and many more participating in the Mahila Samitis, women had high visibility in the block. External loans were being accessed even as an equal amount of savings lay in the bank—idle. Several SHGs were in default to Samajik Bank, and some of these had been wound up. The external loans outstanding were less than the idle funds lying in banks. The women of Boden expected external loans. They expected the local bank and/or Lokadrusti to bring in external funds, and wanted to keep their funds parked in the bank, either for their own security or as collateral for the lender. Boden had a large number of very articulate women, with a vision, who were acknowledged as leaders by the women and men of the block. Women, however, were not familiar with bookkeeping or accounting, and were dependent on local men or Lokadrusti staff for management of their accounts. With the village 'institutions' not registered, problems were likely to crop up later about the ownership of the properties (such as the storage units) being set up for and used by the women.

In Khariar, large numbers of women were participating in SHGs in each village, as in Muthi Chawal, even though only one of the SHGs in the cluster was over a year old. New SHGs were also being formed. Women of all castes were SHG members and were comfortable dealing with one another. Women from the BC and ST communities were a little wary of women from the SC community. Visiting hamlets other than their own was a new phenomenon for the women. The women expected, on the whole, to be self-reliant in fund mobilization. They wanted a permanent arrangement in their control to meet their financial needs. Unlike Boden, they did not have financial expectations, either of the local banks or of Lokadrusti. There were some examples of successful group businesses. Joint activities actually impacted on local traders and the manner in which the traders conducted their business. Women had not thought through the rules for lending, though they certainly did have the capacity to evolve appropriate rules for themselves.

In Sinapalli, almost all the groups were formed after November 2000; they were one to five months old, as of 31 March 2001. In spite of that, at a meeting in Bhooliyabhatta (Khandapara cluster), there was a spirit of camaraderie, solidarity, and trust among the women. On the other hand, at Sardhapur (Khairpadar cluster), where the SHGs were of more or less the same age, the women were wary of one another, and left it to the Lokadrusti staff to 'own' the meeting. Where Khandapara had 182 members from eight villages, Khairpadar had 148 members from its eight villages. The numbers of women engaged in SHGs, and perhaps the distances between the villages in a cluster, appeared to affect the vibrancy of the groups and their members. While having cluster meetings in different villages is important for building solidarity and articulating a larger vision, the choice of cluster headquarters (in terms of location in relation to other villages), too, is important, it would seem, for vibrancy. As with women in Khariar, those in Sinapalli were not forming SHGs to access external funds. They reported that they were forming them to work with one another for more self-reliance and greater visibility. However, here too, as in Khariar, the women had not adequately thought through the rules related to their SHGs.

Women leaders of Khariar and Sinapalli were not as articulate as women of Boden, as work in both these areas was of more recent origin. However, what was remarkable was that unlike the women of Boden, who expected external finance as a right, women in both these areas did not see SHGs as a means of accessing external finance; they saw SHGs as tools on which to build their own self-reliance. Given the fact that the savings of the SHGs lying idle in the banks were more than the loans outstanding to the banks, this was probably a good beginning. However, as Table 6.2 indicates, much of the savings of the clusters in Khariar and Sinapalli, too, lay idle in the banks, instead of being used for on-lending to members. The larger picture of flight of capital from the district may well get repeated in the case of SHGs, too, if care is not taken.

Changes in the Lives of Individual Women because of Micro-credit

Access to Savings and Credit

Although Lokadrusti began its work in the area much earlier, the oldest SHGs were around three years old. When asked why SHGs had been set up in the first place, women said that they needed the SHG to save up for difficult times. In Boden, there was also an expectation in several villages that the savings would then help them access larger loans from external sources. All the same, savings alone—even without external loans—were valued by the women and their families. They were equated with staying power in times of need, and with creditworthiness. Almost every woman wanted her pass book to be seen; it was equated with wealth and flaunted in most meetings.

Where women had borrowed from their SHGs (whether from the SHG's own funds or external funds), it was often the first new loan from a 'formal' lending agency for the family, after several years. Numerous men had become defaulters to the local bank, and had not been able to access credit from the banks. While on the one hand, it could be argued that the men were supporting the women to access funds because of their own interests, the women were using the loans accessed for a range of purposes chosen by themselves; the family farm was only one of the many purposes. There was a strong emphasis on borrowing for income generating activities, but women borrowed for other purposes, too, such as for their own health, children's health, children's education, and so on. As the Muthi Chawal provided an opportunity to 'borrow' for food, borrowing for food from the SHG was not common, even in years of drought.

Even though women had access to credit, they tended not to rotate their own funds much, with the result that they did not access as much credit as they potentially could. There was an underlying emphasis that borrowing was sensible only for income generation; as a result, women tended to treat their own savings as funds 'to fall back on' in emergencies, even though their own idle funds exceeded external borrowings. The other reason for funds lying idle in the bank was perhaps the perception that more funds in the bank might result in larger loans from the bank. Women in areas that did not access external funds spoke of the burden of remitting savings in banks, and said that they would prefer to rotate their own funds among themselves. They already had experience of the Muthi Chawal growth, and expected similar growth for their cash savings. Women who had accessed loans from external sources spoke of the need to borrow from only one source, and argued that their own funds were mainly for emergency needs.

Increase in Income

Women had entered the rice and *moori* (puffed rice) business and set up shops for the first time, enabled by loans from the SHGs. In these family businesses, women raised the finance and also undertook most of the production and marketing. However, when more distant and/or larger markets were sought, when the goods could not be sold locally or carried in headloads, then men took over the marketing with the use of bicycles. Women still walked distances for their own work: be it the attending meetings or selling produce.

While the rice and *moori* businesses as well as some shops increased individual incomes, women engaged in them at an individual level did not exceed 5–6 per cent of the total number of women in the SHGs. On the other hand, many more women were engaged in or had tried to enter collective businesses, such as *mahua* procurement. These did not have the same success rate, it appeared. They had succeeded in some areas, where the women had fewer expectations of Lokadrusti or banks, and did not expect to be bailed out if in loss.

New Skills

Where joint businesses had succeeded, they had opened a whole new world for women, in the fields of strategic planning, negotiation with tough traders, procurement, storage, weighing and marketing. Even though women's literacy and numeracy skills had not undergone any significant change (except for women learning how to sign their names), women did remember most of their transactions. The transactions, however, were rather simple in most cases, as the transactions were few. Many groups had done very little on-lending of their own money. Many that had borrowed from Samajik Bank tended to share the amount equally among members. Interest on savings was not being credited to members' accounts at the year end. Therefore, most tended to be able to keep in memory most transactions.

The account books were not kept by the women. Men in the village or the Lokadrusti staff helped maintain them. The women felt that if they were trained they could possibly maintain the books. The SHGs could have provided women with learning opportunities in the fields of finance management, bookkeeping and accounting, but even the recognized leadership had little knowledge or skill in these areas. Large numbers of women did have the capacity and the interest to learn on all these fronts, and to manage and control their own organizations. Women said that they understood money better, that they enjoyed discussing rules and procedures, and that just meeting and working with women from other villages was enriching.

Most women, however, did not relate their own savings to opportunity for growth. They saw their own savings as capable of meeting ad hoc and/or emergency needs, and as a sign of increase in their creditworthiness. Most also had not questioned the depleting value of their savings lying idle and earning low or no interest in the banks. As already mentioned, most had not noticed that their combined savings lying with the bank were more than the combined loans from the bank via Lokadrusti.

Women also had not acquired organizational management skills of any significance, as the performance of the SHGs, or of the members vis-à-vis their SHGs was not being monitored with the objective of organizational development, at any level within the system. Much of the monitoring was with a view to preparing statistical reports. The sheer numbers of SHGs made it very expensive to monitor performance and standards of accounting and management.

In Mirdhapada of Tetalpara cluster, for example, a loan of Rs 2,000 was taken from Samajik Bank, and given to nine of the 14 members. The decision to lend was not taken at a meeting where all the members were present. As a result, there was conflict and drought was being cited as a reason for non-repayment. One member had borrowed Rs 400 for treatment of illness and now says she cannot repay. Of the nine members, some have repaid part of the loans. The president said that repayments amounting to Rs 500 were lying in her house for some months, and that she would wait till all the members paid before giving it to Samajik Bank. Her right to hold back and keep repayments in her home had not been challenged. Even though several cluster meetings had been held in the area, the matter was not discussed.

In Tetalpara, on the other hand, a member had a problem with repayment; but the group did not want to default to Samajik Bank. Therefore, after discussion, the rest of the members paid up on her behalf, and she was expected to repay later to the SHG. Samajik Bank has a manager who looks after the accounts and a five-member committee that looks at default. Notice was sent to Mirdhapada. There is not, however, a systematic follow-up on defaults.

The SHG in Arjuna village of Baklighunti cluster was formed in December 1999. Members' thrift stood at Rs 310 in June 2001. Apparently, the president had gone out of the village in search of work and had kept the passbook with her. The SHG members did nothing. One remittance of Rs 210 was made in December 1999, and another of Rs 100 in January 2000. The SHG's defunct status was not known to the other SHGs in the cluster. SHG functioning is not a part of the cluster discussion, though loans from Samajik Bank are discussed. The members appear not to know that they could have changed their president or the signatories to the bank account. On the other hand, in an SHG in Tutupada village, members changed their leader because she was difficult, and they could not understand why the SHG in Arjuna did not do the same.

SHGs are financial institutions and, as in any financial institution, unless care is taken to have sound accounting and management systems in place—and unless the leaders and managers are helped to equip themselves with the necessary skills and systems—default, mismanagement, even fraud, are inevitable.

When women leaders at cluster meetings were asked why these issues were not discussed at cluster meetings, they reported that in the interest of a more democratic set up, SHGs are represented by different members at each cluster meeting. Therefore, most women were not familiar with the problems in their cluster. While changing women delegates to meetings is good for the individual woman delegate, it is not helpful for institution building. Where the savings and credit activity is not institutionalized, there the reins remain with the promoting organization, and that denies the women the opportunity to learn finance management, organizational management, and conflict management, skills not beyond the competence of most leaders in the Lokadrusti area.

It is often argued that savings and credit can bring but some financial relief; that they can be only so empowering. However, if savings and credit services are used to help build strong, visible, inter-generational financial institutions that are designed, owned and controlled by women and are sensitive to them, then they could be very empowering. If village after village had a strong women's financial institution managed by them, gender relations could change very significantly in the area. The savings and credit services are instead led by ad hoc arrangements and ideas.

Mobility

The mobility of large numbers of women involved in the SHGs (as also in the Mahila Samitis) had increased. Members and leaders had stepped out of their own habitats, to neighbouring ones. Lokadrusti was attempting to form clusters of SHGs in small compact areas, and encouraged regular meetings within the cluster. These meetings were valued by the women and had (a) increased their mobility; (b) increased their contacts; and (c) made them think for and contribute to a larger world—one beyond their own families, even beyond their villages.

As many villages did not have bus connections, women tended to walk across the hills to most meetings held in other villages. In spite of the large numbers of women involved in Boden, women inevitably reported that they walked with other women or on occasion, travelled with their husbands on their bicycles.

The SHGs appeared to have contributed significantly to expanding the mental and physical spaces available to large numbers of women. Apart from visiting one another's villages, many women had been to the local bank because of the SHG, and to the block headquarters, for discussions and negotiation with government officials on getting contracts, seed procurement (available on subsidy and/or for cash/credit purchase), and other specific issues relating to individual women in distress. Key leaders had travelled and interacted as resource persons for meetings organized by the government and other agencies. The bank manager of SBI, Boden branch, said:

> SHG leaders come on their own to the bank to deposit the group monthly savings. For the opening of new accounts, men usually accompany them. Initially, women opened these accounts jointly, in the names of two leaders. Now we have changed those accounts to the names of the groups. We drafted a simple resolution and once the SHGs come to us with that, we make the changes. Signatories to these savings accounts, too, have changed on occasion. The women are very vocal and assertive. Earlier, when we visited their villages, the women would ask their husbands and children to speak to us. Now they come forward themselves and are at ease with us.

The women and men in the villages visited had also made similar statements about their interactions with bankers and others. Almost all women spoke of the widening of their world because of the SHG. They said that it was not as if they had not been out of their villages earlier. More than the geography, it was the agenda for which they now travelled, and the fact that they travelled, not with family members, but with friends from other castes, that made them feel that their world had become larger.

Where different caste groups lived separately in nearby hamlets, or in clearly demarcated spaces, there the women reported that the SHG had helped them come together across caste lines around issues. In such places, the SHGs tended to have 'homogeneous' membership; all members in an SHG were from the same caste group. In one such village (Chandgiri), when women were asked if they knew one another before the SHG, women said about the other castes, 'Oh yes, we have always called them "mama", "kaka" (uncles) and so on'. References were made only to male relations; women appeared not to have been familiar with women from other castes. In Palma village, where the hamlets were half a kilometre away from one another, women reported that they started visiting one another's hamlets only after the formation of the SHGs.

In many villages, however, the habitats were not caste-based. In all such villages, each SHG in the village had membership from different castes. In all three blocks, women from such villages reported that caste was not a big issue for them, and that even before the SHGs, they did visit one another and did participate in one another's feasts.

Status in Family and Community

During the course of individual interviews and village-level meetings, women members of SHGs appeared self-assured and confident. Men and children watching the meetings looked on with respect and, in most places, did not interfere with the proceedings.

The 15-year-old son of one of the leaders spoke with great admiration for his mother. He said that earlier, if he needed money, he would never think of going to his mother. He said that now he would go as often to his mother as to his father for his needs. He added that he felt great pride in the way his mother moved about in the village. Some other younger children said that they recognized that their mothers were important in the village, but perhaps because of their age, could not remember a time when it was different, and assumed that this had always been the case.

The sheer numbers of women engaged in SHGs in Boden as a whole, and the numbers engaged in SHGs in each of the villages visited in Khariar, appeared to have made the SHG an important organization in the lives of the women.

At the very first set of village meetings at Amlabahili and Nangpara in Boden, the self-assurance of women members of the SHGs, as against those who were not members or were unsure of becoming members, was striking. Men in these villages appeared to have prevented the formation of more SHGs, even though membership in the Muthi Chawal and the Mahila Samiti was encouraged. When questioned about family attitudes to the different organizations, women (non-members) said that the Muthi Chawal helped the whole family, and the Mahila Samiti helped bring work to the village. However, the SHG required a discipline in lean and good months and, more important, it required travel outside the village (to cluster meetings, Samajik Bank, etc.). Men concurred that that was why they discouraged women from their families to join SHGs.

Workload

Women who were not members were so because of their husbands. Those who were members spoke of supportive husbands and families. Almost all SHG leaders said that their husbands cooked for their families when they went out of the village for cluster or Samajik Bank meetings. Some said that their daughters cooked when they were away. They, however, also reported that as all adults went out to work every day, even on normal working days, whoever (husband or wife or mother) came in first from work, tended to cook the evening meal. Yet another practice mentioned by some women was that of the man cooking during the women's menstruation. It appeared that men cooking a meal at home was not a new phenomenon; however, cooking by men when women were out attending meetings (as against out working for a living) was new, said the women.

When asked about the increase in workload because of participation in the SHG, woman after woman expressed annoyance and said that the SHG was an educational experience, and that if there were a price to be paid for it, they would pay it. Many laughed and said that participation at the meeting, thinking through issues and getting hot freshly cooked food at the meeting were all a pleasure; these made the morning at home rush by and the long walk to the cluster or other external meetings worth it. Some women said that the cluster meetings were therapeutic, as they felt that they had a day off from all work.

When asked about the loss of a day's wage to attend a meeting, the women said that those who did not regularly attend meetings found that their villages paid the price for it, as other villages got the public work contracts and other benefits. This was one of the instances where it appeared that women did not distinguish between the SHG (cluster/federation) and the Mahila Samiti meetings. On the other hand, in relation to remittance of savings amounts in banks, women were conscious of loss of wage and/or time. The walk to the bank was treated as a burden in most instances. Where attendance in meetings was clearly seen as an investment in themselves and their village, the walk to the bank was equated with loss of wage and/or energy.

Education of Children

Most women sent their girl and boy children to school, although most tended not to educate girl children as much as the boys. Very few reported that they did not send their daughters to school; a few also reported that their eldest sons had not been sent to school as the family, for various reasons, had needed their earnings.

The bank manager of Kalahandi Anchalik Gramya Bank (KAGB), Khariar branch, felt that girls went to school because of the mid-day meal scheme introduced three years ago:

> Of 180 school days, they attend 80 days, which enables SCs and STs to get stipend, at Rs 1,000 per day-scholar. They also get jobs after matriculation; this too is a reason for schooling. If they get appointed as *anganwadi* teachers, they get Rs 500 per month for doing some work in their own village.

In the schools visited during the study, there were more older girl children than boy children, perhaps because these were schools aimed at preparing dropouts to return to school, and there was a higher incidence of older girl children dropping out. The children attending these schools appeared to be there for the sheer joy of it, and even though a single

teacher handled a wide age range, the children were helping one another learn.

The presence of girl children at school was more because
of Lokadrusti's multi-pronged approach when working with
women and the local community than because of the micro-
credit intervention. The only link with micro-credit perhaps
was that women trusted Lokadrusti more because it helped
them on the economic front, and, therefore, when Lokadrusti
set up schools and asked that girl children, too, be educated,
the community was willing to do so.

Infant Mortality

During the course of discussions and interviews, especially
in Boden, it appeared that the family sizes were quite small.
In some villages, women spoke of the whole village consciously having taken to family planning. However, many
women had also reported the death of a child after birth,
during infancy, or during pregnancy. When in village after
village women reported miscarriage, infant deaths and small
family sizes, some attempt was made to find out whether
there was any bias against girl children.

In Jambahalli in Boden, 17 women present at the meeting had among them 15 living sons and five living daughters.
Seven sons and four daughters had died at different times
after birth. Boden has a large ST population. In Palma in
Khariar, 32 women had among them 58 living sons and 37
living daughters, while 16 sons and six daughters had died
during pregnancy, infancy, or childhood. In Chandgiri, also
in Khariar, with no person from the ST class present, a similar stocktaking of conceptions indicated a happier story. The
38 women present at the meeting had 40 living sons and 47
living daughters, while they had lost 13 sons, 10 daughters,
and four others (sex not determined) during pregnancy.

Orissa is one of the states where the female population
as a percentage of the total population is decreasing. In both
Palma and Jambahalli, for the group present at the meetings, fewer girl children were conceived compared to boy
children. In Jambahalli, four of the 17 women had not conceived any children.

Women expressed outrage when it was suggested that perhaps girl children were not wanted. Their response in Jambahalli and Palma was that they yearned for children and were grateful for any they had. The figures of deaths of boy children, too, did not suggest any anti-girl child sentiment. A more thorough study on the subject of gender ratio, beginning with conception, especially in the tribal belt, may be needed, to assess whether these cases are exceptions, or whether indeed this is a serious problem for the area as a whole. While SHGs had made some interventions in the field of health, infant mortality was not yet on their agenda.

Position and Status of Women's SHGs within their Villages

Women's Visibility

If the individual woman's mobility had increased, the sheer number of women moving around, especially in Boden, appeared to have impacted on the role of women in the area. SHG/Mahila Samiti leaders reported that they had been invited to give talks at meetings organized by local universities, banks and governmental agencies. Although probably only a handful of women were giving these talks, the fact that they were being invited to educate others about their interests indicated that women's groups and their leaders were being taken seriously, not just in the immediate Lokadrusti area but in the district too. At the DRDA office in Nuapada, the officers requested the Lokadrusti chief executive to participate in a meeting on SHGs called by the collector, and appeared quite at ease when Lokadrusti offered to send one of the women leaders to participate instead.

Women's Groups in the Consciousness of the Village

In all small villages in Khariar and Boden, where there were more than one SHG, the SHGs (again perhaps along with the Muthi Chawal and the Mahila Samiti) had a strong village presence. Most adults were aware of their existence and even of their rules, procedures and meetings. Men in the village knew the names of the leaders, the age of the group, and the quantum of monthly savings. The SHGs were not seen as nominal associations. They were perceived as being of value to the village. The women's groups were often the only functional 'institutions' in the village. In comparatively larger villages, which had just one or two SHGs, the SHG did not have the same presence.

Women as Village Leaders

Women leaders of the SHGs of Boden were acknowledged as leaders, not just for the SHG, but also for the village. In Khariar, where the work was not as old, women leaders were yet to be recognized by the village as its leaders, even though there appeared to be admiration for them. In Sinapalli, the SHGs were far too young for the leaders to be acceptable as leaders for the village as a whole. In Boden, the large membership of women from a small geographical area had made the SHG a force in the village and in the block. Moreover, in this area, excluded by external financiers because of high loan default, external credit had once again been accessed because of the women's groups.

Lokadrusti had initially promoted men's SHGs in some villages, but then decided against it as more men than women tended to migrate for labour. All the same, in many villages, men spoke of their interest in promoting their own SHGs, although in some they narrated earlier experiences of mismanagement and fraud in men's SHGs, and said that women were better at thrift and credit. In some villages, men came forward just to exchange experiences about the SHGs that they had promoted, after seeing the success that the women had had with theirs. The men saved higher amounts each month than the women. There was acknowledgement in the villages of women's success with the SHG, and acknowledgement too of following their lead.

Capacity of the Women's Groups to Protect and Promote Women's Interests

Basanti of Maharajor cluster in Boden reported that in their cluster, they had 240 women and Rs 33,000 of own funds in the SHGs. She then went on to explain that because of drought, a woman in her village had been in starving condition. Her brother had migrated for work and she was left with no money or food. She was allocated some land because women went to the block to appeal on her behalf; she now had an asset base with which to meet her own needs. Although this was probably undertaken by the Mahila Samiti, it was mentioned in relation to a discussion on SHGs and their impact. There were other instances of women deserted by their husbands, or widowed, and the women reported action taken by them to help the individuals. The women in Tetalpara said that they had taken a stand to put a stop to heavy drinking in their village, and now most of the men did not drink. The local distillery had been shut down.

In Bhaisadani cluster, Sagidihi village was central to the cluster. Women leaders said that they came from the surrounding hills to Sagidihi for their cluster meetings. A dispensary was to be built in that village. The men of the area had wanted the dispensary in some other village. Women said that as they held meetings in Sagidihi, and as women from all villages came there regularly, the dispensary ought to be situated there. 'All of us got together and we won the battle,' said a leader with seven daughters and one son.

Consciousness of Combined Strength

In Tetalpara, one of the more saturated villages in Boden, a leader said:

> We already have five SHGs. We'll probably have two more within the year. Therefore, of 83 houses in our village almost all will be covered by the Mahila Samiti, the Muthi Chawal and the SHGs. We first started with the Muthi Chawal, then had the Mahila Samiti, and then the SHGs. We have three quintals of

rice in the first, Rs 500 in the second, and a lot of savings in the SHGs. We think of every non-member woman as if she were a potential member and extend the services to her.

What neither the women nor Lokadrusti was conscious of was that the total savings that lay in the bank were probably a significant portion of the total deposits mobilized by the bank branch, and that their combined savings exceeded their total borrowings. Even though they were doing and could do more for themselves than the external financiers, they had not yet understood their collective strength. They still believed themselves to need help, when it was their money that probably boosted the branch's deposits!

In one village, the local priest had felt threatened by the SHG and warned the women of tragedy befalling their children if they continued to work as an SHG, or used the community-cum-storage centre built for them by Lokadrusti. The women, despite their collective strength, felt overwhelmed, and were unwilling to challenge him. They did, however, work on him with Lokadrusti's help, did overcome their fears, and finally began to conduct meetings inside the new centre. They continue to work as a cohesive group.

Women who had organized joint marketing of *mahua* successfully were conscious of the strength of collective action, and had made the local traders conscious of it. There were, however, quite a few examples of unsuccessful attempts at collective marketing.

The SHGs of Khariar and Sinapalli held cluster meetings but did not have a federation (a Samajik Bank for their block). The women, unlike those in Boden, expected to be fully self-reliant, and did not seek or expect loans from Lokadrusti. When women were asked in each block about whether they knew the combined strength of the SHGs in their village, and whether they would like to work as one, the response in Khariar and Sinapalli, where Samajik Bank money had not reached, was one of pleasant surprise at their combined strength. Most said that they would like the small SHGs to become one large organization. In Boden, in villages where SHGs had not become defaulters to the Samajik Bank (and the Samajik Bank had many defaulter SHGs), there was a similar response. However, in villages that had defaulters to the Samajik Bank, the response was that managing small groups was difficult enough, and managing a large, village-level organization would be even more difficult.

Village Caste Consciousness and SHGs

Homogeneous membership in SHGs is believed to help group cohesiveness. In Lokadrusti area, even though most groups had a happy mix of castes, the very first defaulter groups to be met were SHGs with homogeneous membership, and indeed the cohesiveness was visible, if for the wrong reason. In Jamgaon of Boden, which has five SHGs, two were in serious default to the Samajik Bank. At least one of them had also drawn out all its money from its savings account and lent it all out, so that recovery from the group's own funds became impossible. Both the groups had membership drawn from SC, and both used drought as a reason for default, even though the remaining SHGs in the village, living and working in the same conditions, were regular in loan repayments. When the other SHGs in the village were asked what they intended to do to help recover amounts from their village, they said that it would be very difficult for them to do anything as the defaulting members took a common stand on the matter. To make matters worse, the president of one of the defaulting SHGs was also a key leader of the Samajik Bank. In Maharajor cluster, again in Boden, the women said that they had been one large group of mixed castes, but then broke into smaller groups when some sections defaulted. The splitting did not bring back the defaulted amounts.

The Larger Environment and Women's SHGs

Banks and SHGs

The branch manager of SBI, Boden, said that there were around 2,000 savings accounts in his branch. Of these, 15 per cent were those of SHGs. The actual number of SHG accounts was found to be 125, and the percentage mentioned did not appear correct. However, when asked what the total deposits in the branch were, given that the women had around Rs 300,000 in the branch, the branch was reluctant to provide information. The bank manager mentioned that the SHG–bank linkage had begun the previous year. Prior to that, the branch had given loans only to individuals:

Now we lend to SHGs and require that the group be small and homogeneous, that it not be registered, that it be flexible, that the members belong below the poverty line (BPL) list, that they not be defaulters to the bank. The women's expectation is that each borrowing will be larger than the previous one. In SHGs they seem to be taught that they will keep getting larger and larger loans. Therefore, when they first deposit their savings with us, the expectation is that they will be given a large loan at the end of six months. Self-help is not what motivates them; it is the expectation of that larger loan.

We evaluate them after six months, but in our case we found many women and almost all the men in the SHG areas, to have been defaulters to the bank. It is for this reason that we chose not to finance the SHGs directly, but instead to lend through Lokadrusti. We had financed some of these women leaders earlier with Rs 25,000 for their *moori* business. How on earth can the small *moori* business absorb Rs 25,000? The loans did not come back. The terms of repayment, too, are such that there is a moratorium for one full year initially, and the borrowers forget their responsibilities. On the whole, many of the schemes for financing the poor are not well thought through.

In Dhamnapada village in Boden, women said that they each needed credit worth Rs 30,000–40,000. When they and women from other villages were asked what it was that a woman could borrow and repay comfortably, the maximum figure quoted in several meetings was Rs 5,000. They went on to say that although for a few this was a feasible loan in terms of their current needs, for most others, not more than Rs 3,000 was 'digestible'. However, they said:

> The government has taught us to ask for Rs 30,000 to Rs 40,000 under various schemes. When it says that such money is available and that we should try and access it, it is too much to resist, even though we are all conscious that we will not be able to absorb such a large loan. Also, the government has given indications that it does not expect its loans back; so those of us who know the art of accessing such 'loans' do get such loans, and do not think of them as repayable.

Lokadrusti had disbursed the SBI loan through the Samajik Bank to the SHGs. Of the first 60 SHG loan accounts in the ledger, 39 were defaulters of over six months.

Sameshwari SHG of Chitarama borrowed Rs 5,000 on 22 June 2000 and repaid only Rs 1,080 on 7 April 2001. Thakurani SHG of Mahulpada borrowed Rs 2,400 on 29 April 1999 and had repaid nothing even towards the end of June 2001. Jagannath SHG of Makkarbilli borrowed Rs 8,100 on 4 January 2000 and had repaid nothing since. Duarani SHG of Boigaon borrowed Rs 10,000 on 29 September 2000 and repaid only Rs 1,400 on 23 May 2001.

All remittances to the Samajik Bank were first adjusted against the principal. Only the last instalment was adjusted to interest. Default was not frowned upon by Lokadrusti, even though it was worried about it, as was true of many voluntary development organizations and governmental agencies engaged in the promotion of SHGs for savings and credit. Most, including Lokadrusti, do not have a system where a defaulter pays a price for default. Default is explained away: drought, illness, and so on. Default is not monitored or dealt with at the SHG, Samajik Bank, or Lokadrusti levels. Even though many groups had defaulted to the Samajik Bank, Lokadrusti paid up to the SBI. The SBI bank manager said that the bank had lent approximately Rs 5,000 per SHG through Lokadrusti. Although the amount was a cash credit facility available for a year, Lokadrusti preferred to clear the loans fully as if they were short-term loans, he explained. Forty accounts were, therefore, fully paid. Although details of loans to SHGs led by leaders of the Samajik Bank were not looked into, it is likely that the bank lent more to the SHGs that they represent than to others. Jana Kalyan SHG of Tetalpara, whose president had previously been the president of the Samajik Bank, and was still on its board, had received over Rs 80,000 in loans at different times from the bank. It was good with repayment, but then repeat loans were usually given soon after repayment of earlier outstanding loans. Binapani SHG of Jamgaon, whose president was also at one point of time the president of the Samajik Bank, had received nearly Rs 45,000 in loans, and had defaulted fully on the last loan of Rs 12,000.

Of Rs 290,000 lent by the SBI branch, the current outstanding (at the time of the interview) was Rs 130,000. Against this, the SHGs together had over Rs 300,000 in their savings accounts with the branch. The branch was not aware of the SHG loan repayment performance, as Lokadrusti paid on time. The bank's own recovery in the previous year was very poor, the manager said. The Samajik Bank's loan recovery performance, too, was not encouraging, he added.

The bank manager of KAGB, Khariar branch, when interviewed about SHGs promoted directly by the branch, said:

We have lent Rs 753,000 to 36 SHGs over three years. I find that repeat loans make them stronger. In our branch, the total lending in the last three years was Rs 8 million, with a 50:50 ratio for urban and rural loans. Therefore, the Rs 753,000 loan to SHGs is significant. Whenever there is a bank linkage, the first question in everyone's mind is, 'What is the economic activity?' I say, 'Let her consume my loan, if that is her necessity.' For then, she will not need to sell her cattle for consumption purposes, and, therefore, my loan is in fact a contributor to her economic activity. However, as the loan sizes increase, I do need to ask, 'What's the economic activity?'

When asked about KAGB's approach to giving loans to women whose husbands were defaulters, he said that there were a large number of migrant workers in the district. 'If a migrant husband is a defaulter, should we deny the wife a loan?' he asked. External loans, while useful perhaps at the individual level, had not resulted in good banking behaviour or sound banking business for the area.

The Government and SHGs

Even though he did not directly deal with Lokadrusti-promoted SHGs, the bank manager of KAGB, Khariar, was familiar with its work, and specifically mentioned that he appreciated its attempts at federating SHGs. He mentioned that collectors and governmental departments constantly sought information regarding SHGs purportedly with a view to assisting them. He said that he was very wary of governmental role in SHGs:

> The Collector asked for a list of our SHGs, which I refused to provide. I believe that Lokadrusti did give them a list. I'm always afraid that external political forces and interference and populist ideologies will destroy the SHGs. The Swarnajayanti Gram Swarozgar Yojana (SGSY) will destroy the SHGs. We and Lokadrusti organize SHGs over time. Block staff organize them quickly, grade them, place money with them under SGSY, and then our SHGs start to put pressure on us to make similar large loans available. We make loans available to them first on a 1:2 equity–debt ratio, then change this to 1:3 and then to 1:4. SGSY loans are given on much easier terms, and whatever borrower discipline we are trying to inculcate, will be lost if our SHGs received these easy loans.

The DRDA project director, Nuapada, said:

> I am new here. In Khariar block, there are SHGs for women. SHGs need proper guidance and constant visits by facilitators regarding savings, loans, and business. In many cases, women have not entered into any business. Most SHGs seem primarily interested in accessing external loans. Many save, simply to demand a loan later. Their husbands are defaulters; how can

they get bank loans? Facilitators put it into the heads of the members that if they save they will get bank loans. I say that they should build on their own funds. The women threaten that they will break their SHGs if they do not get external loans. Some SHGs are involved in rope-making and other businesses even without governmental support. They are also into animal husbandry, farming, vegetable vending and other trades.

It was evident that neither the women nor the government officials had a clear long-term vision on SHGs. Women could have contributed to the discourse on SHGs but had interacted with the banks and government officials primarily to access external loans.

SHGs as Potential Leaders of Local Markets

SHGs as Potential Leaders in the Local Financial Market

SHGs were already net savers in the local economy, given that their idle funds in banks were higher than their dues to the banks. The SHGs were poised to be leaders of the local financial markets. They were, however, not aware of the possibility and not yet conscious of their combined strength. Given the assumption that what women do for themselves is 'micro', let us examine just how important bank linkages and external borrowings are to a set of SHGs, to a village, for on-lending to women. Let us take an average SHG in Khariar, and see what it could yet mean to the members in the village, and indeed to the village itself. Let us also examine what length of time is needed for the members to access a 3,000-rupee loan, agreed by most as what could be easily absorbed and repaid.

Let us assume that an SHG in Khariar block has 10 members, of mixed castes, mostly small landholders or landless, and that each member saves Rs 20 per month. The group charges 3 per cent per month interest on loans and does not expect to borrow from any external source. Currently, most such groups tend to remit their savings in the bank each month, and the bank is anywhere between 1 and 8 kms away. Two women travel to the bank and all such women report losing their daily wages on the day they go to the bank. While women did not mention loss of wages to attend cluster meetings, they spoke of tired feet and/or wage loss in relation to visits to banks. The local wage was stated to be Rs 25 per day. That is, in order to remit Rs 200, Rs 50 was the 'expenditure' borne by the women with responsibility (which the group did/could not compensate). For each such remittance which when lent can earn only 3 per cent per month, there is a cost of 25 per cent in the very month that the money is raised, that someone is bearing within the group. On occasion, they actually went to the bank a second time in the month to withdraw a part of their savings to lend to one or more members, thereby adding to the costs.

If, however, at each monthly meeting, the women lent to themselves the bulk of the amount raised by them at that meeting, without going to the bank, the leaders would not need to lose their wages. The small amount of idle funds could be kept in the home of one of the leaders, or in a post office account. Loans would of course need to be for any of a number of purposes, and not just for 'income generating' purposes.

If a village has seven SHGs and 70 members, as some villages in the Lokadrusti area do, with each member saving Rs 20 per month, then, the picture for the village could be as shown in Table 6.3.

The average thrift and interest per member shown in the last two columns is, in fact, the average loan size per member (not necessarily per borrower, though, as that will be higher if all members are not borrowers at once). In the middle of the sixth year, with average thrift and interest having crossed Rs 3,000, every member could have access to a loan of that size. For ease of understanding, a uniform 3 per cent per month interest on loans over the years has been shown. However, as it emerged during discussions in

TABLE 6.3
Scenario Projection

Year	Opening balance (rupees)	Thrift during year (rupees)	Interest earned at 3 per cent per month (rupees)	Total funds at year end (rupees)	Average thrift and interest per member at year end, with all the interest earned distributed (rupees)	Average thrift and interest per member at year end after setting aside half the interest earned for expenses (rupees)
1	0	1,6800	2,996	19,796	283	261
2	19,796	1,6800	10,123	46,719	667	595
3	46,719	1,6800	19,815	83,333	1,190	1,049
4	83,333	1,6800	32,996	133,129	1,902	1,666
5	133,129	1,6800	50,923	200,852	2,869	2,506
6	200,852	1,6800	75,303	292,954	4,185	3,647
7	292,954	1,6800	108,460	418,214	5,974	5,200
8	418,214	1,6800	153,553	588,567	8,408	7,311
9	588,567	1,6800	214,880	820,247	11,718	10,183
10	820,247	1,6800	298,285	1,135,332	16,219	14,088

village after village, the interest rates, which were as high as 5 per cent per month in some of the villages, and as low as 1 per cent per month in a few, would most likely keep reducing as loan sizes grew. This would be both because of the incapacity to pay a high interest on large loans, and also because the women would have captured a very large share of the local financial market, and could afford to set the trends and choose rates they wanted.

What the women in the Lokadrusti area can do for themselves in the field of finance in five or six years, most primary agricultural credit cooperatives, and for that matter, most cooperative and commercial banks in the country have not been able to do in over 50 years. For that to happen, however, much more effort has to go into institution building in the area. The SHGs in Lokadrusti area are in a position to get converted to long-term institutions, serving local women and through them, the local communities, over generations. After all, if 70 women from one village can together have Rs 1.1 million plus of their own funds in 10 years, then around 19,000 women can have, in 10 years, the Rs 3 billion mobilized by the commercial banks, over 50 years, in the district, from 100,000 families (as mentioned in the NABARD plans for the district).

SHGs as Potential Leaders in the Local Commodity Market

In village after village in Boden, the women spoke of having entered 'business' with the SHG loans. In Khariar, the women of Shraddhapur village, which had four SHGs, spoke excitedly of their profitable *mahua* business. When questioned how such a small area could sustain so much business, the women presented the economics.

The Rice Business Boden has at least 80 women now engaged in the rice business, whereas earlier it used to have at best 30. The women reported that paddy procurement, milling, and selling usually take up a three-day cycle. Every three days, if each woman has a turnover of Rs 500, and if the business runs for at least 210 days every year (which the women said it did), then total combined annual turnover = Rs 500 × 80 women × 70 (210/3) days = Rs 2,800,000.

That is, about Rs 1.8 million of additional rice business now takes place in the small block because of the SHGs. Assuming profit to be 20 per cent of turnover, profit is Rs 560,000 annually, or Rs 7,000 per woman. At least 50 more women have an additional annual income of Rs 7,000 now. This was a very significant impact of the SHGs, and one repeatedly mentioned by members. In different villages, different sets of calculations relating to the rice business were presented by the women. These calculations indicated that the women did indeed understand their business. One set of calculations presented was as follows:

> One bag of paddy costs Rs 330; this bag of paddy is converted to half a bag of rice and the sale price of half a bag of rice is Rs 450.
> Milling costs = Rs 15
> Therefore, profit per bag = Rs 105, inclusive of the cost of time of the woman.
> Profit = approximately 23 per cent of sales.

When women were asked who the buyers of the rice were, as the area was an agricultural area, they said that initially they sold a lot of the rice in Boden headquarters, where people come in on government service or as traders. Now they search for more distant markets. They said that they carried headloads of rice for sale to some extent. For the more distant markets, their husbands took the rice on their bicycles. They said that without access to loans of Rs 500, they would never have got into the rice business.

The *Moori* Business   A similar, but more complicated, exercise was conducted with the women on their *moori* business.

> 8 *mand* (approx. 4 kg) = of paddy costs Rs 100
> This converts to 24 *mand* of *moori*, as *moori* is much lighter

Moori can be sold for Rs 164

Cost of wood for making *moori* = Rs 20

Cost of milling of the paddy in the first place = Rs 4

Net profit = Rs 40 for every 8 *mand*, or Rs 120 for about Rs 500 of sales, or 24 per cent of sales.

Given Boden's small geographical area, even the few women in just the rice/*moori* business significantly increased business in the locality. The potential for women to capture a major share of the local financial and commodity markets in an organized manner was very high. Lokadrusti's strategy of working with numbers in concentrated clusters could yet change the economy of Boden, Khariar and Sinapalli blocks. Whereas in Boden the figures were quite significant already, more villages needed to be reached out to in the other two blocks perhaps, before a similar impact on the economy could be seen.

Information on deposits mobilized was not forthcoming from local banks, perhaps because of a realization that the SHGs could outstrip their performance. Even though large numbers of women visited bank branches regularly, they had not taken their external borrowings seriously. With governments and donors continuing to push money, it is unlikely that credit behaviour will improve significantly. The SHGs may be more responsible with their own money, and as the projections show, can probably have a very significant presence in the local financial market. The women already have had an impact on the local commodities market, even with so few of them engaged in it. With more focused attention, and more value addition, the women could probably play a leading role in local agricultural produce processing and marketing.

An Overview of the Impact

As a result of Lokadrusti's work in the field of micro-credit, at the individual level, the women appeared to have gained very significantly in terms of mobility, self-confidence, widening of interests, access to financial services, building of own savings, competence in public affairs, and status at home and in the community. What the women still needed to acquire at the individual level was competence in organizational management and long-term vision building and planning.

Within their villages, the SHGs were respected and the women members were visible and sought after at block and district meetings, and accepted as leaders. Women had represented issues of interest to them, and had protected/promoted the interests of women as a class, and of individual women in distress, successfully at times, and unsuccessfully at other times. Even where unsuccessful in relation to their primary objective, they did manage to make their presence felt. Where at the individual level, the women had found their world enlarged with active and purposeful interaction with other castes, this had not as yet translated to a village with less caste consciousness.

Boden's women were not conscious of their own current and potential strength in matters of finance, whereas the women of Khariar and Sinapalli expected little from external agents, wanting only to be fairly self-reliant. The women, if they are not aware of it, have already had an impact on the local commodities market, even with so few of them engaged in it. More focused attention and value addition would help the women play leading roles in local agricultural produce processing and marketing. With savings and credit being managed by formal member-owned institutions at the village level, there was every likelihood that the women could collectively emerge as key players in the local financial market.

The Mahila Samiti, the Muthi Chawal and the SHG may need to invest more in their own design and development, if women are to have even greater influence on their own lives, as well as the larger community. Lokadrusti needs to help with the process. The micro-credit intervention of Lokadrusti has touched individual lives and changed the manner in which villages respond to their women. It has made women visible, mobile, articulate, and impact local markets significantly. With some investment in institutional design and development, Lokadrusti's work could result in strong, viable, inter-generational organizations that will have a life beyond that of Lokadrusti itself.

The Way Forward

Lokadrusti has worked in a concentrated manner with large numbers of women in three blocks of Nuapada. Lokadrusti has on its staff and board, people belonging to the district, who want to have an impact on the development of the district. It has aimed at local women taking responsibility for the development of the area, as more men migrate for work than women. It has reached out to women from STs, SCs, BCs and a few from other classes/castes, and has helped women to work across castes. It has provided three sets of opportunities for women to work constructively with one another for their own development and for the development of their villages: the Muthi Chawal (itself a savings and credit organization), the SHG and the Mahila Samiti.

What Lokadrusti has achieved in such a short time is remarkable. What the women in the area have achieved is very impressive. The women have self-worth, appear to be valued by families and their villages, could well be on their way to becoming leaders of the local financial market, and have even begun to impact business in the area. Lokadrusti has worked systematically at aiming for the inclusion of as many women as possible in any village in the savings and credit activity. It has also worked in village after village in any given area, bringing together numbers of women large enough for local communities and institutions to take cognizance of. By continuing to keep the groups small and distinct from one another (even if federated), it may find that it continues to be rated highly in governmental, donor, banking, and women's circles, which might have a short-term perspective on women and their money. By assisting in the building of strong institutions, it may find itself much less popular with governmental, donor, and banking agencies but it may find that women will truly become designers and managers of long-term financial institutions, far more efficient and resourceful than most other alternatives, serving themselves and their communities with élan.

Lokadrusti is one of the better interventions in women's SHGs, across India. What could further increase the impact of SHGs, in Nuapada or elsewhere in the country, is perhaps a series of steps to systematically work towards institution building, so that women's institutions have lives of their own, unrelated to the capacity of the promoting institution to continue to meet the costs of operation/management of the groups. The following steps could further increase the influence of women on their own lives as well as on their communities and the larger environment.

It might be helpful to encourage SHG members to better analyse each stream of activities (financial services, marketing, advocacy, charity, generating employment, etc.) that they engage in. Each has a very distinct contribution to make to women's development, and while in some, almost all 'members' are involved, in some, they are not; in fact, 'non-members' too are involved. In the first phase of work, the overlapping of different activities, without a close scrutiny of which/how many members are involved, might even be helpful. However, as the numbers and size of work increases for each stream, a much more professional approach may be needed, so that each service takes cognizance of its users/participants, and is sensitive to their specific needs around that service, or set of services. While men have a number of rural institutions that they engage in, women should not have to depend on any one set of organizations to meet all their needs. Levels of self-reliance, leadership and skills required for each stream are quite different. Leaders of advocacy groups need to be vocal, articulate and able to motivate people. Leaders of democratic business organizations need to be prudent, understand finance and accounts, and be committed to high transparency and accountability.

Legal forms of organization available in each state to women, for various types of activities, need to be explored by support agencies. Whereas a trade union might be appropriate in fighting for better wages in areas where the government treats forest dwellers as labourers collecting forest produce, a society might be a better choice for an advocacy group, or one with a strong political or social agenda. Similarly, a cooperative (where cooperative legislation is liberal) might be the best choice for a financial services or a marketing initiative. SHGs were first promoted in the 1980s, when cooperative laws across the country were appalling. With Section 11 of the Companies Act requiring groups engaging in business, with more than 20 members, to be registered under one or the other law, SHGs were deliberately kept small. Since the mid-1990s, however, more and more states have introduced liberal cooperative laws. Engaging in financial services through small scattered groups that cannot easily be monitored is no longer a necessary evil. Savings and credit services can be brought into formal cooperatives of women that will last through generations.

Ad hoc, small, scattered groups, useful as they have been, must lead to multiple village-level, inter-generational, democratic organizations of women that have focused objectives, have developed, or are in the process of developing, a body of knowledge around their chosen field, have body corporate status, have a *sui generis* existence, can hold properties in their own names, and exist to fulfil the aspirations of their members, in a manner decided by them. Micro-credit interventions, in many an area, have already made women leaders in the local financial market. They need to be helped to stay ahead.

7

Social Mobilization and Micro-finance for Women's Empowerment— Lessons from the ASA Trust

Kalpana Sankar[*]

Introduction

To be without assets, underemployed and illiterate, as well as overworked, tired and weak is the lot of most rural women in Tamil Nadu, like in the rest of India. They are often deprived of access to improved means of production and productivity such as land, credit, technical advice, training and marketing skills. Although women are accorded little social status or recognition, their earnings are frequently essential to the survival of their households. In several households in Tamil Nadu, women are the *de facto* heads of the household by virtue of desertion, migration, illness, unemployment, or the addictive habits of their husbands. Thus, though women have lesser access to power and resources, they do play key roles in managing their households and coping with poverty.

* I would like to acknowledge the immense support received from Mr S. Devaraj, Chairperson of ASA throughout the exercise. I would also like to thank all the project staff for their support. I am extremely grateful to the government department staff for their help in data collection. Last, but not least, I wish to express my appreciation and gratitude to the women who set aside their valuable time for the study.

The Indian government, the National Bank for Agriculture and Rural Development (NABARD), and several NGOs are increasingly seeing micro-credit for groups of women as the panacea for reducing poverty and empowering women. Activists for Social Action (ASA), based in Tiruchirapalli in Tamil Nadu, is one such NGO promoting micro-credit among a variety of other programmes for dalit women's empowerment. This case study, commissioned by the United Nations Development Programme (UNDP) and the ICICI Bank, examines the ASA experience in terms of the role of social mobilization and micro-credit for poverty reduction and women's empowerment. It also seeks to throw light on the role of women's economic empowerment through assistance provided to women creditors. A third objective is to see whether greater incomes for poor households translate into a situation where children are removed from work and put into schools.

To examine these three aspects, both primary and secondary data have been used. Primary data was gathered from members of self-help groups (SHGs), non-members, members' husbands, federation leaders, panchayat presidents and other government departments. In addition, branch managers of banks and NGO staff were interviewed. Secondary data was retrieved from the records maintained by the project functionaries. The research methodology drew upon the approach adopted in the mid-term review of the Tamil Nadu Women's Development Project, modifying it to suit the requirements of the ASA study (Murthy et al., 2001).

For gathering primary data on household-level poverty, participatory rural appraisal (PRA) methods such as social mapping and wealth ranking were used. For examining issues of women's empowerment, participatory methods such as focus group discussions (FGDs), mapping of gender division of labour, workload and mobility of women and men, gender-based access and control over resources, and gender-based access to decision-making were applied. These in-depth village-level field studies were carried out in five villages and covered 40 groups and 161 member households. Intra-household impact was examined in depth in 31 member households. Forty non-member households and 27 male relatives of members were also included in the study to gather their perceptions. Care was taken to select villages which represented different degrees of remoteness and different caste and religious compositions. Similarly, SHGs comprising members of different ages and who were part of different kinds of income generation programmes (IGPs) were selected. While selecting members, it was ensured that they included both women in male-headed households (MHHs) and in women-headed households (WHHs) (12 per cent were WHHs[1] and 88 per cent were members of MHHs). Apart from drawing comparisons between the situations of members and non-members, the situation of members before and after joining the group was also compared.

The study cannot claim to be totally representative. In particular, the study of intra-household impact was restricted to 31 households, which is a small sample from which to draw definite conclusions. Time and cost were major constraints. Nevertheless, the study offers major insights and lessons that are presented in this paper. As the findings from the study have to be located within the context of the functioning of ASA, I shall begin with a brief history of the organization, its perspectives, and where the micro-finance programme fits into its overall framework.

Activists for Social Action

ASA was founded in 1986 for empowering women, the landless poor, small and marginal farmers and dalits in Tiruchirapalli and the neighbouring districts of Tamil Nadu. Initially, its approach was to mobilize dalit women to protect themselves against inequity and injustice. In the process of its growth, members of ASA realized that social and political empowerment would be a distant dream without economic empowerment. The trust then started intervening in the

---

[1] Seventy-nine per cent of the women members heading households were widows; the rest were either deserted by their husbands or were heading households because of male migration.

area of livelihoods through a combination of struggles for releasing bonded labourers, increase in wages and for sustainable development programmes such as watershed development and alternative employment for released labourers. Soon, ASA added micro-credit, insurance and savings programmes to its portfolio of development activities, as it believed that such programmes offered the potential for poverty reduction (through income enhancement and risk reduction) and empowerment of rural poor women (through elevating their economic status and collective space to challenge gender inequalities).

By 1993, ASA had transformed itself into a micro-finance institution (MFI) based on the Bangladesh Grameen model of forming SHGs of five members, and federating them into centres (comprising four SHGs), clusters (comprising 20 centres), branches (comprising five clusters), and franchisees (comprising six branches). The micro-finance programme has been named *Grama Vidiyal*, meaning 'Dawn of the Rural Poor', and is currently operational in five districts of Tamil Nadu: Tiruchirapalli, Pudukottai, Sivagangai, Madurai and Dindigul. These districts are known to be drought prone and face declining soil productivity. Problems of migration, bonded labour, contract labour and child labour persist in the area. Socially and economically oppressed groups, as a result of the caste system, constitute 80 per cent of the population and own less than 20 per cent of the total landholding in the area. Twenty-four per cent of the population where ASA works are dalits, who tend to be the poorest of the poor. Across class and caste, women are oppressed, as reflected in high rates of female foeticide, infanticide, child marriage and trafficking for sexual purposes. ASA's major areas of activities to address poverty and gender discrimination now include: (*a*) identification of women entrepreneurs; (*b*) facilitation of timely availability of credit and insurance for various consumption and income generation activities; (*c*) targeting opportunities in both agriculture (land rights of tenants, watershed development) and off-farm income generation activities; and (*d*) supporting networks of women for collective action.[2] Thus, over a period, micro-finance has become ASA's central programme, with other programmes supporting it in different ways, as reflected in its mission: 'To alleviate poverty among the marginalized groups, in and around Tamil Nadu with an effective micro-finance programme and organize, train and network them through participatory processes around issues for economic, social and political empowerment' (ASA, 2000).

As August 2001, through its micro-finance programme of ASA had reached out to 20,340 poor women, mobilizing them into 4,068 groups, 957 centres and 18 branches. By 2005, ASA hopes to extend its financial services to 100,000 poor women; by 2008 to 200,000 women; and by 2010 to 500,000 women. Most of the SHG members are poor, and 35 per cent are dalits. Among the poor and dalits, ASA's micro-finance programme focuses only on women, though the tenant farmers' programme targets both men and women. The main reason for focusing on women is ASA's belief that women are the poorest amongst the poor and discriminated against in gender-specific ways. Women are also seen as more honest and creditworthy than men. ASA feels that it is a myth that poor women cannot save. It believes that poor women will save, provided their savings are kept in a safe place, close to their homes or places of work. Hence, ASA's weekly centre meetings—where savings and loan repayments take place—are conducted in a place where the groups are within a vicinity of 3–4 km. ASA believes that the fact that disbursing loans to women increases their status and strengthens their position in the household. Further, through enterprise loans, it hopes that women will shift from unpaid/waged work towards self-employment. It is ASA's conviction that the collective space of a group fosters collective action against oppression and hence fosters women's empowerment. It

---

[2] ASA is a member of the New Entity for Social Action (NESA) and the Indian Network of Micro-credit Practitioners (INDNET). NESA comprises 40 development organizations and grassroots networks in south India that focus on empowerment of dalits and tribals. INDNET, whose office is located within ASA's premises, is involved in training member NGOs and members of SHGs started by other organizations, as well as networking them.

firmly believes in building leadership skills among women through training programmes and awareness camps. Women members of ASA elect their own leaders and representatives at centre, cluster, branch and franchise levels to evolve and implement micro-finance policies, as well as to take up socio-economic development issues in the community.

A unique feature of ASA is that not only its programmes, but also its governance and staffing, reflect sensitivity to dalit oppression. Fifty per cent of the ASA's board and 30 per cent of its 179-strong workforce are dalits; the organization itself is headed by a person from the dalit community. Representation of women in the organization stands at 45 per cent, being higher at managerial levels and lower at the field level.

Eighty-six per cent of ASA's staff focuses on the micro-finance programme, reflecting the centrality of this programme within its various strategies. At the village level, the field officer plays a key role in supervision of the micro-finance programme. Each field officer has to manage one cluster serving approximately 400 women. S/he has to attend centre meetings in every village to collect savings and repayments. The branch office is headed by a branch manager, supported by five field officers (one for each cluster) and an accountant. The franchise is the next level in the hierarchy, comprising six branches headed by a chief executive officer (CEO). Currently, there are three franchises. Each franchise is affiliated with ASA and the project management unit of ASA located in Tiruchirapalli. Most staff members are qualified and experienced and the staff turnover has been very limited, being reported only at the level of field officers. ASA has given importance to staff development through various training programmes and exposure visits within and outside the country. All senior staff members have been trained in PRA, micro-finance and watershed development, and have attended gender sensitization workshops.

The micro-finance programme is fully self-sufficient and is generating positive returns on investment. The financial costs of the operation are also covered. The capital for lending is raised through commercial banks (CBs) and the income is sufficient to cover the cost of lending. Around 90 per cent of the overall expenditure of ASA is on micro-finance.

Operational Aspect of the Micro-credit and Insurance

Membership and Participation

A 16-point housing index has been adopted for identifying the poor; households that score below four points constitute its target group. Another criterion is that members should have less than 2 acres of land. Most of the groups visited were homogeneous in terms of economic background. Members were in the age group of 20–45 years.

In each of the five villages taken up for in-depth study, the wealth ranking exercise was conducted in a representative portion of the village (Table 7.1). This revealed that only 58 per cent of the members were very poor or poor at the time of the exercise. This need not be viewed negatively, as there is evidence that some of the members currently moderately off were poor before the group formation.

TABLE 7.1
Profile of Members and Non-members as per Wealth-ranking Exercise

Economic category	Number of members	Percentage of members under each category	Number of non-members	Percentage of non-members under each category
Very poor	23	14.29	20	14.29
Poor	70	43.48	62	44.29
Moderate	49	30.43	22	15.71
Rich	16	9.94	29	20.71
Very rich	3	1.86	7	5.00
Total	161	100.00	140	100.00

The data on caste composition of members gathered from 40 SHGs reveals that 33 per cent of the members were dalits. Though this figure is slightly lower than the project figure of 36 per cent, it is higher than the proportion of dalits in the project area. This indeed is commendable.

A point of concern, however, is that 12 per cent of the current members are rich or very rich, as per the criteria of the members. It is highly unlikely that the poor would have moved up so significantly after joining the group, and this perhaps reflects the need for better targeting. The exercise also suggests that 47 per cent of the very poor or poor households in the village are yet to be covered under the groups. These households include those where women are disabled, unskilled labourers, or above 45 years or below 20 years (17–20 years). Some of the households do not fall in these categories, but possess more than 2 acres of land and are hence outside the membership criterion. Some of the women non-members with infants not only lack independent income, but also the time to attend meetings. Yet another reason for not joining was lack of cooperation from husbands. Thus, inability to save (in the case of disabled and elderly women), lack of time (young mothers and unskilled labourers), ineligibility to join groups (owning more than 2 acres of land and aged below 20 years) and social hierarchies (between parents and adolescent girls, or between husbands and wives) are the key reasons for exclusion.

As per the data furnished by ASA, only 1 per cent of the members have dropped out after joining the group. This has also been confirmed during the study. The low dropout rate can be attributed to efforts to strengthen the group. The main reasons for dropouts include death of members, sudden fall in household income, inability to save, inability to contribute to the centre fund (elaborated later), lack of time to attend meetings and migration in search of employment.

The attendance of members in group and centre meetings is of a high order. Nevertheless, the economic background and literacy levels of the members do have a bearing on the levels of participation in group and centre meetings.

Participation was higher amongst the better-off than the very poor, and amongst the literates when compared to the non-literates. This is particularly true with respect to holding positions as group or centre leader.

Yet another concern is the role of members and NGO staff in decision-making. The day of meeting, time of meeting and amount to be saved per week are all decided by the NGO. Similarly, the quantum of loan and loan instalments are decided by the NGO, not by the group. Details of savings fixed for the group and selection of leader of the group are as yet not supported by a group resolution.

Access to Training

ASA organizes several training programmes for SHG members. These include (a) five-day training prior to group formation on vision, mission and objectives of ASA and micro-finance programme called the Continuous Group Training (CGT); (b) gender training to some SHG members, selected at random (financial constraints come in the way of extending training to all members), and their husbands; and (c) Panchayati Raj training for elected panchayat leaders. Inputs on enterprise selection, cooperatives, value addition of produce, community action programme, functional literacy and numeracy and gender-based violence could further strengthen the capacity building programme.

Group leaders are given training on economic development (enterprise promotion, market linkages, savings and credit), social development (gender issues and social security), and leadership development (in credit groups at different levels and PRIs [Panchayati Raj institutions]). Leadership training has been given to only a few groups, and the leaders of the groups covered under the study were yet to take part. This training perhaps needs to be extended to all leaders, as well as members of SHGs, to strengthen democratization and sustainability.

In addition to classroom training, ASA facilitates exposure of members in two ways. The first is through *padayatras* under which group leaders of one branch go to the area of another branch to campaign on a particular issue. So far, *padayatras* have taken up issues such as gender equality, child rights, equal wages for men and women, hygiene and sanitation, and child education. Groups are also exposed to the functioning of SHGs of other NGOs in Karnataka and Kerala. One SHG member even went to Durban to discuss the issue of caste discrimination in the World Conference against Racism.[3]

Savings

In all the 40 groups surveyed, savings have been fixed at a minimum of Rs 10 per week, with members having the option of saving more (voluntary saving).[4] Members are allowed to withdraw money from voluntary savings for making the fixed savings during lean periods and for repaying loans during such times. ASA offers 6.5 per cent interest on the voluntary savings made with the group. In addition, each member contributes Re 1 per week to the centre fund, which is used by the group to pay savings of any defaulted member. All savings are deposited on the same day into the bank in which ASA's branch has an account. An impressive increase has been achieved in mobilization of savings, as savings are retained as collateral for issue of loans. The higher the savings amount, the greater the loan amount that can be raised. In the 40 groups surveyed, 55 per cent of the members save Rs 10, 30 per cent save Rs 15, 10 per cent save Rs 20, and 5 per cent save Rs 25 per week. The members had saved (fixed savings), on an average, Rs 830 on a cumulative basis. However, the fixed savings per week excludes the very poor from joining the group. Further, the rule of linking the amount of loan with the amount saved may further exacerbate inequalities.

---

[3] The World Conference against Racism, Racial Discrimination, Xeno-phobia, and Related Intolerance was held in Durban, South Africa between 31 August and 7 September 2001.
[4] Although the minimum savings per week are fixed as Rs 10, members can save more if they can afford it. This amount is accounted for as part of the centre fund and is rotated as loan to members.

It was observed that 35 per cent of members save outside the group, either in banks or at home in the form of cash, assets and/or grain. The main reason cited for saving outside the SHG was the difficulty faced in withdrawal of voluntary savings with the group. While banks are safe, keeping money or assets at home poses risks when husbands are alcoholic.

Rules Governing Lending

No loan is given during the first three months of group functioning. It is treated as an observation period, during which the financial discipline, regularity in attending meetings, and cohesiveness of the group are examined. If the group functions well, then it is considered for a loan. As a rule, loans are not given to all the beneficiaries in one go. Two out of the five members get their first loan 12 weeks after the group's inception. If they repay on time, then the other members get the loan. A 15-day period is allowed for purchasing the said asset, failing which the loan is to be returned to the branch office. Also, the borrower cannot sell off the asset until the loan is cleared.

Aspects that are taken into account before disbursing a loan to a member are type of house, monthly earning capacity of household members, and amount required for purchase. In instances where a woman in an MHH applies for a loan, the application is considered only if the husband jointly signs the loan application form in the branch office. This is done, according to ASA, to ensure joint responsibility towards loan utilization and repayment. Once the group decides which two members' loans are going to be forwarded, the two applications are submitted by the group leader to the centre leader, countersigned by the remaining members of the SHG. Only if the group leader approves the loan application is it handed over to the centre leader. The centre leader then forwards the loan request form to the field officer. Thus, the collateral for the loan is essentially 'social' in nature, with the group taking responsibility for repayment (though the savings of the member reduces the risks).

The first loan amount is normally Rs 3,000, and the pre-requisite is a minimum savings of Rs 10 per week. The size of the loan increases from Rs 3,000 to Rs 5,000 for the second loan. The size of the third loan varies from Rs 5,000 to Rs 10,000. Members who opt for a higher dose of credit have to pay increased savings per week (Rs 5 more for the second dose). In the early stages of the scheme, an interest rate of 48 per cent per annum was charged to recover costs; this has been currently reduced to 36 per cent per annum (18 per cent interest at a flat rate)[5] because of the increase in membership and consequent viability of low-interest margins. Though the interest rates charged by the SHGs are much lower than those charged by moneylenders, they are higher than the norms of NABARD on interest rates for lending to the poor.

On the whole, easy loan documentation procedures, timely disbursal of credit (normally within 48–72 hours), and multiple doses of credit are the key strengths of ASA's micro-finance programme. The openness and accountability with which ASA's centre meetings are conducted prevent certain members of the group colluding with field workers over credit allocation. There are, however, some areas for strengthening. In most cases (80 per cent), it was noticed that the amount disbursed as loan is not sufficient to meet the entire cost of the productive asset or activity, and the member needed to mobilize credit from outside to meet the balance. This was particularly true of the first dose of loan. Sixty per cent of the members felt that it should be increased from Rs 3,000 to Rs 5,000. Yet another concern is that in most groups, the leader is one of the first two beneficiaries.

Actual Lending Operations

As of August 2001, 16,549 members (81.36 per cent) out of a membership of 20,340 have availed loans. Disaggregating further, around 51 per cent of ASA's borrowers obtained the first loan, 26 per cent obtained a second loan, 12 per cent

---

[5] Flat rate of interest implies that interest is calculated on the original loan amount and does not get reduced on subsequent loan repayments.

obtained a third loan, and 11 per cent obtained a fourth loan. The study of 40 groups revealed that between 1996 and 2001, each member of the 40 groups studied had received 1.92 loans, of an average amount of Rs 9,712. There was no bias or preference reported in accessing subsequent loans; access mainly depended on the individual's capacity to repay. As per ASA's reports, three types of loans have been availed by members: loans for non-farm income generation (87 per cent), seasonal loans for agriculture (8 per cent), and loans for consumption (5 per cent). Consumption loans, though small in number, have been given for a variety of purposes such as medical expenses, household celebrations, education and funeral expenses (together 4.9 per cent), as well as housing (0.2 per cent) (Table 7.2). The small proportion of consumption loans may be one of the reasons why some members still depend on moneylenders.

TABLE 7.2
Purpose of Loans

Type	Number	Percentage	Amount (Rs)	Percentage
Non-farm income generation programmes	27,500	87.28	112,572,545	86.79
Consumption loan (non-housing)	1,538	4.88	4,306,870	3.32
Seasonal agriculture loans	2,408	7.64	10,696,300	8.25
Housing	62	0.20	2,135,000	1.65
Total	31,508	100.00	129,710,715	100.00

Around 35 per cent of production loans are for household enterprises (self-employment) such as gem cutting, ayurvedic medicine preparation, quarrying, leasing of land, charcoal-making and brick-making. How far women retain control over the loan and income generated in such cases is a moot question. The rest of the loans are for women-managed enterprises, particularly livestock and petty industries such as food vending, vegetable vending, small grocery shops and rice shops. Women primarily take up these enterprises because they are familiar with them, these entail low risks, and tend to lead to regular income. There is a need for training women on taking on new enterprises that lead to higher returns. The productivity of the existing economic activities depends greatly on the status of the assets and its quality. ASA's field staff closely monitors the creation of assets through loan, but training for members is currently inadequate in ensuring that the asset is of a good quality when it is purchased, and to maintain it subsequently.

The credit–savings ratio per group for 2000–2001 was 11.70 (average loan of Rs 48,558 against a savings of Rs 4,151). The ratio has decreased with the age of the group. The NGO investment per branch has also reduced. The reason for higher credit–savings ratio over 1998–2000 (at 12.69) is that higher amount of loans had been given in the initial stages since the absorption capacity of the groups is higher. Also, with time and repeated doses of credit, the group members require lower quantum of loans.

A heartening observation was that the repayment of ASA loans is 100 per cent in four of the six branches, which is a contrast to the performance of nationalized banks. In the other two branches, repayment is around 98 per cent. These branches were the first ones to be started and it was difficult to change women from the then pervading grant culture to a repayment one. Linking the salaries of field officer, branch accountant and branch manager with repayment has yielded fruitful results. Further, members feel that it is their social responsibility to repay loans on time. The fear of criticism by other members has also yielded fruitful results. The loans taken from the group were paid through members' regular income, accessing husband's income, reduction of consumption of tobacco and tea, working overtime, borrowing from friends and relatives without interest, and sometimes borrowing from moneylenders. The last three ways of repaying may go against the interest of the poor in the long run.

Insurance and Social Security

All members of ASA who have taken a loan have been insured under ASA's social welfare security scheme. The members pay a capital fund of Rs 700 for life or an annual premium of Rs 150. ASA's members are also insured under the Janashree Bima Yojana (JBY) of the Life Insurance Corporation of India where the annual premium is Rs 125. In case of natural death of the member, the household is paid Rs 20,000; on accidental death, Rs 50,000 is paid. In case of partial or total permanent disability due to accident, the benefit to the member ranges from Rs 50,000 (total disability, or two eyes, or one eye and one limb) to Rs 25,000 (loss of one eye or one limb). Forty-four per cent of members have been linked under the JBY scheme. Other insurance schemes that ASA could consider mobilizing are life covers under the Oriental and General Insurance for the Poor (premium only Rs 15 per year) and the Raja Rajeswari Mahila Kalyana Bima Yojana.[6]

Since 27 per cent of the women have taken loans for livestock, all the assets bought under this category are insured to provide risk cover in case of unforeseen eventualities. However, members who have taken agricultural loans (8 per cent) have not taken crop insurance. Good housing facilities have been the unmet need of many poor households in the villages. ASA has helped 62 members from SHGs to obtain housing loans through the Housing and Urban Development Corporation (HUDCO).

Planning, Monitoring and Recording

The ASA follows a bottom-up process to plan financial and non-financial aspects. Prior to the launch of the micro-credit

---

[6] There are many micro-insurance avenues open for SHGs. The Raja Rajeshwari Kalyan Mahila Yojana scheme of four nationalized insurance companies offers personal accident insurance while the Jana Shree Bima Yojana scheme of the Life Insurance Corporation offers personal accident and natural death coverage.

programme in any village, the field officers and branch managers undertake a complete socio-economic survey of potential villages. As mentioned, a housing index is then followed for identifying the poor. Rules on whom to give loans to, rates of interest on loans from groups' own resources and those borrowed from outside, rate of repayment of loan, and amount of savings and interest to be paid on savings are arrived at through a process of gathering feedback from the members themselves. Non-financial aspects such as size of staff, coverage, targeting, and expansion, are also derived through a participatory process. Planning has been restricted to micro-finance interventions so far, leaving out issues such as atrocities against women.

Attention to planning for backward (skill upgradation) and forward (marketing) linkages is at a nascent stage. Support for skill diversification and upgradation of quality and design of products is not provided as yet. Women are involved in economic activities such as production of candles, soaps, ready-made garments, pickles, food products and leather products that require technical and marketing support. It appears that the annual Women's Day celebration on 8 March is the main occasion to facilitate marketing of products.

ASA has excellent infrastructure with computerized branches and a head office for efficient monitoring and retrieval of data. It has developed software specifically for the micro-finance programme. Performance at each level—group, centre, cluster, branch franchise—is monitored by the respective leaders and officials of ASA. Branch officials also make surprise visits to groups, centres and clusters to monitor programmes and records. Daily figures on cash transactions are reported from branches to franchises, and from franchises to head office for the information of the managing director. The head office audits the records of the branches on an annual basis. Monitoring of social indicators is under development. ASA has introduced two diaries, at the centre and group levels, based on the Impact Learning System, a tool for monitoring progress on social indicators (Naponen, 2003). Training to groups on recording data is currently under way. Although progress in social and economic empowerment can be obtained from the diaries, it could perhaps be less structured and more flexible leaving more scope for members to document the events.

On a day-to-day basis, several books, records and vouchers are maintained at each level. At the SHG level, these include a 'minutes' book, individual loan and savings books, attendance register, a copy of the loan withdrawal slip, and a copy of the loan repayment slip. At the branch level, the savings ledger and loan ledger of each village and original copy of the denomination and collection slips are maintained. These records are currently maintained by the NGO staff, not by members themselves. As of now, mainly the details on savings and credit transactions are recorded in the 'minutes' book, not discussions on social issues. This may be useful for tracking impact on social changes.

Sustainability

ASA has been able to cover all administrative costs through the interest charged to borrowers for the past five to six years; the system is becoming more financially sustainable with a larger number of borrowers receiving loans. The cost of borrowing from the Small Industries Development Bank of India (SIDBI), Grameen Trust, Friends of Women's World Banking (FWWB), Grameen Foundation and others amounts to 7.32 per cent, and it lends it to members at 36 per cent (18 per cent at a flat interest rate). In fact, it may be in a position to charge lower rates of interest and still be viable. Another issue in financial sustainability is the need for the groups to have linkages with banks. There should be an exit policy from ASA for the groups to become sustainable. A group that has received multiple doses of credit should be allowed to function independently, rotate its savings, and gain access to bank credit at a cheaper interest rate of 12 per cent. Only two members from the 40 groups studied had accessed bank loans. Bank loans may be necessary for housing and other purposes that require large amounts of money and low interest rates. With respect to social sustainability, the emergence of collective leadership is a sign of sustainability.

Rotation of the leader on an annual basis will enable wider sharing of responsibility, leading to better capacity building and participation of each member. Although it was reported that it was ASA's principle to rotate two-thirds of the group leaders annually, as per our study none of the groups have rotated their leaders.

Changes in Lives and Situations of Women

Sixty-eight per cent of the members of the 40 groups studied reported that their households had completely stopped taking loans from moneylenders after joining the group. Even the 32 per cent that reported having taken loans, had done so in the initial stage of group formation and mainly for emergency consumption needs. Further, a comparison between project and non-project members shows that the proportion of non-members who borrowed from a moneylender stood at a higher figure of 46 per cent, and they had taken loans not only for emergency needs but also to acquire assets.

Another economic benefit was increased income. Of the 161 member households covered in the study, 97 per cent experienced an increase in income because of the IGPs of the ASA. The remaining 3 per cent had gone in for low quantum of loans as they were single and could not take high risks. The in-depth study of 31 members reveals that the increase in household income because of IGPs was over Rs 1,000 a month in the case of 54 per cent of the members. Though non-members also experienced increased income in the last five years, it was a lower proportion that reported an increase (only 34 per cent of the 26 non-members covered reported an increase in household income).

The average household income of member households was Rs 3,351 per month as of August 2001. A comparison of number of loans taken and the loan amount with household income (Table 7.3) indicates that there seems to be a direct correlation between the number and size of loans and household income, showing the need for repeat loans and higher investment for poverty reduction.

TABLE 7.3
Average Savings, Loan per Member

Year of formation	Average number of loans	Average loan per member	Average household monthly income per member (Rs)	Average savings per member (Rs)
1996–98	2.82	15,680	5,422	1,483
1998–2000	2.06	10,589	3,253	835
2000–2001	1.07	4,257	2,004	357
Average of 40 groups	1.92	9,712	3,351	830

Whether increased household income leads to reduction of women's poverty and improvement in the status is a key question. To understand the implications that delivering financial services has for relations between men and women, gender-differentiated impact at the household level was studied in 31 households. The findings are as follows.

Access/Control over Private Assets

All loans related to micro-enterprises have led to the creation of an asset for the member household since the member has to return the loan if no asset is purchased within 15 days. ASA's housing loans (to 1 per cent of the members) have also strengthened the asset base of members. In addition, assets have been created through increased incomes. Details of the assets created after the launch of the programme were obtained from the members during the field study. Twenty-seven per cent of the 161 member households had acquired milch animals, 40 per cent had acquired jewellery, 18 per cent had taken land on lease, 2 per cent had acquired their own houses, 7 per cent had purchased television sets, 2 per cent had purchased cycles, and the remaining 4 per cent had purchased wet grinders and fans.

The extent to which women legally or normatively own the assets was examined in the 31 households. Although property rights for women have been established by an Act in the State of Tamil Nadu a decade ago, land is leased in the husband's name as the husband is perceived to be the cultivator. Bullock carts are seen as belonging to men, though legally the loan is in the name of the woman. All the livestock given through ASA's credit linkage programme as well as jewellery and tailoring machines are seen as women's property. The insurance of animals in women's names also helps create a sense of ownership. Assets related to gem-cutting are seen as jointly owned. Houses acquired/built through the housing loan are seen as belonging to women,[7] but not necessarily those created through increased household income. On the whole, 65 per cent of the household assets created through joining SHGs are perceived by women to be owned by them.

Income: Contribution and Control

In all member households, women share the burden of earning to run the household. Twenty-eight per cent of the members, who were not contributing in cash in the past, have started doing so after taking on a loan for productive purpose. Sixty-two per cent of the women members reported an increase in their financial contribution to the household. As of now, 62 per cent contribute 75–100 per cent of household income, 35 per cent contribute 50–75 per cent, and 3 per cent contribute 25–50 per cent. Ten per cent of the households—mainly women-headed—are run solely on women's earnings. However, their entrance into the labour market, made inevitable by inadequate incomes of males or absence of male earners, is still seen as deviant behaviour and reflected in the attitude of husbands that they are supplementary earners.

---

[7] In a particular incident, a woman member of a village refused to leave the house (as demanded by her husband) during a quarrel with her husband, claiming right over the house.

An examination of who controls the cash generated through the IGPs revealed interesting data. In 61 per cent of the households, women retain control over household incomes, that is, they either receive cash themselves and keep it (19 per cent), or their husbands receive cash and hand it over to them (42 per cent). In the rest of the households, either the husband (29 per cent) or older women members retain control over income (10 per cent). The practice of members handing over income to older women is common, mainly in the case of young members. The degree to which women exercise control over income depends to some extent on the nature of activity, being higher in women-managed activities and lower in men-managed activities. Muslim women appear to have lesser control over household income than women from other communities, perhaps due to restrictions on mobility and interaction, but this needs to be verified through a larger sample.

Another, and perhaps a more important, dimension of control over income for women is the say they have in spending it. In 61 per cent of the households surveyed, women have complete control over household expenditure. In the remaining 39 per cent of the households, husbands or elder women relatives take decisions on expenditure. The proportion of income used by members for personal needs varied from 2 to 20 per cent, averaging around 5 per cent. Expenditure was normally on clothing, bangles, jewellery and luxury utensils.

Division, Nature and Hours of Work

It appears that child care, domestic work, cooking and cleaning continue to be done by women, like in many parts of India. At times, men help in fetching water and collecting fuel. However, centre meetings held in the early hours of the day seem to push the men in member households to temporarily look after children and serve food for themselves and the children. In 4 per cent of the 31 households, men have started cooking when women attend meetings. The extent of help offered by men for reproductive work depends on the health and physical well-being of the women members. It is higher when women are sick or pregnant, and lower when they are healthy and not pregnant. Other factors that influence assistance by men for reproductive work are literacy, age, caste, household type (joint or nuclear) and gender and age of children. If literacy levels of women members are high, the assistance offered by the spouse is higher. It is higher in nuclear than joint households. Assistance offered by male members is less when girl children are present.

A comparatively greater change in the gender-based division of so-called productive tasks could be observed. Fifty-four per cent of the women who had taken a productive loan recorded marked change in gender-roles related to productive activity. Women manage all the activities pertaining to loans like filling forms and going to branch office for loan collection. The spouse accompanies the woman member at the time of loan disbursal to the branch office due to the procedure followed by ASA. In the past, purchasing and selling used to be the domain of men entirely but there is a slight shift now. Thirty-two per cent of women independently purchase and sell produce. Ten per cent of the women purchase and sell along with their husbands. In women-headed households, the percentage of women who independently handle purchase and markets is higher. In the case of Muslim households, 5 per cent of the women independently purchase and sell, and 3 per cent do it jointly with their husbands. In the remaining Muslim households, men manage it.

Eighteen per cent of the members and their husbands, who were working as labourers, have moved from worker status to manager or self-employed status through the loans taken. However, women members continue to engage in wage labour to supplement their income, earning lower wages than men. ASA currently supports struggles on the issue of higher and equal wages.

The time spent by women on economic activities varies with the type of activity. A woman agricultural labourer spends 6–8 hours per day during the peak enterprise season and three to four hours per day during the slack season. Women engaged in construction activity work for 10 hours per day. In the case of household enterprises, women's average time spent on enterprise activity is limited to six hours per day and there is flexibility in the timings and working hours. In addition to enterprise work, women members also have to engage in domestic work. If one takes into account both reproductive and productive work, the workload of women has increased in 61 per cent of the member households, which has a bearing on women's health and the quality of child care.

There is no leisure time for agricultural labourers and construction workers. Self-employed women, on the other hand, do have some leisure time. Sixty-two per cent of ASA's beneficiaries covered during the study had leisure time varying from two to three hours. This time was spent in taking rest, visiting friends, reading books, shopping or watching television (including in neighbours' houses).

Girl Child Labour

The extent of prevalence of child labour, as per its official definition, is around 8 per cent in the project area, with the incidence of girl child labour being higher like in the rest of Tamil Nadu (if one defined child labour more broadly to include housework, 50 per cent of girl children of members would belong to this category).[8] Beedi rolling, gem cutting, and handloom weaving are cottage industries in which largely girl children of member households work, and largely during out of school hours. Three out of 200 members met, however, had pulled their children out of school to contribute labour to the IGP initiated through the loan activity. The hours of working varied from two hours for school-going

---

[8] Data from the 1991 census reveals the presence of over 6.06 lakh (606,000) child labourers in the main and marginal worker category in Tamil Nadu. In urban areas, in the age group of 5–14 years, 2.4 per cent of girl children are classified as workers as against 5.9 per cent boys. In rural areas, 10 per cent of the girl children in the age group 5–14 are workers, as against 4 per cent of boys (National Sample Survey, 49th round). Dalit children constitute a significant proportion of child labourers in rural areas.

children to 8–10 hours for dropouts. Persistence of child labour is due to seasonal variation in levels of poverty and cannot be attributed to increased economic activity under the programme. The absence of good quality education and adequate number of women teachers is another influencing factor. In some areas, the absence of exclusive high schools for girls has led to adolescent girls dropping out. Dropouts were higher in Urdu schools run by the government for Muslims because of vacancies in the post of the teachers.

Women's Control over Physical Mobility

The household-level study covering 31 households reveals considerable expansion in mobility of women across caste, religion, headship and age group. Forty-seven per cent of women members interviewed had visited new places and travelled a longer distance than earlier. Centre leaders visited branch offices weekly. They also visited the Village Administrative Officer for getting insurance claims in the event of death or loss to members' property. Expansion in mobility was lower amongst women heading households due to higher domestic workload and absence of child care support. The degree of expansion in women's mobility and interaction was also lesser among Muslim women, who had to take the permission of the Jamaat (religious committee) leaders before travelling outside the village.

Another dimension of mobility is whether women travel alone or with their spouse. Ninety per cent of the women reported that they visit ration shops, other shops, schools and hospitals alone. Husbands or sons escorted 40 per cent of the women members when they went to the theatre or to their parents' houses. Seventy per cent of the women members whose parents lived in the same village reported that they have freedom to visit their parents any time they wished.

The mobility of women members was restricted during the night, other than for shopping or visiting temples. Like elsewhere in India, Hindu women members are prevented from entering temples during menstruation. They cannot go close to the temple deity on all days because of social gender norms. Muslim women members in the project area are prevented from worshipping in the mosque on these days. Across communities, women continue to be prevented from visiting burial or cremation grounds at times of death in the household. Yet another issue is the persistence of caste hierarchies, restricting mobility and interaction. Fifteen per cent of women from backward classes mentioned that they were forbidden to visit group members in dalit colonies.[9]

Access to Food, Health Care and Fuel

An analysis of access to food in 31 member households indicates that, in all the households, consumption of food has increased with increase in household income. Prior to joining the SHGs, women faced the brunt of food shortage. Ninety-two per cent of member households access three meals a day, in contrast to 60 per cent before the commencement of the micro-credit programme. Most members can even afford luxury foods such as meat during weekends. All members, except new migrants, have access to ration cards and hence the public distribution system for essential food items such as grains, sugar and oil. During the lean season, poor members take consumption loans to ward off starvation. No inequality was reported in distribution of special food among male and female children in 98 per cent of member households. However, the nutritional status of members and their children is still an issue of concern. Forty per cent of the members' girl children in the age group 0–3 years were malnourished in comparison to 20 per cent (of girl children) amongst non-members. A similar disparity was also noted with respect to boy children. Twelve per cent of boy children of members were in

---

[9] Dalits are the lowermost in the caste hierarchy, oppressed for generations and regarded as untouchables. Backward castes, though marginalized economically and socially, are not considered untouchable and are well within the caste system; they are considered one level below the upper castes.

the severe malnourishment category in contrast to 2 per cent in the case of non-members. Given that there was no marked variation in the poverty profile of members and non-members, it appears that the increase in workload of members may be accompanied by a decline in attention to young children.

However, higher malnutrition among children in the 0–3 age group was not necessarily leading to higher deaths, pointing to the possibility that the member households had greater incomes to meet emergency health costs of children. On checking the records available in *anganwadi* centres, it was observed that six infants had died in non-member households in the five villages studied, but only two had died in the case of member households.

Immunization practices among members revealed that children born after group formation had received BCG, oral polio, DPT, and measles vaccines as per schedule, due to the awareness generated through inputs from the ASA staff. Pregnant members were found to take immunization against tetanus. Nevertheless, it does appear that women's health problems get addressed only if they become chronic or life-threatening, partly because they themselves do not accord adequate attention to their problems, but also because male members respond to women's illnesses only when the household gets affected as a result. On studying the expenditure pattern of women members, it was found that, on average, they were spending only 4 per cent of their monthly income on personal health. Pregnant members found it difficult to avail maternity benefits of Rs 500 per delivery from the government because of corruption and lengthy procedures.

Most members and their husbands are unaware of healthy practices with regard to nutrition and hygiene. In some instances, members had taken loans for cultivation or selling greens but their intake of greens routinely and during pregnancy was limited to once a week, leading to anaemia. All births of children of members after group formation have been registered. Sanitation facilities have not improved after enrolment under the project. None of the member households studied had access to toilet facilities. Around 72 per cent of the households covered in the study had not adopted the small

312 ◆ Kalpana Sankar

household norm. Members with children with cerebral palsy were not aware about the special support facilities schools run by government for children with this ailment. Domestic air pollution and fuel shortage are two other problems facing members of ASA. With rural firewood being the single largest source of energy, respiratory infections in newborn and children, adverse pregnancy outcomes, chronic lung diseases, and cancer in women are common in the project area. As of now, ASA and the SHGs have not intervened on these issues. They can motivate members to take consumption loans for liquefied petroleum gas (LPG) stoves or promote smokeless and low-firewood-intensive *chulhas*. Occupational health hazards are also seen as important factors that impact on women workers engaged in occupations such as *beedi* rolling and gem cutting; they need to be sensitized on preventive measures.

Education and Child Care

A study of education and literacy levels of 200 members in 40 groups covered during the study suggests that 50 per cent of women members are illiterate (though they have learnt how to sign after joining the group). Forty-six per cent of the women had studied up to the primary or middle level, and 4 per cent had studied till the higher secondary level. Restrictions on mobility after puberty and early marriage were two reasons for discontinuity. It is also a concern that 50 per cent of members are non-literate, as literacy and numeracy skills are necessary adjuncts to ensure that group members are aware of the details of their savings, loans, and repayment as well as to ensure control and transparency with respect to records. Only with enhanced literacy and numeracy skills can members take over the role of maintaining records from field officers.

If one examines children's education, an issue that needs to be looked into is subtle enhancement of inequality in access to quality education. Twelve out of the 200 women members reported that because of increased incomes they have enrolled their sons in private convent schools (run by

Christian institutions). None reported having enrolled their daughters into such schools.

Closely related to girls' education and women's economic participation is the issue of child care. All the SHG women have access to an *anganwadi* or a *balwadi*,[10] which offer child care services within their village premises. Seventy-six per cent of the SHG members with children in the 0–5 age group sent their children to *balwadi* centres. The rest complained about the poor services and upkeep of *balwadis* and preferred to use the services of their mothers, mothers-in-law, aged sisters, or daughters. SHG members should be motivated to monitor the general upkeep of *balwadi* centres, as well as fetch water/contribute locally available vegetables to nutrition centres.

Control over Body

One of the aspects of women's control over their bodies is whether they have a say in whom they want to marry. Since the beneficiaries of micro-finance intervention are married women, existing or proposed practices with regard to marriages of daughters were examined. In 60 per cent of the households, the elders collectively decide whom the girls should marry. The mother exercises choice in 10 per cent of the households, and the father or brother (in the case of widows) in 20 per cent of the households. Only in 10 per cent of the households girls exercise choice themselves, that too in the context of proposals put forward by their parents.

Issues of reproductive decision-making were discussed with 21 members, with respect to their own lives. Husbands or in-laws make decisions on the number and spacing of children, contraceptive use, and abortions in 52 per cent of the households. In the rest of the households, members and

---

10 *Anganwadi* and *balwadi* centres are both child welfare centres and perform similar functions. Earlier, the term 'balwadi' was used to refer to these centres; currently, the term *anganwadi* is used throughout the country to refer to child welfare centres.

their husbands take decisions jointly. Sixty-five per cent of
the women and 30 per cent of the men have undergone
sterilization; 5 per cent have not taken any measures because of poor health condition.

Another aspect of control over body is the right over one's
sexuality. Women seem to consider the fulfilment of their
husbands' desires as their social obligation. Women seem
to give in to their husband's sexual demands irrespective of
their health condition, simply to prevent their husbands
from having extramarital affairs. Seventy per cent of the
members said that their husbands decided when to have
sexual relations with them; in the case of the remaining,
decisions were taken jointly.

A high 45 per cent of the interviewed women experienced
verbal abuse, 12 per cent reported wife battering, 18 per
cent suffered negligence and 22 per cent experienced emotional abuse. Thus, domestic violence continues to be high,
though rates of wife battering are lower than figures reported in Tamil Nadu from other studies.

Intra-Household Decision-making and Political Participation

ASA's micro-credit programme has resulted in the enhancement of intra-household decision-making powers of women
in MHHs. Women dominate decisions on food preparation
(100 per cent of households) and whether to take a loan
from the SHG and for what (77 per cent). Decisions with
regard to land and asset purchase are decided jointly in 58
per cent of households, and on production and selling of products in 33 per cent households. However, actual selling is
mainly in the hands of men. There has been an overall
increase in decision-making powers because of asset creation and control over income. The decision-making power
of women who head their households (in particular widows,
constituting 12 per cent of the sample) is higher than
women in MHHs. The decision-making powers of Muslim
women, on the other hand, seem low, pointing to the need
for greater attention to this group. Again, this inference
needs to be validated with a larger sample.

It is a concern that in 33 per cent of the households, decisions on whether to take a loan is taken by others, that is women become conduits of loans for others, mainly husbands. In some instances, mothers-in-law used the membership of their daughters-in-law to access loans for their enterprises; in such instances, the member had control over neither the loan nor the income.

Apart from who takes decisions, is the issue of what decisions are taken within the household. Only 10 per cent of the women members openly admitted their preference for male children, but adverse and declining sex ratio and juvenile sex ratio in the project area, especially Madurai and Trichy districts, point to gender discrimination and prevalence of female foeticide. Whether women members are forced by other household members to endorse female foeticide, or they themselves havé internalized such values is an issue worth exploring.

Moving on to the public space, an impressive 90 per cent of the women members have access to voter identity cards. Women decide whom to vote for in 40 per cent of the households, while in the rest of the cases, the husbands take the decision. Muslim women reported that they vote for the candidate recommended by the Jamaat.

Seventy-five per cent of ASA's women members (1 per cent) contested the local body elections in October 2001, supported by loans from ASA for the initial deposit. Ninety of them (51 per cent) got elected, 85 as ward members, two as councillors, and three as panchayat presidents. However, poor members do not come forward as much as the (comparatively) better-off to contest elections, as they cannot afford to lose their wages or income (no salary is provided for panchayat members). Women's collective engagement in the gram sabha is discussed in the following section on collective empowerment.

Collective Empowerment

At the collective level, women members have begun to engage with community structures, land and labour markets, government bodies, and banks. They use these interactions to demand that their needs and concerns be addressed. There is, of course, room for building upon this foundation in the coming years.

ASA, for example, has organized men and women tenants into tenant groups. Most women members of the tenant group are also members of the SHG. The tenant group has taken up the case of enforcement of the Tenancy Act and filed litigation for obtaining electricity connection in the name of tenants. Both men and women who are tenants have benefited from this legal action, which was started prior to the launch of the micro-credit programme. Women members are also waging struggles to demand higher and equal wages, though results are not as yet visible. As yet collective activities for selling and purchase of grains and enterprise products have not begun.

At the community level, the presence of women's groups is being felt, particularly after the formation of federations in 1990 at the branch level. Rallies on International Women's Day and padayatras have brought visibility to women's groups at different levels. However, traditional village or caste panchayats, which normally uphold gender norms of society, do not call upon women's groups to mediate in disputes involving women's interests.

As of now members as a collective do not attend Gram Sabha meetings of the statutory panchayats regularly.[11] This is a space that groups should enter and influence in the coming years, and strengthen allocation to basic amenities like water, toilets, roads and transport. Panchayat presidents seem enthusiastic about the participation of SHG members. If given training, SHGs could also play a role in making gram sabhas accountable to poor women through monitoring revenues and expenditures.

The SHGs and ASA have established contacts with the state forest department. Linkages with other line departments including nutrition, health, education and agriculture may need to improve in the coming years, as also with commercial banks. Currently, SHGs are not linked to the

---

[11] Members from the group elected as ward members or presidents of course attend the meetings, but in their individual capacities.

Tamil Nadu government's state-funded micro-credit programme covering the entire state.

Another key aspect of collective empowerment is how far
the groups can function without the support of ASA. Different SHGs are at different stages of development: some can
conduct meetings, take decisions, and resolve internal conflicts independent of ASA; others cannot. As of now, the ASA
supports the weaker groups in conducting meetings. Federations at the cluster and federation level are not called
upon to strengthen the weaker groups. In older branches,
networking amongst SHGs through cluster and branch meetings is strong, but this is yet to take place in ASA's groups
in new branches. Irrespective of how mature the groups
are, they are dependent on ASA for maintenance of records
and accounts.

Changes in the Larger
Socio-economic Environment

At the wider level, some changes in the poverty profiles of
villages are visible. The availability of employment has increased in member households through activity initiated/
expanded through the loan. In 36 per cent of the households, the increase has been stark. Further, because of the
increase in income in the hands of member households,
their purchases from the PDS have increased. The members are less dependent on moneylenders now than earlier.
To that extent, the turnover of lending by moneylenders may
have reduced. Through their collective power, groups have
been able to prevent malpractices among village institutions.

As the coverage of dalits is higher than their representation in the population, it is also likely that the caste profile
of people in poverty in the village has changed slightly.
Caste-specific dimensions of poverty are less stark than
earlier. Dalit and non-dalit members visit each other's
houses, share food, celebrate festivals together, and drink
water from the same tumblers. In the four centres and 15

groups visited, the community has accepted a dalit woman as a centre or group leader, which by their admission was not possible initially.

Given that ASA's coverage of the poor in each village ranges from 20 to 50 per cent, it is, however, difficult to say that the poverty profile of the village has totally changed. A significant proportion of the poor is still outside the purview of SHGs. Consequently, a reduction in number of operating moneylenders could not be observed. Neither could any reduction in interest rate charged by moneylenders be seen; it continues at 120 per cent. Similarly, though caste feelings within the group are declining, the same cannot be said of the village as a whole. Twenty-five per cent of dalit women still reported that they could not fetch drinking water from wells in upper caste areas.

Moving beyond the village, some positive changes can be seen in wider institutions. ASA's micro-finance programme has positively influenced the attitudes of SIDBI and ICICI Bank towards lending to the poor. Notwithstanding this change, the attitudes of commercial banking institutions at the block and district levels remain anti-poor. This is mainly because the linkage between SHGs and commercial banks has not been strong. Neither is the groups' influence on policies of different government departments (rural, municipal administration, health, or the Tamil Nadu Corporation for the Development of Women [TNCDW]) their strong point.

The micro-credit programme has also influenced other NGOs, particularly dalit NGOs in south India, through the training and exposure it offers. Many NGOs who have visited ASA have commenced similar programmes in their project areas.

Conclusion

Going back to the first of the three questions raised in the introduction—whether micro-credit is adequate for poverty reduction and women's empowerment—the ASA case study suggests that micro-finance interventions alone are not enough for poverty reduction and women's empowerment. An integrated strategy for poverty reduction and women's empowerment is important, which while including micro-finance as a component, goes beyond. Micro-credit, insurance, enterprise development training, asset creation and marketing support are all part of the strategy required for poverty reduction. For fostering women's empowerment, women SHGs should be encouraged to discuss not only savings and credit, but also gender-specific interests (rights of women to land, equal wages for work of equal value, etc.), leading to an annual social action plan. Literacy and numeracy skills are necessary, though not sufficient, for women's empowerment. It is essential to form federations of small groups and strengthen their linkages and bargaining powers vis-à-vis the government (particularly child care, agriculture, health and education departments), PRIs and banks. Creation of special funds, such as what ASA has done, for enabling poor women to contest elections seems crucial.

On the role of economic empowerment in the total empowerment of women, the case study indicates that economic empowerment is a good starting point for furthering empowerment in other spheres, but it is not an adequate strategy. Additional interventions, outlined in the chapter, to further social and political empowerment may be essential.

On the issue of whether greater incomes for poor households translate into greater education of children and girl children, the study highlights that expansion or launching of new economic enterprises by women and their husbands through SHG loans may increase the work burden of children, particularly girl children (due to double burden of increased enterprise-related work, and increased domestic work and child care responsibilities with mothers being busier). This may lower the educational attainment of children and, in some cases, lead to children being pulled out of schools. Strengthening child care facilities, as also raising awareness on the importance of children's and girl children's education, is essential to combat this trend.

Apart from throwing light on these three key issues, the ASA case study points to some operational lessons for pro-poor, pro-dalit and pro-women social mobilization and micro-credit interventions. It points to how a housing index could be used for effective targeting of the poor. Focusing on dalits, as done by ASA, seems another effective strategy to reach out to poor, as most dalits are poor. ASA experience suggests that while a pro-dalit orientation is necessary, dalits and poor non-dalits need to be brought together in groups to break caste hierarchies. Ensuring attendance, promoting consensual decision-making, and investing in training are essential components of social mobilization. Training needs to be imparted to members on the concept of SHGs, gender issues, social and community action programmes, and skills in numeracy, literacy and record maintenance. Inputs on health, nutrition, education and hygiene seem essential if improved income is to lead to improved well-being.

Reaching credit to poor women requires meticulous planning, easy documentation procedures, and timely credit disbursal. There is a need to pay attention to the purpose of loans taken by members, as different loans have different implications for women's economic empowerment. Loans for enterprises controlled by women, as per social norms, lead to greater control of women over the income than loans for enterprises controlled by men. Loans from banks to meet large-scale credit needs are necessary for women's empowerment. Merely relying upon internal resources is not adequate.

Savings need to be flexible (but regular) rather than fixed to reach out to the poor. To develop confidence in the system of savings, members should be allowed to withdraw savings after some time, or dividends should be declared. Savings need to be rotated as loans among members. Over and above regular savings, members should ideally be allowed to save money as deposits when they have excess money to capture all the savings among members.

For financial sustainability, high repayment rates and rotation of capital are essential. Costs can be lowered by training women members with some basic education to take up recording and accounting responsibilities. Social sustainability, however, requires several additional strategies: rotation of responsibility to go to banks, building skills amongst group members to maintain and monitor minute books and books of account, and building skills to negotiate with banks and other organizations. ASA's strategy of insisting that the loan should lead to some asset creation/expansion before the first 15 days of taking loan has paid off, and strengthened asset creation. Financial monitoring of groups is also important. There is also a need for monitoring gender and social sensitivity of group processes and impact. The case study also throws light on the institutional requirement for dalit and women's empowerment. Representation of dalits and women in intermediary organizations/MFIs at leadership levels seems essential if micro-credit programmes on the ground are to be dalit and gender-sensitive. Given the difficulty of getting women staff at the field level, the strategy of training and appointing federation members as cluster leaders seems effective. It also strengthens the leadership and mobility of women members. The strategy of linking the salaries of field staff to repayment performance of groups in their areas seems helpful for ensuring high levels of repayment. A similar system of linking staff salaries to gender/social sensitivity and group performance may be essential.

References

ASA (Activists for Social Action), 2000, *Annual Report*, Tiruchirapalli: ASA.

Murthy, R.K., Rajaraman, Sankar K., D'Souza, W., and Valsarajan, A., 2001, 'Gender and Poverty Impact Evaluation of Micro-credit', *Newsreach*, April.

Naponen, Helzi, 2003, 'Internal Learning Systems: A Review of Existing Experience', in L. Mayoux (ed.), *Sustainable Learning for Women's Empowerment: Ways Forward in Micro-finance*, Kolkata: Sanskriti.

8

Conclusion: Analysing the Link

Ranjani K. Murthy and Joy Deshmukh-Ranadive*

The six case studies have provided significant findings regarding the potential of micro-credit and the effort of intervening organizations in reducing poverty and empowering women. This concluding chapter draws lessons from these findings, placing them within the analytical framework of poverty and empowerment presented in the introductory chapter. The lessons are valuable in ascertaining both the potential and limitations of micro-credit in alleviating poverty and empowering women. They also throw light on the methods that can be used by organizations to increase the efficacy of their interventions.

Can Micro-credit Alleviate Poverty?

As discussed in the introductory chapter, poverty can be seen as an interlocking failure of ownership, exchange and consumption entitlements and outcomes, shaped both by the domestic and macro environments. The case studies support the view that reducing poverty entails addressing these failures. Each of the intermediary organizations

* We are grateful to the participants of the January 2002 workshop on *Social Mobilization, Micro-credit and Women's Empowerment* for pointing to several of these lessons, while others emerged through the post-workshop analysis by the authors.

studied has attempted to address one, or a combination of, failure(s). The impact of interventions on reducing poverty is better when an attempt has been made to address all three kinds of failures, than only one. Activists for Social Action (ASA), Lokadrusti, Swayam Shikshan Prayog (SSP), and the South Asia Poverty Alleviation Programme (SAPAP) in Andhra Pradesh have sought to expand ownership of assets by the poor (land lease), returns to their labour and produce (through credit, watershed development, wage struggles), and access to state rations. These organizations have had a greater impact than those that have focused only on micro-credit. Expanding the ownership of immovable assets—land and house—by poor households seems particularly important for poverty reduction, yet also the most difficult to achieve. The extent of poverty impact of the SAPAP project, for example, varied with the economic backgrounds and land ownerships of members at the time of joining the group, being higher among those who had marginal or small land to begin with, and lower among the totally landless. While some new immovable assets have been created for poor households through the project, it has not been able to make a marked dent on the existing land distribution in villages.

The case studies suggest that a combination of two strategies is required for effective poverty reduction: development and struggle.[1] Some organizations have adopted only the development path (SHARE Micro-finance Limited [SML] and DHAN), while others have straddled a combination of development and struggle (for example, ASA, Lokadrusti, SSP and SAPAP). ASA, for example, has not only initiated credit programmes (a development intervention) for the poor in its project area, but also supported their struggle for land and wage rights. The impact upon poverty of ASA is perhaps higher than those organizations that provide only development support. As many as 97 per cent of the members of ASA experienced increases in income, compared to 77 per cent in the case of SML's members. There is also a requirement

---

[1] Also see Carr et al. (1996) for a similar conclusion from case studies that they reviewed.

of directing struggles to the needs of the elderly and the chronically ill among the poor and the differentially abled who cannot earn. Normally, such people are outside the ambit of collectives formed by the intermediary organizations, as they cannot save or attend meetings regularly. Such social groups need access to welfare programmes or social security provided by the government. Except SAPAP, which works with the differentially abled, none of the intermediary organizations has helped these social groups to mobilize welfare programmes. As a result, these groups have either been excluded from the programmes and benefits, or have remained at the fringes. Put in another way, waging struggles to make the state accountable to the poor is central to poverty reduction.

Further, the case studies point to the need for directly attacking both the dimensions and causes of poverty. As Kabeer and Murthy (1999) argue, one needs to adopt both an 'ends' and 'means' perspective to poverty reduction. In the context of poverty, 'ends' refer to the satisfaction of basic needs while 'means' refer to the resources necessary to meet basic needs like income, land, livestock and employment (ibid.). Improved income does not always lead to improved well-being, due to leakages on excessive alcohol consumption, gambling, drug consumption and consumption of luxury goods. The strength of the SAPAP and Lokadrusti programmes, for example, has been the fact that they have not only sought to increase the asset bases and incomes of the poor, but also to improve food security and children's access to education. As a result, the impact on human poverty[2]—health, nutrition and education levels—has been

---

[2] The term 'human poverty' was introduced in the *Human Development Report*, 1998, as distinct from 'income poverty'. Income poverty refers to lack of income to meet basic needs. The underpinning assumption is that increased income will lead to improved well-being. Human poverty, on the other hand, captures direct well-being in terms of literacy, life expectancy, nutrition and access to health and safe water. The focus on income poverty is on (some of the) means of poverty reduction, while human poverty focuses more on the 'ends' (UNDP, 1997).

more marked in these two organizations. On the other hand, in the case of the ASA, which did not focus so much on the 'ends', malnutrition was higher among children of members than those of non-members (though of similar economic backgrounds).[3] But even in the case of SAPAP, the net[4] percentage of poor households reporting an increase in income was higher than those reporting an improvement in well-being. This can be partly attributed to the leakages of male, and in some instances female, income on alcohol consumption.

Poverty reduction programmes need to not only enhance access to basic needs and means to meet it, but also arrest expenditure leakages. The case studies point to two kinds of leakages: leakages on social evils, and leakages due to diseconomies of small-scale and scattered consumption. Falling under the first category are leakages on alcohol consumption, *beedi* consumption, dowry, puberty rites and elaborate death ceremonies, which have been noted in almost all the case studies. In particular, leakages such as expenditure on dowry can plunge households which had improved through participation in livelihood programmes back into poverty, while the impact of leakages on excessive alcohol consumption and gambling are more chronic and gradual in nature (see the SAPAP study). None of the case studies has systematically sought to address the impact of such leakages on social evils. A few organizations, like Lokadrusti and SAPAP, however, have sought to redress the diseconomies of small-scale purchases of consumption goods. Lokadrusti's 'Muthi Chawal' programme has not only reduced outflow of food grains from the village but has also

---

[3] Unlike case studies from Bangladesh that have pointed to children's nutritional enhancement with women's participation in micro-credit programmes (Pitt et al., 1999), the ASA experience as well as the experience from Mahalir Thittam in Tamil Nadu brings out that, at times, women's participation may be at the cost of nutrition of children (see Murthy et al., 2001). This aspect needs to be examined through a larger sample size and more case studies.

[4] The difference between the percentage reporting improvement to those reporting deterioration.

reduced the price of food grains for food-deficient households, which otherwise would have had to pay high prices because they cannot purchase in bulk. The programme has also reduced the time-to-market for the consumption of items from far-off markets. In addition to promoting grain banks in some areas, in one of the districts, SAPAP is supporting groups for bulk purchase of grains, pulses and oil for members from wholesale markets as well as government godowns.

It is definitely possible for group-based micro-credit interventions to reach a section of the poor, expand their access to resources, increase self-employment opportunities and reduce poverty, provided adequate investment is made in social mobilization, capital formation, capacity building, and pro-poor programme design. However, this potential can be realized only if the state continues to play an active role in the delivery of essential services (health, education, public distribution system [PDS]) and pro-poor policy formulation.[5] Without a pro-poor macro-policy environment, micro-credit programmes cannot be successful in poverty reduction.

Almost all the case studies showed that some ultra-poor[6] groups like elderly poor households, chronic distress migrant households and households with severely disabled people (who cannot earn) often fall outside the ambit of such programmes. To reach them, it is necessary to combine micro-credit with welfare programmes (for elderly, differentially abled who are unable to earn) and strategies to expand wage employment and land rights (chronic migrants). The latter set of added interventions, as well as collective interventions in labour and commodity markets, may also

---

[5] Based on UNICEF-supported country case studies covering Nepal, Vietnam, Egypt, India and Kenya, Nigam (2000) also points that micro-credit can reduce the worst manifestations of poverty only when it is combined with basic social services and key social development messages.

[6] Term first used by Lipton (1990) to refer to those whose access to resources, due to lack of land and skills, is so low that they are at significant risk of undernutrition.

be necessary to make a significant dent on poverty of the poorest members (among those earning) who have joined groups. To that extent, micro-credit programmes need to be located within a broader sustainable livelihoods framework.[7]

The case studies support the view that as a significant proportion of the poor are dalits, it is central that poverty reduction strategies target them. The case studies also point out that like gender-specific aspects, there are caste-specific dimensions and causes of poverty. As illustrated by the SAPAP, ASA and SSP studies, whether all caste groups (economically) benefit equally through the micro-credit programme depends on how far the rules of the group are pro-dalit, that is, whether dalits are adequately represented as members and leaders, whether they have equal or greater access to credit (number and amount of loans), and whether strategies are woven to expand the asset base of dalits. Also, even when the increase in household income is similar across caste groups, whether the increase in income leads to similar access to basic needs such as nutrition, education and health depends upon the elimination of caste biases in different institutions. As illustrated by the Lokadrusti study, caste barriers are easier to break within the group than outside. Thus conscious strategies have to be added to micro-credit interventions to address caste discrimination existing in *balwadis*, schools, health centres, etc.

---

[7] The most commonly cited definition of livelihood is the one outlined by Chambers and Conway (1992): 'a livelihood comprises the capabilities, assets (stores, resources, claims and access) and activities required for a means of living: a livelihood is sustainable which can cope with and recover from stress and shocks, maintain or enhance its capabilities and assets, and provide sustainable livelihood opportunities for the next generation: and which contributes net benefits to other livelihoods at the local and global levels and in the short and long term'. The livelihood approaches adopted by different agencies, however, differ, based on their ideologies and orientations. For a comparison of livelihood approaches of CARE, OXFAM, UNDP and DFID, see Carney et al. (1999).

Can Micro-credit Address
Gender-specific Poverty?[8]

The question of whether women constitute a large proportion of the poor has been debated upon in the recent years,
though with no global consensus (Lockwood and Baden,
1995). The case studies support the view that women may
constitute a disproportionate proportion of the Indian poor.
Both ASA and SAPAP provide strong empirical evidence to
support the view that amongst the poor, women-headed
households (WHHs)[9] are poorer than male-headed (couple
composed) households (MHHs) in terms of both income measures and measures of access to basic needs such as housing, electricity and water. Single-men-headed households
may be exceptions, but they are few compared to WHHs in
India. As per women's own perceptions, households with
more girls are poorer than those with more boys; pointing to
another aspect of the feminization of of poverty.

The Lokadrusti, ASA and SAPAP case studies also highlight the fact that women are not only more in number among
the poor, but also face poverty more intensely. Within poor
households, women and girls have lesser access to education, nutrition, health and rest than men and boys. As a
result of the interventions of the organizations, the intensity of gender inequalities had been reduced but not eliminated. In fact, most of the case studies have had greater
impacts on reducing collective household poverty, than on
reducing gender differentials within access to basic needs.
Hence, to eliminate gender disparity in access to basic
needs, interventions are required to alter inequalities in
entitlements within households.

---

[8] For a review of the complex relationship between gender and poverty in the international or/and Asian context, see Baden and Milward
(1995), Beneria and Bisnath (1996), Buvinic (1993), Cagatay (1998),
Jackson (1995), Kabeer (1997), Kabeer and Murthy (1999), Lockwood
and Baden (1995) and Murthy and Sankaran (2003).
[9] Not all WHHs are poor. Those with access to remittances from migrant husbands or relatives abroad, or good inheritance through their
late husbands are not necessarily poor.

Faced with poverty, women used more adverse strategies to cope than men. As highlighted by the SAPAP study, women cut down on their own consumption of essentials such as food and clothing more than men to provide for their family in times of stress. In one area,[10] it was observed that some poor women—across castes—were selling their bodies to help their families overcome poverty. Though such adverse practices have declined in the project area due to its interventions, they have not been eliminated. Any effort to reduce women's poverty has to combat such adverse coping strategies.

The case studies also point to the fact that poverty affects men and women differently. In the DHAN project area, it was found that, though few in absolute terms, more women in poor households were unmarried than men for want of dowry. Some poor households married their daughters to elderly men (the latter's second marriage) to reduce expenditure on dowry. In South Asian societies, marriage lends social respectability to women and life without the support of a man can be difficult at different levels for a woman. While one is not endorsing such a social norm, it has also to be acknowledged that in a society where unmarried women and sex outside marriage are frowned upon, lack of access to the institution of marriage disadvantages poor women. So far, access of the poor to sex has been taken for granted because all poor men have access to it; consequently it does not come under the normal list of basic needs of human beings.

Related to the above, what constitutes basic need itself may be defined differently by men and women. The SML, ASA and SAPAP case studies suggest that for women, gas and toilets are part of the definition of basic need; for men, they are not. The SAPAP research team in fact makes a valuable distinction between generic basic needs and gender-specific basic needs. The presence or absence of generic basic needs affects both men and women to similar extent (example, electricity, roof over head) while the presence or absence of

---

[10] Studied by one of the two authors of the conclusion subsequent to the SAPAP study.

the latter affects one gender—here women—more than the other (for example, toilets and gas). To reduce poverty, it is important to expand access to both generic and gender-specific basic needs.

It can be seen that women slip into poverty in gender-specific ways. The DHAN case study captures how a woman slipped into poverty through the death of her husband (and though her husband had gone in for life insurance, the money became a site of contestation between his relatives, her father, and herself). The death of the wife on the other hand does not affect the husband's poverty as much, as chances of widower's remarriage are higher than that of widows (among Hindus), and further the wages of men are higher than that of a women in much of India. Households also slip into poverty due to gender-specific reasons, such as dowry for a daughter's marriage, male alcoholism, and so on. Thus addressing the feminization of poverty entails addressing these gender-specific processes that cause women and households to slip into poverty. As pointed out by the SAPAP research team, 'dowry' is not just a women's rights issue but also has a direct bearing on collective household poverty. Though the poverty impact of the single-women's group in Kurnool was not systematically assessed, it seems an intervention in the right direction. This group is taking up cases such as maintenance and property rights of divorced/abandoned women and property rights of never-married, single women in their natal families, and has been fairly successful.

Apart from gender-specific reasons for women *suddenly* slipping into poverty, there are structural gender-specific factors that have a bearing on why women *chronically* face poverty more intensely than men. The SML and SAPAP case studies point to several of these deep-rooted structural causes of women's poverty: unequal land and housing rights, unequal wages for work of equal value, gender disparities in allocation of resources and responsibilities within household, unequal control over body leading to ill health (low and restricted mobility, violence and high fertility), socio-cultural norms restricting women's work and mobility, and unequal access to political spaces. Thus, it is important to tackle not just the gender-specific dimensions and intensity of women's deprivation, but also the causes.[11] Otherwise there is a danger that improvement in women's lives resulting from improved household income will be contingent upon their continuation in the institution of marriage, that is, in the event of a collapse of their marriage through divorce or desertion, they would be plunged back into poverty. Addressing these structural factors is going to be the challenge for development organizations in the coming years.

The case studies suggest that micro-credit programmes that target women, bring them into leadership positions, and adopt pro-women rules do play vital roles in reducing the feminization of poverty. Micro-credit programmes should be combined with efforts to consciously monitor distribution of food, health care and education within households. Further, strategies to sensitize men on gender-specific basic needs of women (gas, toilets, child care, etc.) are important.[12] Otherwise, there is a danger that increase in income through micro-credit will lead only to improvement in access to generic needs, and not the gender-specific ones. Similarly, strategies are required to strengthen women's

---

[11] See Baden and Milward (1995); Beneria and Bisnath (1996); Cagatay (1998) and Murthy and Sankaran (2003) for a similar argument. Baden and Milward (1995), for example, point to the need for addressing gender discrimination within the household, in labour markets, and in public administration for effective reduction of women's poverty. Beneria and Bisnath (1996) point to the need for reducing women's poverty through expanding their entitlements, rights and capabilities. Cagatay (1998), apart from holding similar views as the earlier authors on reduction of women's poverty, points to the need for engendering macro-economic and trade policies, and budget allocations at the national level.

[12] The evidence from SAPAP suggests that in MHHs, increases in household income translate into enhanced generic basic needs, but not into enhanced gender-specific basic needs. This is not true in the case of WHHs. For example, 77 per cent of women from MHHs participating in the SAPAP programme reported that they were able to access three meals round the year, when compared to 66 per cent in the case of women from WHHs participating in the programme. However, only 9 per cent of women from MHHs had access to gas when compared to 20 per cent in the case of WHHs.

independent access to income and land and housing rights, combat dowry, promote equal wages for work of equal value, increase returns to their produce, and increase women's participation in political processes. Further, along with increasing women's access to independent income, men need to be sensitized to not abdicate their roles in sharing responsibility for contributing to the household income. They also need to be sensitized to share the burden of domestic work and child care. Else, there is a danger that the burden of earning for the household will fall disproportionately on women (see SAPAP), without any change in their reproductive work, leading to an increase in their workload.

Can Micro-credit Empower Women?

The case studies strongly support the position that enabling women to remove constrictions and expand spaces is central to their empowerment. All intermediary organizations have created forums for women to come together and challenge some dimension of the inequitable realities of their life. Some (for example, the SML and DHAN) have sought to challenge mainly economic inequities by expanding economic spaces. Others have endeavoured to support women to challenge inequities in all spaces, though with varying degrees of success. For example, the SAPAP, ASA, SSP and Lokadrusti have organized poor women around multiple issues, such as domestic violence (body space), savings and credit and livelihoods (physical and economic spaces), contesting elections for local self-governance institutions (political space), and caste and tribal atrocities (socio-cultural space). Wherever organizations have attempted to support women's struggles to simultaneously expand several spaces, the impact of the empowerment has been higher.

The case studies also reveal that there are many elements to each space; and expanding access and control over each element is central to women's empowerment. For example, women's economic space can be enhanced through interventions in the areas of finance, land rights, wages, number of days of employment, prices of commodities, and so on. The empowerment impact is better when access to more elements of each space is expanded, rather than just one. For example, through a combination of micro-credit programmes, grain banks, watershed development and women's own banks, SSP, Lokadrusti, SAPAP and DHAN have had greater impacts than organizations that have focused only on micro-finance.

Related to the above observation, the process of empowerment unfolds best when expansion of one space or one element is not achieved at the cost of another. This is however not always easy. In almost all case studies, the expansion of women's economic space within and outside the family has been accompanied by an increase in their workload, thus cutting into their time to expand socio-cultural and political spaces. Though not emerging from the case studies, Khan (1999) observes in the context of Bangladesh that in a few instances women beneficiaries of a micro-credit programme shifted from wage to self-employment, which in itself is an expansion of element of economic space; but where the self-managed enterprise was actually run by the husband, women's control over income in fact reduced. Thus, it is important to distinguish between access and control in discussions around spaces, and expansion of both is important.

This reinforces the need to intervene not just in the macro environment but also in the domestic environment. In fact, the extent of empowerment unleashed by different interventions has been shaped by the extent of emphasis placed on expanding spaces in the household or the domestic environment. All intervening organizations have placed more emphasis on intervening in the macro environment than directly in the domestic, as the former is easier to change than the latter. In particular, private political spaces (intra-household decision-making) are difficult to change, which in turn are determined by socio-cultural spaces (position within the family or household). Other spaces—economic (private and public), physical (private and public)—can be changed to some extent with intervention in the macro environment. However, for socio-cultural (private and public) and domestic political spaces to change, there has to be a change in women's (and men's) mental spaces first. Hence, when attempts are made to alter perceptions on gender relations, these stubborn spaces expand. While some organizations have totally bypassed the domestic sphere, others have intervened selectively in the domestic sphere to ensure that women have command over resources acquired through the programme or to combat instances of domestic violence (ASA, Lokadrusti and SAPAP). The impact of empowerment has been stronger in the latter cases than in the former, though none has been able to totally change the private socio-cultural or private political space, reflected in the persistence of son-preference among women members.

Intervening in the domestic sphere is also necessary to ensure inter-generational and inter-relational equity and sustainability of gains. In some instances, the expansion of women's space has increased the space available to girls as well. For example, with greater awareness and economic means, women across all projects are now more willing to invest in their daughters' education than earlier (though not always equal to sons). However, there need not always be a positive relationship between expansion of women's space and that of their daughters. When asked to whom they will pass their newly acquired property, some of the women members of SAPAP pointed that they would give it to their sons. In most case studies, the expansion of members' economic spaces had been accompanied by an increase in the workload of their children (in particular girl children, during out-of-school hours), cutting into their access to recreation and play (socio-cultural space). In a few instances, the brunt of middle-aged women's participation has been borne by daughters-in-law.

Women's empowerment is also about institutional change. Different institutions shape the domestic and macro environments. The domestic environment is shaped by the rules and norms governing institutions of marriage, family, and household. The macro environment is shaped by multiple institutions: the community (caste and religion), markets (local to global), and the state (bureaucracy, legislature and judiciary). As pointed out by Kabeer (1994), women's empowerment thus entails changing the rules, norms and allocation of resources within different societal institutions in favour of women. Marriage, family, household and community are perhaps the most difficult of these institutions to change. At different times in the savings and credit group's life-cycle, particular institutions may assume importance. For example, in Lohara village of the SSP project area, the savings and credit group took up the case of a woman who was driven to commit suicide due to violence in the family. The process of taking up this issue strengthened the group immensely. Only later did other issues such as malfunctioning of the PDS run by the government become important. Thus, the trajectory of empowerment processes cannot be pre-planned.

Within different institutions, gender relations are only one axiom of inequity confronting women from marginalized sections. Social relations of caste, class, ethnicity, age and physical ability are the other variables. Thus, women's empowerment entails expansions of spaces not only for women as gendered groups, but also as members of other oppressed groups. Both ASA and SAPAP have attempted to expand spaces of both women and dalits, and their impact on dalit women's empowerment is more visible. Lokadrusti has similarly focused on issues of gender and ethnicity, and their impact on tribal women's empowerment is more visible. Given the diversity among women, care should be taken to ensure that the spaces of the most oppressed groups among women are expanded first, and at no cost is their space eroded. In worst cases, expanding spaces for the relatively better-off women may constrict spaces for a more vulnerable group of women. A classic example, though not from the case studies, is credit support for rice mills and mechanized harvesters, which may reduce drudgery or lower labour hiring costs for the upper-class women but adversely affect the livelihood of women from the labouring class.[13]

An analysis of the inequities that have been reduced, and those that have not, reiterates the view that expanding mental space is central to expanding other spaces. Because women members of DHAN have started to challenge their socially internalized perception that the public is the men's

---

[13] See Bangladesh case study in Moser (1993).

domain, they are negotiating confidently with bankers, government officials and traders, thereby expanding economic spaces. On the other hand, perceptions on gender division of domestic work are yet to break among DHAN members, leading to increase in women's workload with their economic participation. The nature of socially conditioned blocks that women break down, shapes the pace and direction of empowerment in their lives, as well as that of their daughters. Where the mental map on son-preference and girls' chastity persists, the daughters' physical and sociocultural spaces may not expand with the expansion of that of their (member) mothers (see SAPAP study). Equally essential for women's empowerment is an expansion in the mental spaces of other members in the family, particularly the men. The SML case study points that fathers- and mothers-in-law influence the number of children that their daughters-in law have. The latter are expected to produce children till they deliver a male child.

The case studies also point to several strategies for expanding the mental spaces of women. The first is organizing collectives of poor women of similar socio-economic backgrounds and, through them, creating room for critically questioning and challenging inequalities. All the organizations studied have formed women's collectives, though the organizational strategies have differed.[14] Another key strategy for expanding mental spaces is 'transformative capacity building', which challenges gender, caste and other social relations.[15] Training in capacity building is therefore crucial to

---

[14] In the case of ASA and SML, primary-level groups have been small, comprising five members each. The groups formed under the SAPAP, Lokadrusti, SSP and DHAN have been larger, comprising 15–30 members.

[15] This concept is used by Kannabiran (1996) and Murthy (1998). Kannabiran distinguishes between transformative gender training that integrates an analysis of issues of power, privilege, culture and tradition with access to and control over resources; and project-oriented gender training, which is limited to project implementation and aims at achieving a more efficient delivery of gender equity. Murthy opines that at a bare minimum gender-transformative training seeks to provide an understanding of gender at an analytical rather than descriptive level, emphasizing the political point that women occupy a subordinate position not because they are themselves the problem but because of the socially constructed power relations between men and women played out within different institutions of society.

changing mindsets. However, not all training programmes transform gender and social relations. Much depends on how far gender concerns are institutionalized within the training. ASA and SAPAP have included issues such as women's subordination, women's legal rights and government's programmes for women's empowerment within the training provided to members of groups, and the empowerment impact of such training is visible. SSP has drawn upon several non-training strategies for gender-transforming capacity building, like organizing gender-aware study tours, peer group exchanges, *melavas*, information camps and learning fora including different stakeholders.[16] Adopting a range of transformative capacity building strategies, rather than one, for expanding mental spaces seems important.

While collectives are important for the expansion of women's mental and other spaces, not any kind of collectives can lead to such a transformation. Equitable access to space *within* the collective is essential. Each collective, like the domestic and macro environments, can be seen as comprising political, socio-cultural, physical and economic spaces. The process of empowerment unfolds better when marginalized members have equitable access to such spaces. In almost each organization studied, some collectives have fostered such equity, while others have not. The very poor, extremely sick and elderly tended to participate less in some collectives, and assumed fewer leadership positions. Other than ASA and SAPAP, this was also true of dalits when compared to upper castes. Adult, but young daughters and daughters-in-law (below 25 years of age) had lesser access to socio-cultural and political spaces within some collectives when compared to middle-aged mothers and mothers-in-law. The SSP, DHAN and ASA case studies illustrate how literate women—with primary, middle or higher levels of education—dominate leadership positions and maintain records and accounts for groups. This vests

---

[16] For another example of networking as a strategy for transformative capacity building, see the experience of the NGO Anandi in Gujarat elaborated by Dand (2003).

in them the power to represent the groups at cluster meetings, training programmes and workshops and access information to a greater extent than non-literate members. Even among members of the same socio-economic and age strata, some members had greater access to leadership positions than others. Though all intermediary organizations studied espoused leadership rotation, this was difficult to practise in reality.

Equally, economic and physical spaces within the group can be a contested issue. The SAPAP case study shows, for example, that women who were extremely or ultra-poor[17] had access to lesser quantum of loans than the poor. Whether this is due to discrimination, or self-exclusion, is debatable. In some collectives formed by ASA, the leaders had first access to loans due to their higher position in the self-help group (SHG). Moving on to the issue of physical space, the SSP and ASA case studies stress that the physical location of where the collective met is also an important determinant to equity in access. Rotation of meetings in different members' houses and in different villages, for example, ensures equitable access to physical space. On the other hand, when meetings were held in the *sarpanch*'s house, the ultra poor members did not participate in discussions (see the Lokadrusti and ASA case studies). Temples again are not appropriate venues to locate meetings as dalit and menstruating women often are not allowed inside.

Yet another variable that has a bearing on the empowering influence of women's collectives is whether the collective is in reality a women-managed one. Most of the collectives formed by SAPAP, Lokadrusti, SSP, ASA and DHAN were not only officially 'for' women, but also women-managed in reality. There were, however, a few exceptions. In remote villages of the area where Lokadrusti works, it was found that women were subdued in front of men, and men in fact equally occupied the physical and political spaces of the collective. The chances of expanding mental spaces of women

---

[17] Term first used by Lipton (1990) to refer to those whose access to resources, through lack of land and skills, is so low that they are at significant risk of under-nutrition.

were much lower in such instances. In the case of SML, however, the meetings were conducted by its staff, not by the women themselves. How far such a process facilitates women's empowerment is questionable. Collectives may be required at different levels to initiate a process of empowerment. Small collectives (5–20 members) can help only to expand spaces in the economic sphere. Larger collectives at the village, cluster, block, *taluka* and district levels are essential for expanding women's spaces in the macro environment, as well as women's physical (including their own bodies), political and socio-cultural spaces at home. All intermediary organizations studied have formed collectives at the habitat, village, cluster and higher levels. Village-level collectives have helped women negotiate more spaces vis-à-vis village organizations such as panchayats, the PDS, schools, nutrition centres, village health sub-centres, as well as village-level commodity, labour and financial markets. Collectives at the cluster and block levels have played similar roles. For example, in the case of Lokadrusti, they played key roles in strengthening the ability of poor women to engage strategically in the food grain and commodity markets. Collectives initiated by SAPAP at the *mandal* level played important roles in enabling poor women to contest elections to gram panchayats in 2001. SSP collectives at the cluster (10–15 villages in the case of SSP) and larger levels have engaged with government officials in local planning exercises, thus engendering development processes. Equally, the backing of a large collective strengthens women's bargaining power within the household and reduces the incidence of domestic violence. Because of pressure from village-level women's collectives in Tetalpura village in the Lokadrusti project area, the men in the entire village were forced to stop drinking excessive alcohol and the local arrack shop was subsequently closed. The SAPAP collectives at the *mandal* level have reduced the incidence of domestic violence in both members' and non-members' households, through the formation of domestic violence protection committees. However, merely forming collectives beyond the level of the habitat is not enough to expand women's spaces. As observed by the SAPAP research team, such social capital generated through collectives needs to be directed towards making claims on social institutions.

Collectives of different kinds may be required to compensate for institutional failures at domestic and macro environment levels. The habitat-based collective often enhances the bonding and emotional capital of women, which a marital family may or may not provide. In the case of SML, it was observed that members visit their parents less frequently after joining the group. While this was so partly because of time constraints, it was also because they could look up to the group for emotional support. Moving to the macro environment, Mahila Banks (women-run banks) play key roles in compensating for the failure of banks to cater to the credit needs of women. Both DHAN and SAPAP have formed Mahila Banks mainly to bridge this gap. Lokadrusti has formed the 'Muthi Chawal' group to offset the failure of the government-run PDS in meeting women's needs. Labour cooperatives, *agarbatti* collectives and quarry worker collectives have been organized by SAPAP in parts of its project area to address the failure of the labour and commodity markets. Though not illustrated through the case studies, the Mahila Samakhya groups in Gujarat have set up women's courts to render justice to women victims of violence and exploitation who had failed to secure justice from the government's legal machinery (Sharma, 2002).

Finally, the case studies point to the fact that even in instances where the above preconditions for empowerment are taken into account in time-bound project interventions, it would be inaccurate to expect that women will reach a state of 'total empowerment', where no gender inequities exist. In the best of the case studies, a son-preference still persists, property ownership is by and large unequal, and violence against women is yet to be eliminated. Empowerment is hence better understood as a long-term process, rather than as a condition or an end that can be reached in a short span. This brings us to the relevance of the discussion on women's empowerment and spaces to the reduction of women's poverty. Expanding women's physical, economic, political and socio-cultural spaces in the domestic and macro-environmental domains is central to address gender-specific dimensions and causes of poverty. Women's access to and control over physical space of their houses and mobility is again central to combating the feminization of poverty. Where women have been more mobile, as in SSP, they have been able to access information better and bargain more effectively vis-à-vis the government and markets.

Women's economic space is again central to poverty reduction, in particular their independent control over economic resources of the household and outside. Women's ability to partake in decision-making within the household (domestic political space) may influence whether increased income enables enhanced access to gender-specific basic needs such as gas and toilets. Their ability to expand the public political space influences the extent to which local institutions address gender-specific needs and causes of poverty. Expanding the socio-cultural space determines whether improved income and assets in their own names lead to improved well-being through challenging norms on access to food, clothing and education within the household. Given the close relation between gender, poverty and empowerment, it is not surprising that the expansion of spaces is not just central for initiating the process of empowerment but also for addressing gender-specific dimensions and causes of poverty.

Micro-credit is essentially an intervention to expand women's access to economic space in the macro environment. An expansion of this space has, however, not automatically led to that of political and socio-cultural spaces. For example, micro-credit groups have not been able to make a dent into caste panchayats that continue to be male strongholds. Except in instances where a conscious decision has been taken to work on political rights, micro-credit groups have been unable to make local self-governance institutions accountable to women. For example, women's participation in the micro-credit programme of SML has had little impact on women's ability to negotiate their collective interests in gram sabha meetings (though individually, with their families' backing, a few women have contested elections).

Further, the case studies suggest that micro-credit need not automatically lead to expansion of spaces in the domestic environment. The domestic environment is less amenable to change than the macro environment, in particular, elements of body space (for example, violence against women, reproductive rights)[18] and socio-cultural spaces (for example, social norms on gender division of labour). Though women's intra-household access to economic resources has expanded through micro-credit, it has not always been followed by greater control. In almost all the cases studied, agricultural loans and loans for family enterprises have often been managed by men in the MHHs. The fact that across most case studies empowerment impact has been higher among WHHs than MHHs, points to the resilience of the domestic environment. On the whole, in none of the case studies has gender inequalities in the domestic or macro environment disappeared with this single intervention. Neither can it be assumed that with greater time, this result would be automatically achieved.

Strategies to Realize the Potential of Micro-credit

Accepting that micro-credit interventions by themselves have some impact on women's empowerment, there are credit and non-credit strategies required to propel the process of empowerment. Micro-credit programmes should be preceded by a process of social mobilization. That is, a group comprising women should be formed first, common issues confronting members should be taken up, and cohesion should be achieved, before taking on micro-credit activities. DHAN, for example, started its micro-credit interventions only after a process of forming groups of poor women

---

[18] There is evidence from Bangladesh that participation in microcredit programmes enhances contraceptive use through greater access to information and income (Sidney et al., 1997), but this does not automatically imply greater control over reproduction.

around issues concerning the village such as the absence of drinking water, roads and transport facilities. Starting lending operations from day one may lead to a collapse of the group, like in the case of artificially created groups under some government programmes.[19]

It is important that loans and finance be put to strategic uses, which challenge the distribution of resources and power in different institutions: markets, communities, family and state. Loans given through micro-credit programmes should ideally support collective action to change rules and norms of market and state organizations, rather than involve themselves in merely isolated individual activities. Some Lokadrusti groups have eliminated the male middlemen who controlled the local *mahua* trade and changed the gendered nature of this domain. Some women's groups organized by SAPAP have come together as labour co-operatives and taken contracts for construction works of the government. Most private individual contractors, on the other hand, have been men.

Yet another use that loans and group resources should be put to is provision of support to women to overcome barriers that prevent them from assuming equal spaces in public decision-making domains. The micro-credit programme of ASA created a separate credit fund for poor women to contest elections in local self-governance institutions, since poor women rarely have enough funds to submit as election deposits.[20] Unlike women from better-off sections, they cannot rely on the financial support of their husbands in their endeavours.

---

[19] Target-driven methods led to the hasty formation of a majority of DWCRA (Development of Women and Children in Rural Areas) groups. As a result, there was little cohesiveness, and members joined the groups with the sole purpose of availing loans. The policy of identifying 20 eligible women at times led to women from different villages being brought together in one group, which made it difficult to meet periodically. Giving loans immediately after formation is another reason cited for collapse of some of the DWCRA groups (Kabeer and Murthy, 1999).

[20] In India, candidates contesting elections to local self-governance institutions have to place a non-refundable deposit with the Election Commission. If they lose the elections, they cannot claim the deposit.

Another kind of support that poor women require to contest elections is day-long child care services of good quality. The government child care services operate only till 2.30 p.m., which is not adequate. The SAPAP groups put aside money to start *ammavadis* or child care centres to enable women to work, and enter the public decision-making domain. In the case of SSP, the groups used the interest earned through lending to demand better provision of essential services such as food rations from the government. At the same time, care needs to be taken to ensure that such interventions do not enter the domain of the state and shift responsibilities for service provision from the state to poor women. As observed in the synthesis workshop, there is a line of thought that group-based micro-credit interventions are part of a larger globalization and privatization agenda whereby the state is gradually handing over provision of services (such as PDS and maintenance of roads and infrastructure) to SHGs. As most SHGs comprise poor women members, the burden is indirectly being shifted to poor women. In such a context, one needs to examine whether herbal gardens promoted by NGOs through SHGs (as in the case of Lokadrusti) is an example of self-help or of shrinking health services provided by the government.

The management of finances and accounts should be placed in the hands of women themselves. In the SAPAP and SSP groups, the operations were managed by women themselves, from writing minutes, keeping accounts, to keeping track of finances. In the case of DHAN, ASA, SML and Lokadrusti, this was not the case. Outsiders managed these functions. This not only created a dependency on outsiders (mainly men) but also perpetuated the perception that management is a male domain. The low literacy levels among members played a role in the case of Lokadrusti. But such problems can be surmounted by appointing members' daughters or training neo-literates to manage accounts. Thus, it seems critical to balance gender-transformative inputs with managerial skill building.

Yet another solution is the rotation of the responsibilities for visiting banks, travelling out and meeting officials among the members, thus enhancing the mobility of hitherto restricted groups such as Muslims and the upper castes. One more lesson emerging from the DHAN experience is the need for financial accountability of federations to the lower units of SHGs at the village level. The system of interest accumulation only at lower levels ensures that financial decisions of federations are in the interest of primary groups.

Changes in the domestic arena arising out of the micro-credit programme should be monitored. In particular, attention must be paid to who controls the credit and income, and who bears the onus of work and repayment. Wherever micro-credit interventions are not accompanied by attention to changing power relations within the family, women may at times act as conduit of loans to men, for activities that the latter manage. The case studies suggest that around one-third of loans seem to fall under this category. But even here, the onus of work and repayment falls more on the women. In some instances, women cut down on their own expenses or borrow from outside to repay. The case studies reveal that it is not uncommon for women's workload to increase through micro-credit interventions. In SML, there was an attempt to get husbands or relatives to sign on the loan agreement form before a woman raised a loan, but this need not necessarily mean joint sharing of the burden of work or repayment. In Lokadrusti, the NGO seemed to bear the onus of repayment as members perceived that the money belonged to the NGO rather than themselves.

Even if these prerequisites are taken into account, micro-credit interventions by themselves cannot foster the entire gamut of women's empowerment. Several non-credit interventions are required to alter power equations within the family. Protecting bodily integrity[21] is imperative, and there is need for strategies to combat domestic violence and reproductive rights of women. Though several case studies

---

[21] Bodily integrity refers to the right not to have one's body or person interfered with by the state, medical professionals, community, or family. The 1993 World Conference on Human Rights held in Vienna in 1993 explicitly recognized that violence against women and violation of their reproduction and sexual rights are violation of women's bodily integrity (UN, 1998).

support the view that violence has reduced as a result of micro-credit interventions, the reduction has been minimal when compared to other improvements in spheres such as mobility and access to resources.[22] Strategies to combat domestic violence may include the formation of watchdog committees to prevent domestic violence, initiation of women's courts to facilitate extra-legal redress; sensitization of boys, youth and men on gender and masculinity; working with teachers to identify and address girl child abuse; and establishment of dowry-free marriage bureaus.[23] The SML case study amply highlighted the gap between desired and actual fertility among member households, and hence the need for specific strategies to strengthen reproductive health and choice of women.[24]

An important intervention is the promotion of sharing of reproductive work and child care responsibilities. As highlighted by the DHAN case study, changes are easier to bring about in the productive arena through micro-credit interventions rather than the reproductive one. As a result, women's participation in such programmes has increased their workload and that of their children, and in the long run may have a bearing on their educational attainment. Gender sensitization of men and their initiation into public child care services are essential (while it is also important to safeguard against child sexual services in such public facilities). In addition, advocacy to increase the timing of government child care centres so that they provide full day care is necessary. While community-managed child care centres are good, they cannot be seen as alternatives to

---

[22] There are, in fact, examples from Bangladesh that point to increase in scale of male violence in response to women's increased access to resources through micro-credit programmes (Schuler et al., 1998).

[23] See ICRW (2002), Poonacha and Pandey (1999) for case studies on such strategies.

[24] Sabala and Kranti (2001) share their experiences in facilitating self-help training programmes on women's bodies and their health with women members and women NGO staff in parts of Andhra Pradesh, Maharashtra and Gujarat between 1993 and 1997. The process of self-help entailed understanding one's body, realizing how it is controlled by different institutions of society, and exploring strategies to gain control over the same.

government ones. It is of paramount necessity for the government to undertake the responsibility of caring and schooling of children in the 0–6 age group.

Yet another non-credit intervention in the social sphere that is necessary is expanding women's access to literacy. The ability to read and write is necessary for group members to effectively monitor records and transactions. It is also a prerequisite for enabling women to access critical information, and to ensure that they are not exploited by middlemen. On the other hand, the ability to read and write does not automatically ensure that they will monitor finances and access critical information, or will not be exploited. Many well-educated women face domestic violence and are disempowered. Thus, the content of literacy programmes is of as much importance as is the implementation. Gender and social concerns have to be woven into the literacy manuals and how the programme is organized.[25]

Though micro-credit interventions target the economic sphere and have the potential to empower women economically, they can at best lead to incremental change in women's control over resources. For example, at best micro-credit programmes can ensure that assets created through the programme are in the women's names, but they cannot make a dent on ownership of ancestral property or marital family's property which may be more substantial than assets created through the micro-credit programme even in poor families. It is hence absolutely necessary to promote rights of women to property in general, and to provide legal support to women who want to avail rights to natal or marital property.

Finance to purchase land in the name of women's groups is another strategy that seems important, especially given

---

[25] See REFLECT for an example of one such gender and socially aware methodology. The term REFLECT stands for Regenerated Freirean Literacy through Empowering Community Techniques. This methodology emerged out of an action research project initiated by ActionAid to explore possible uses of participatory rural appraisal techniques within adult literacy programmes tried out in Uganda, Bangladesh and El Salvador. It is now used in several developing countries (ActionAid, 1996). For an example of its use to promote adult literacy with tribals in Andhra Pradesh, India, see Madhusudhan et al. (2003).

the fact that many women are not in a position to (or sometimes not willing to) pass their property to their daughters against their husband's wishes. In the case of totally landless households, strategies are required to form women wage labourers into labour unions and co-operatives to struggle around equal wages for work of equal value and avail of protection available under existing legislation.

Several non-credit interventions are also essential in the political sphere. These include advocacy strategies to give more powers to local self governance institutions and mainstream gender concerns into their budgeting and decision-making processes; training of women who want to contest elections about their political rights; provision of security to women who wish to contest elections; training of elected women and men representatives on gender concerns; formation of networks of elected women members, and so on.

Institutional Processes that Facilitate Poverty Reduction and Empowerment

While poor women have an inherent potential for transformation, an external stimulus seems necessary to unleash the process. In all the case studies reviewed, the process of empowerment was fostered by an intermediary organization from outside. The process occurred not through a top-down but a bottom-up strategy that released the creative potential of poor women and other oppressed groups. However, it is not as if any intermediary organization whatsoever has the capacity to nurture such a process. Intermediary organizations themselves occupy a space within the macro environment, while trying to challenge inequalities within it and in the domestic environment. How far the institutional processes facilitate empowering and poverty reducing processes depends on whether its perspective, programmes, internal organization and systems are gender-, caste- and class-transformative.

It is apparent from the case studies that intermediary organizations seek to work with women for a variety of reasons. Some like SML seek to work with women because they are better managers of finance and because improving women's condition improves the condition of their families. Others like DHAN and SAPAP seek to work with women because they are the poorest of the poor. Still others like SSP seek to work with women because they are the most oppressed. The empowerment impact of the micro-credit programme has been higher when the main reason for choosing to work with women has been the fact that they are oppressed and need support to be empowered. Even in the latter case, the empowerment impact depends on whether different dimensions of empowerment—social, economic, and political—receive equal emphasis. In the case of SSP, though the main purpose of working with women was to promote women's empowerment, the focus was more on the economic aspects. Similarly, the impact of different organizations on addressing feminization (and dalitization) of poverty has depended not only on how far they recognize that women (and dalits) constitute the poorest, but how far they recognize the gender- (and dalit-) specific dimensions and causes of poverty. The positive impacts of SSP, SAPAP and ASA on reducing women's poverty can be attributed to the attention to the gender-specific dimensions.

A significant finding that emerges is that for intermediary organizations to be in positions to play empowering roles, they should be non-profit or autonomous in nature. The SML experience suggests that there are limits as to how far 'for-profit' organizations can foster women's empowerment, or reduce poverty. The cost of building the capacity of members on gender, arranging for exposure trips, and setting up funds for groups to lobby with the government may make the enterprise unviable. This brings us to another question. While the organization should be non-profit in nature, does it matter whether the intervening agency is a government or a non-government body? The SAPAP study suggests that whether the organization is governmental or non-governmental is less important, but it should function autonomously and in a non-bureaucratic way, have the freedom to draw its staff from both government and outside and its programmes, and its internal organization should be sensitive to gender and social issues. A line department may have much less freedom in this regard than a semi-autonomous government body.

Moving on to the programmatic orientation of empowering organizations, one key lesson emerging from the case studies is the need for role transformation of intermediary organizations with time. Intermediary institutions should work towards making the groups at different levels function independent of them. This can be achieved through building their capacity and linking them with banks and government, and with social movements. In the case of DHAN, over a period, the task of forming and monitoring new groups (that it did in the beginning), was taken over by the older groups. Equally, intermediary organizations should strive towards establishing grass-roots structures so that the women themselves (rather than intermediary organizations) can represent their interests vis-à-vis policy-makers and planners. SSP's multiple stakeholder workshops wherein government planners, women members and NGOs came together on a common platform are a good example in this direction. Whether this role transformation over time implies withdrawal of the intermediary organization is a context-specific question, but gradual weaning of dependence of groups on such organizations is a must.

At the internal organizational level, the impact of intermediary organization on unleashing empowering and poverty reducing processes also depends on how far the physical, economic, political and socio-cultural spaces within the organizations are distributed equitably in terms of gender and caste. It also depends on whether the organization functions in a gender-/social-sensitive manner. The leaders of SAPAP and ASA were well-known for their dalit and social sensitivities, of Lokadrusti for their sensitivity to issues of ethnicity, and of DHAN and SSP for their class and poverty sensitivity. The sensitivity of the leader of the intermediary organization to gender, caste and class shaped the extent to which political and other spaces within the organizations were equitable. More than the biological sex or ascribed caste and class of the leader of the organization, their sensitivity appears to be important.

Given that decisions of leaders are implemented through those at the middle and field levels, the presence of women and dalit staff in significant proportion at all levels does seem to have a bearing on outcomes. At the level of field staff, ascribed sex and caste identity does seem to make a difference as women (and dalits) in the community are more comfortable with staff of the same gender (and caste). In the case of the SSP, the presence of women staff in large numbers did have an impact on the outcomes of women's empowerment. With respect to ASA, the presence of dalits to the tune of 50 per cent of the board and 30 per cent of staff played a role in its impact on poverty reduction and empowerment of dalit women. However, the mere presence of women and dalits in the organization does not automatically translate itself into empowering or poverty-reducing outcomes. Their sensitivity to gender and social issues seems to matter, as well as their continuity in the organization for a long time. For example, though women constituted a greater proportion of field staff in the case of the Development of Women and Children in Rural Areas (DWCRA) programme (Murthy et al., 2002) than SAPAP, the impact of empowerment was stronger in the case of the latter as they had undergone several gender sensitization programmes. Rather than recruiting outsiders whose sensitivity can be questioned, ASA has started recruiting experienced and sensitive women group leaders as field staff. DHAN, on the other hand, has invested in recruiting staff with professional qualifications who are committed to development issues. The pros and cons and the cost-effectiveness of these two approaches may be well worth studying.

An institutional space that seems to facilitate greater gender and social sensitivity within intermediary organizations is the setting up of special focal points or structures to coordinate activities pertaining to gender and social issues. In SAPAP, gender focal points were set up in each district; in one district, a social discrimination focal point was also set up to address dalit issues and facilitate their empowerment. Recently, gender resource groups have been set up in each district to enlist support of other stakeholders to the empowerment agenda of the organization.

However, actual mainstreaming of gender and social concerns should not be the responsibility of the focal points; their role should be coordinating and supporting such integration by line staff. Hence it is important that gender and social concerns be integrated into the job descriptions of all programme and relevant administrative staff.

The other necessary institutional feature is the placing of monitoring and evaluation systems that track not just the delivery of inputs (staff appointed) and processes (groups formed, loans given, training imparted) but also trace whether inputs have led to desired outputs (increases in income) and impacts (women's empowerment and reduction in poverty). Gender-specific indicators need to be evolved for women's empowerment. Poverty indicators need to capture both whether access to basic needs has increased, as well as whether means to overcome poverty has been strengthened for both women and men. Equally important is the need to involve women members in arriving at indicators for monitoring, and in actually tracking changes. DHAN has started such a process.[26] As pointed out earlier, the indicators used by women themselves might be different from those used by staff drawn from the middle class. Furthermore, such indicators may also change with time.

In Conclusion

Therefore, there is no linear link between micro-credit, poverty reduction and women's empowerment. Collective strategies beyond micro-credit to increase the endowments of the poor/women enhance their exchange outcomes vis-à-vis the family, state, markets and community, and expand socio-cultural and political spaces (in both the domestic and macro environment) are required for poverty reduction and women's empowerment. Mental spaces of both women and men need to expand to enable such a process.

---

[26] See Mayoux (2003) and Viswanath (2001) for other efforts in this direction in India.

It is true that women members point that their access to economic resources and generic basic needs has improved through their participation in micro-credit programmes, and that gender disparities in access to basic needs has reduced, though not eliminated. They now travel greater distances without male accompaniment and at hours prohibited before. They now have access to independent sources of savings and credit. When the loan is for their own purposes, women exercise control over the income generated. Women have started entering new economic domains in the macro environment like marketing, procurement and financial management. Wherever women have been provided with capacity building inputs from the intermediary organization they have also started entering local self-governance institutions.

However, such positive impact comes with qualifiers. First, these are dependent on the poverty and gender sensitivity of the programmatic and institutional strategies adopted by the intermediary organization with respect to micro-credit. Second, even if micro-credit interventions are sensitive to issues of poverty and gender discrimination, there are limits to how far micro-credit interventions can by themselves reach the ultra-poor, enable them to improve their economic position, and lead to the elimination of gender inequalities in the domestic and macro environment. Inequalities in access to socio-cultural and political spaces and in control over resources within economic spaces are very difficult to eliminate (in particular in the domestic environment). Third, the extent of positive impact varies across household headship, caste and religion. Further, initial gender relations in the household mediate the extent to which participation in micro-credit programmes result in positive outcomes. Fourth, a strong presence of the state—which is eroding in the context of privatization, liberalization and globalization—is required to regulate the private sector and to sustain the benefits of social service provision.

References

ActionAid, 1996, 'Action Research Report: The Experiences of Three Reflect Pilot Projects in Uganda, Bangladesh and El Salvador', available online at http://www.reflect-action.org.

Baden, S. and Milward, K., 1995, 'Gender and Poverty', BRIDGE Report No. 30, Stockholm: Swedish International Development Agency.

Beneria, L. and Bisnath, S., 1996, Gender and Poverty: An Analysis for Action, Publications for Beijing+5, Gender in Development Program, New York: UNDP.

Buvinic, M., 1993, 'The Feminization of Poverty: Research and Policy Needs', Washington, DC: International Center for Research on Women.

Cagatay, Niloufer, 1998, 'Gender and Poverty', Working Paper No. 5, Social Development and Poverty Alleviation, New York: UNDP.

Carney, D., Drinkwater, M., Rusinow, T., Neefjes, K., Wanmali, S., and Singh, N., 1999, Livelihoods Approaches Compared: A Brief Comparison of the Livelihoods Approaches of the UK Department of International Development (DFID), CARE, Oxfam and the United Nations Development Programme (UNDP), London: DFID.

Carr, M., Chen, M.A., and Jhabvala, R., 1996, Speaking Out: Women's Economic Empowerment in South Asia, New Delhi: Vistaar.

Chambers, R. and Conway, G.R., 1992, 'Sustainable Rural Livelihoods: Practical Concepts for the Twenty-First Century', Discussion Paper #296, Brighton, Sussex: Institute of Development Studies, University of Sussex.

Dand, Sejal, 2003, 'Anandi: Addressing Gender Constraints: Learning from Each Other', in L. Mayoux (ed.), Sustainable Learning for Women's Empowerment: Ways Forward in Micro-finance, Calcutta: Sanskriti.

ICRW (International Center for Research on Women), 2002, Men, Masculinity and Domestic Violence in India: Summary Report of Four Studies, Washington, DC: ICRW.

Jackson, C., 1995, 'Rescuing Gender from the Poverty Trap', Gender Analysis in Development Series, No. 10, Norwich: University of East Anglia, School of Development Studies.

Kabeer, Naila, 1994, Reversed Realities: Gender Hierarchies in Development Thought, London: Verso.

———. 1997, 'Tactics and Trade Offs: Revisiting the Links between Gender and Poverty', IDS Bulletin, 28 (3).

Kabeer, Naila and Murthy, R.K., 1999, 'Gender, Poverty and Institutional Exclusion: Insights from Integrated Rural Development Programme (IRDP) and Development of Women and Children in Rural Areas (DWCRA)', in Naila Kabeer and R. Subrahmanian (eds), Institutions, Relations and Outcomes: A Framework and Case Studies for Gender-aware Planning, New Delhi: Kali for Women.

Kannabiran, Vasantha, 1996, *Sharing the Fish Head: The Philosophy and Practice of Gender Training in South Asia*, Asian South Pacific Bureau of Adult Education and Food and Agricultural Organization, New Delhi: Freedom from Hunger Campaign.

Khan, M., 1999, 'Microfinance, Wage Employment and Housework: A Gender Analysis', *Development in Practice*, 9 (4): 424–35.

Lipton, Michael, 1990, *Who are the Poor? What do They do? What should We do?*, DS-4, Center for Advanced Study of International Development, Michigan State University.

Lockwood, M. and Baden, S., 1995, 'Beyond the Feminization of Poverty: Gender-aware Poverty Reduction', *Development and Gender Brief No. 2*, Poverty Reduction Strategies, Brighton, Sussex: Institute of Development Studies, University of Sussex, and Bridge.

Madhusudhan, S., Seethalakshmi, S., Ramdas, R., and Mayoux, L., 2003, 'Literacy as People's Communicative Practice: An Experience with the People's Organization', in L. Mayoux (ed.), *Sustainable Learning For Women's Empowerment: Ways Forward In Micro-finance*, Kolkata: Sanskriti.

Mayoux, L., 2003, 'Grassroots Learning: Methodologies and Innovation', in L. Mayoux (ed.), *Sustainable Learning For Women's Empowerment: Ways Forward in Micro-finance*, Kolkata: Sanskriti.

Moser, C., 1993, *Gender Planning and Development: Theory, Practice and Training*, London: Routledge.

Murthy, R.K., 1998, 'Regional Perspectives: South Asia in Gender, Society and Development', in *Gender Training: The Source Book*, The Netherlands: Royal Tropical Institute, Kit Press, and London: Oxfam Publishing

Murthy, R.K., Rajaraman, K., Sankar, K., D'Souza, W., and Valsarajan, A., 2001, 'Mid Term Review of Mathi in Cuddalore District', Chennai: Tamil Nadu Corportion for Development of Women (Mimeo).

Murthy, R.K., Ramachandran, A., and DWCRA Research Team, 2002, 'Towards Women's Empowerment and Poverty Reduction: Lessons from the Participatory Impact Assessment of Development of Women and Children in Rural Areas in Andhra Pradesh, India', UNDP (Mimeo).

Murthy, R.K. and Sankaran, L., 2003, *Denial and Distress: Gender, Poverty and Human Rights in Asia*, London: Zed books.

Nigam, Ashok, 2000, *Give Us Credit: How Access to Loans and Basic Social Services Can Enrich and Empower People*, New York: UNICEF.

Pitt, M., Khandker, S., Chowdhury, Osman H., and Millimet, D.L., 1999, 'Credit Programmes for the Poor and the Nutritional Status of Children in Rural Bangladesh', *Working paper* WP98-01, Population Studies and Training Center, Providence: Brown University.

Poonacha, V. and Pandey, D., 1999, 'Responses to Domestic Violence in Karnataka and Gujarat', in *Domestic Violence in India 1: A Summary Report of Three Case Studies*, Washington, DC: International Center for Research on Women.

Sabala and Kranti, 2001, 'To be or Not to be: A Self-help Experience in Women's Reproductive Health', in R.K. Murthy (ed.), *Building Women's Capacities: Experiences in Gender Transformation*, New Delhi: Sage Publications.

Schuler, S., Hashemi, S.M., and Badal, S.H., 1998, 'Men's Violence against Women in Rural Bangladesh: Undermined or Exacerbated by Micro-credit Programmes?', *Development in Practice*, 8 (2): 148–57.

Sharma, Kalpana, 2002, 'Indian Women Pioneer Informal Justice Courts', Women's e-News, 21 September, http://www.womensenews.org/article.cfm/dyn/aid/357/context/archive.

Sidney, R., Hashemi, S.M., and Riley, A., 1997, 'The Influence of Women's Changing Roles and Status in Bangladesh's Fertility Transition: Evidence from a Study of Credit Programmes and Contraceptive Use', *World Development*, 25 (4): 563–75.

UN (United Nations), 1998, 'Violence, Gender and Bodily Integrity: Vienna Plus Five NGO Forum', available online at http://www.hri.ca/vienna+5/review/index.shtml.

UNDP (United Nations Development Programme), 1997, *Human Development Report 1997*, New York: UNDP.

Viswanath, Vanitha, 2001, 'Product to Market Assessment: The Experience of Udyogini', in L. Mayoux (ed.), *Sustainable Learning for Women's Empowerment: Ways Forward in Micro-finance*, Calcutta: Sanskriti.

About the Editors and Contributors

The Editors

Neera Burra is Assistant Resident Representative and Senior Social Development Adviser at the Sustainable Energy and Environment Division (SEED) of the United Nations Development Programme (UNDP), India Office, New Delhi. A sociologist by training, she obtained her Ph.D. from the Delhi School of Economics, University of Delhi. She has previously been with the International Labour Organization (ILO) as National Expert in its women's programme (1988–93) and with the United Nations Volunteers (UNV) as Programme Manager for South Asia (1993–95). Dr Burra has been closely involved with NGOs and CBOs working on micro-credit and women's empowerment for the last 15 years. She has also worked extensively on the issues of child labour and education and was recently awarded a post-doctoral fellowship by the Globalization and Human Rights Programmes of the University of Chicago to study the impact of globalization on child labour.

Dr Burra's current interests are in natural resource management for poverty eradication with a strong thrust on micro-credit, women's empowerment and poverty eradication. She has published extensively in the field of child labour, and has also written on watershed development, women's empowerment and micro-credit.

Joy Deshmukh-Ranadive is Senior Fellow at the Centre for Women's Development Studies (CWDS), New Delhi. She incorporates a multidisciplinary approach to theorizing issues in gender studies, and following her Ph.D. dissertation—which was on 'Power in Economics: A Study of Classical and Neoclassical Thought'—in the mid-1980s, she has remained interested in the concept of power. Her book, *Space for Power, Women's Work and Family Strategies*, presents a conceptual framework for analysing power and empowerment in the context of gender. Another area of her interest is human rights, and Dr Deshmukh-Ranadive has worked on issues related to the Human Right to Food and the Right to Housing, besides writing concept papers that deconstruct the meanings of these rights and conducting workshops and training on economic, social and cultural human rights.

Dr Deshmukh-Ranadive has done considerable work on micro-credit and self-help groups in India, particularly in the state of Andhra Pradesh, as also worked on issues of structural adjustment and globalization.

Ranjani K. Murthy is an independent researcher based in Chennai whose areas of interest have been gender, poverty and health for the past two decades. Through her work with MYRADA (1984–88) and with Initiatives: Women in Development (IWID, 1991–94), as well as by conducting independent research, she has gathered grassroots knowledge along with experience in policy analysis, capacity building and impact assessment. She has carried out policy and impact assessment studies with a focus on gender and poverty in India, Bangladesh, Nepal, Vietnam, Moldova and Sudan (for UN organizations and for national and international bodies which fund NGOs), and has prepared a global literature review on reproductive health service accountability within health sector reforms (for the former Women's Health Project, South Africa). Ms Ranjani Murthy was also a Visiting Fellow at the Institute of Development Studies, University of Sussex (1994). Her published books include *Indian NGOs and their Capacity Building in the 1990s* (1997, co-author); *Building Women's Capacities: Experiences in Gender Transformation* (Sage, 2001, editor); and *Denial and Distress: Gender, Poverty and Human Rights in Asia* (2003, co-author).

The Contributors

Amitha Kamath is Project Officer at the Centre for World Solidarity and looks into the gender aspects of development projects, like watershed development, joint forest management and dalit programmes. She did her post-graduation in social work and emerged a university topper. She has also secured gold medals in courses on farm management and soil water conservation. Ms Kamath has previously worked with Watershed Support Services and Activities Network (WASSAN) and as Project Secretary (Gender) for the Society for Elimination of Rural Poverty (SERP).

Veena Padia has over 25 years of experience in the development and the banking sectors. Beginning her career at the Indian Institute of Management, Ahmedabad and the UTI and Dena Banks, she has been the State Program Director of Mahila Samakhya, an autonomous body under the Education Department, Government of Gujarat, and has also worked in earthquake-affected areas as Project Director for the Women's Livelihood Restoration Project, supported by the Asian Development Bank and implemented by the Commissioner's Office, Women and Child Development Department.

Soma Kishore Parthasarathy obtained her M.Phil. in social planning from the Centre for Environmental Planning and Technology (CEPT), Ahmedabad, where her pioneering work on community participation won her accolades. She has worked in various capacities to integrate gender concerns in development over the past two decades, including a stint with the Government of India as a gender trainer and policy specialist. Her work ranges from capacity development to organizational strategy and advocacy in South Asia related to gender, education, natural resources, livelihoods and organizational development issues. She currently advises Nirantar, a feminist NGO based in Delhi, on its research and advocacy initiatives and remains deeply associated with hill women's issues through the SKS Women's Forum in Uttaranchal.

Shashi Rajagopalan is an activist and an organizational development consultant, who has worked for nearly three decades among disadvantaged rural and urban communities in India and abroad in the fields of health, education, disaster management, race relations and financial and commodity cooperatives. She has also been a member of the Brahm Perkash Committee which initiated cooperative legal reforms in the country.

Anuradha Rajivan currently works with the United Nations Development Programme. She has previously worked in the Indian Administrative Service (IAS) and taught courses in Economics at the Universities of Delhi and Southern California, besides being involved in the implementation of micro-finance and related policy in Asia and Africa. Her interests are in the areas of human nutrition and food security, and trade and regional integration. She has authored books and articles on development issues and written features and short stories for young children.

K. Raju is an IAS officer of the Andhra Pradesh Cadre and is currently Commissioner, Rural Development, Government of Andhra Pradesh. Over the past decade he has made significant contribution to poverty reduction strategies and programmes in the state. As National Project Coordinator of the UNDP-assisted South Asia Poverty Alleviation Programme (SAPAP), he initiated sustainable approaches to poverty reduction through the social mobilization of the poor. Mr Raju is also the CEO of SERP, and has scaled up SAPAP's strategy of social mobilization and community empowerment for poverty reduction in Andhra Pradesh.

Kalpana Sankar is Chief Executive Officer of Hand in Hand, Tamil Nadu, an NGO based in Sweden, which works in the field of elimination of child labour and women's empowerment. She has been involved with the self-help movement of women for nearly a decade and has worked as Monitoring and Evaluation Officer under the IFAD-assisted Tamil Nadu Women's Development Project. She has also prepared the concept note for the Tamil Nadu Empowerment and Poverty Reduction Project, which has been included in the World Bank's lending programme.

Index